P.E.T.

P.E.T. (Parent Effectiveness Training) is a national movement—and a major one. More than 250,000 parents have taken Dr. Gordon's P.E.T. course; nearly 8,000 professionals teach it in every state. And the movement continues to grow because parents keep telling other parents: "It works!"

P.E.T. IN ACTION

Dr. Gordon's in-depth interviews with P.E.T. parents show precisely what goes right—and wrong—when P.E.T. goes to work on the hang-ups, emotions, problems, and resistance of families. Step by step, he explains how such P.E.T. techniques as "Active Listening" and "I-Messages" get results: less fighting, more mutual respect and warm feelings, rules are established and followed, and parents are neither dictators nor doormats.

Here, at last, are practical answers and solutions—an extraordinary inside look at parent-child relationships that breaks ground untouched by Spock, Gesell, or Ginott.

P.E.T.
IN
ACTION

Dr. Thomas Gordon
with
Judith Gordon Sands

BANTAM BOOKS
TORONTO · NEW YORK · LONDON · SYDNEY

P.E.T. IN ACTION

*A Bantam Book / published by arrangement with
Peter H. Wyden, Inc.*

PRINTING HISTORY
Wyden edition published October 1976

Bantam edition / March 1978

2nd printing . . . . March 1978	5th printing . . . . March 1980
3rd printing . . . . . May 1978	6th printing . . November 1980
4th printing . . . . . July 1979	7th printing . . . January 1982

ISBN 0-553-20973-6

Published simultaneously in the United States and Canada

PRINTED IN THE UNITED STATES OF AMERICA

16 15 14 13 12 11 10 9 8

Contents

Acknowledgments

In my book, *P.E.T.: Parent Effectiveness Training*, published in 1970, I began my dedication page with "To my Judy . . . who provided me the opportunity to learn about parenthood." Once again, I acknowledge my daughter, now Judy Gordon Sands, for her substantial part in the creation of this book. First, Judy and I collaborated in the design of the various methods for collecting incidents, dialogues, reports and narrative accounts from the parents who had taken the P.E.T. course. Judy conducted all of the interviews and designed the questionnaires. She then took on the laborious job of doing the content analysis of all the materials collected from the parents. For her careful and thorough efforts, which provided me with the rich data on which to build this book, I sincerely thank her.

I acknowledge the substantial contributions of my wife, Linda, who reshaped my thinking about the organization and focus of this book and suggested its title. She also expanded my thinking about I-messages and their use to prevent conflict.

I am particularly grateful for the help of those P.E.T. instructors who suggested parents to be interviewed to us, and submitted tapes and case histories. Obviously, without our cadre of dedicated instructors, who do such a competent job of teaching the P.E.T. course, there would be no P.E.T. graduates!

I wish to acknowledge the helpful suggestions of

my publisher and friend, Peter H. Wyden, who first encouraged me to embark on this project.

Special thanks are due to Karen Gleason, my secretary, who not only typed the manuscript but did a lot of my work for me so I could be free to work on the book.

Most important, I thank all those parents who took their valuable time to be interviewed or to submit questionnaires, tapes, and personal stories showing P.E.T. in action.

T.G.

P.E.T. IN ACTION

I

INSIDE P.E.T. FAMILIES

When *The New York Times* described Parent Effectiveness Training as a "national movement," my initial reaction was a vague feeling of discomfort with what seemed to me a journalistic exaggeration. On further reflection I am more willing to accept that P.E.T. may have some of the characteristics of a movement. I know that in fifteen years 250,000 parents have taken the P.E.T. course. As of this writing, more than one million copies of the first P.E.T. book have been sold. Nearly 8,000 professionals from every state (and several foreign countries) have enrolled in training workshops to become qualified as P.E.T. instructors in their communities. Judging solely on the basis of such expansive growth, one might certainly view P.E.T. as a kind of movement.

Yet I derive little satisfaction from the realization that I may have started a "movement." Far more important is whether P.E.T. has brought about constructive effects on family life. Taking a course is not necessarily equivalent to learning something, let alone changing one's behavior—not any more than going to school is the equivalent of getting educated.

Have the parents who took P.E.T. increased their effectiveness as mothers and fathers? If so, to what extent? What do they do differently? And how does it affect their children? Has P.E.T. improved the quality of parent-child relationships? Do parents, after exposure to P.E.T. methods and skills, treat their kids more decently? Does P.E.T. make parenthood a less difficult experience? Do P.E.T. parents actually raise more responsible and more cooperative kids? Can parents become more effective in dealing with the inevitable parent-child conflicts and value collisions by attending a P.E.T. course only one night a week for eight weeks?

Such questions deserve to be asked—and must be answered—to make a proper assessment of P.E.T. and its impact on family life, rather than how far or how quickly it has "moved." And where better to find answers to these questions than inside the families of parents who have taken P.E.T.?

In the pages of this book P.E.T. graduates report their own personal experiences as they try to put their newly learned P.E.T. skills to work in their homes. Along with their successes, they share their struggles and problems. So you'll meet families who make such admissions as these:

> "We haven't always done as well with P.E.T. as we should have, especially with our older daughter."

> "It turned out to be a lot harder to practice in everyday situations than it seemed reading the book."

> "With our youngest it was just like talking to a chair."

> "When I use P.E.T. right, it works, but when Jimmy is really agitated, I don't always send the proper messages."

> "I still have some reservations about P.E.T. You know, 'Is this really going to work? Am I leaving too much responsibility with my son? Maybe we should be guiding him more.' "

But readers will also find themselves inside other families that clearly demonstrate how P.E.T. skills can be used effectively, often with dramatic success:

"It has revolutionized our family life."

"Our problems don't seem to be big ones anymore."

"Now somehow I feel like my kids most of the time think of me as a trustworthy and accepting person—like they don't have to hide a lot. . . . It works because we trust each other."

"P.E.T. saved our marriage."

"Lee and I now have a daughter who mostly loves her parents, mostly loves her brother, and more importantly mostly loves herself. She just happens to have a slightly bent spine, and I wonder what indeed she would have had if I had remained being the responsible, all-knowing, all-providing, all-powerful father."

From the actual incidents and dialogues reported by both types of parents—those who ran into problems and those who achieved remarkable successes—I believe that readers cannot help but derive valuable insights about their own parenting. Also, as I studied the transcriptions of our tape-recorded interviews with P.E.T. graduates, I found I could explain why some parents encountered difficulties with the P.E.T. methods. So throughout this book I have added my own interpretation and analysis of why things went awry in various situations. My intent, of course, is to help the reader avoid some of the pitfalls parents have experienced in their application of P.E.T. skills on the firing line—at home with real kids.

Frequently I am asked, "Dr. Gordon, have you changed any of your ideas or concepts since you wrote *P.E.T.?*" And parents often ask more specific questions, such as:

"Do you still feel parents shouldn't use power and authority?"

"Are you still adamant about trusting kids to find their own solutions to their problems?"

"Would you now admit that parents should punish kids for certain grossly unacceptable behavior?"

"Are you still against parents using praise or giving rewards?"

Such questions reflect legitimate concern about whether my early definition of parent effectiveness has withstood the test of time and greater experience. I answer these and many other searching questions in these pages. Meanwhile, you're entitled to know that over the years P.E.T. has continually changed. Through the creative contributions of P.E.T. instructors, P.E.T. teaching methods have improved in significant ways. Periodically, I discovered (or had it called to my attention) that there were gaps in my early theoretical model for parent effectiveness. So important additions have been made that provide a deeper understanding of the dynamics of the parent-child relationship. From our analysis of the vast data in the interviews and questionnaires on which this book was based, further new ideas and improvements emerged.

Readers who are already familiar with P.E.T. principles and skills will welcome such improvements and additions as these:

1. We know now that the P.E.T. skills can be used successfully with very young children—infants and toddlers—long before they develop verbal language. One mother reported how she used the Active Listening skill to quiet down the vigorous squirming and screaming of her baby during diaper changes!

2. We now can relieve parents of a lot of their anxiety over trying to avoid Communication Roadblocks in conversations with their children. Often parents don't need to control how they talk to their kids; they can relax their vigilance and even send warnings, commands, solutions, interpretations, questions or preachments. The key is knowing *when* these responses are harmless.

3. We have enlarged our understanding of why it can threaten and inhibit children when you ask them questions.

4. We have developed new guidelines for parents who turn off their kids by doing too much listening—overdoing the parent-as-a-counselor role.

5. We have developed new guidelines for parents that will be useful when their children ignore appeals for help and consideration.

6. We have added some new applications for I-messages—a way for children to be told exactly what their parents need, so conflict can be avoided in the future.

7. We have discovered that lenient (permissive) parents and strict (authoritarian) parents are very much alike—perhaps cut from the same mold! They really aren't as different as we thought they were, because they both talk in the "language of power."

By no means, then, has P.E.T. remained static. Consequently this book is not a rehash of the skills and methods described in the first book. Readers who are already familiar with the P.E.T. model will not only find the present book a refresher and an "additional shot in the arm" (which many graduates said they needed); they will also find in these pages many elements of an "advanced course" in parent effectiveness.

My first book, *P.E.T.: Parent Effectiveness Training,* now available in paperback (New American Library), is the only basic text for the P.E.T. approach —the complete prescription or blueprint for better relationships with children. Although I rebel somewhat against the concept, it was a "how-to" type of book. The present companion volume, *P.E.T. in Action,* on the other hand, is a book about *people doing it:* mothers, fathers, and their children. This is a companion book that takes the reader inside real families where the mothers and fathers are using the P.E.T. blueprint to build better relationships with their children and with each other.

While the first P.E.T. book included many incidents and dialogues from family life, they were used primarily to illustrate specific P.E.T. skills and methods. Furthermore, many of these incidents involved parents still taking the P.E.T. course. This book explores what happens to parents after they walk out of the P.E.T. course and are on their own—some immediately afterward, some one year later, some four years later, some as long as nine years later.

In these flesh-and-blood families you'll catch intimate glimpses of parents—all very different from each other, yet all using the same blueprint—putting P.E.T. in action.

You'll meet parents without partners, going it alone, and two-parent families in which the partners do not apply their new skills with equal effectiveness. You will also read incidents submitted by parents who had combined their children from a previous marriage into a new family unit.

Some parents took P.E.T. when their children were very young; others had to start building better relationships with teen-agers who already were exhibiting resentment, rebellion, and retaliation.

You'll watch P.E.T. in action with apparently normal children and with kids who are not. Some are hyperactive, some handicapped, some have serious illnesses, some are into drugs.

Information about these parents and their families was obtained from questionnaires, short stories, and interviews. Data collection and data analysis were under the direction of my daughter, Judy Gordon Sands. In addition, Judy also worked closely with me in designing the basic outline for this book. A more complete description of the entire project is given in the Appendix.

One thing is certain from our analysis of all the data: P.E.T. does give parents skills they can use to cope more effectively with everyday problems. You'll see these skills in action throughout this book as parents deal with such nitty-gritty problems as chores, dirty bathrooms, removing food from refrigerators, kids being late for school, making excessive noise, emptying the garbage, handling guns, potty training, eating vegetables, TV. watching, muddy feet in the house, washing dishes, hating to go to school, bedtime hassles, where to ride bicycles, and many others.

One mother summed up her feelings when she said, "P.E.T. sure helps parents get a new perspective for looking at the world."

I agree, and I'm also more convinced than ever that P.E.T. is helping many parents get a new perspective on a lot of things that are close to home: What parents are for, the capacity of their children to solve their own problems, the importance of parents' rights in the family, the value of a democratic and nonpower climate in the home, and the rewards of building relationships with their children that will bring feelings of mutual respect and love—so all members of a family can become what they are capable of being.

II

TOOLS ARE NOT ENOUGH:
Fundamentals Foremost

High on the list of the most important lessons we've learned from our experience is that if parents are to become effective in using the skills they've acquired, they must understand the basic P.E.T. theoretical model. Tools are not enough—parents need to know when to use them and why. And for this, they need to know some fundamentals.

This should not be too surprising. To become competent at sailing a boat, under all weather conditions and in different waters, requires more than the skills of handling the tiller or changing the sails. Competent seamen must know the fundamentals of navigation, as well as the theory of vectors. To fly a plane competently and safely, a pilot must be grounded in the theory of aerodynamics, as well as have a basic understanding of meteorology (weather), to say nothing of knowing how engines work. In fact, the simple skills the pilot needs to take off, fly straight and level, and land an aircraft are so simple that a child of eight can learn them.

It's no different with becoming an effective parent:

it requires certain fundamentals about human relationships. Parents must understand the overall picture—
what goes on between two people in a relationship.
They can do the job of parenting only by working
from a sound theory or blueprint—what scientists call
a "model." Failure to understand the model inevitably
leads to using their skills inappropriately.

I was not as aware of the importance of this when
P.E.T. was in its infancy. What later convinced me of
the importance of the P.E.T. model was observing
parents in the P.E.T. classes and listening to the P.E.T.
graduates. Before enrolling in P.E.T., many parents,
for example, have already read one or more books on
parenting from which they learned specific skills, such
as how to respond to children's feelings. Yet we found
that few parents understood the basic theory they need
to know to decide when to use the skill and when not.
Also, it's a rare parent who could explain *why* the
skill was to be used.

In our interviews with parents we frequently heard
such statements as:

> "I already had some familiarity with what is
> taught in P.E.T., but the course took all these un-
> related skills and ideas and put them all together into
> a 'package.' "

> "P.E.T. helped me know what I was doing and why."

> "I feel now that I understand what's happening in
> every situation with my kids. I'm on top of it, and I
> feel I'm competent to know what to do."

Once a parent talked to me about her response to a
popular book on child rearing which she had read
prior to taking the P.E.T. course:

> "When I read the book by Dr. _____, I really
> liked what he told you to say to kids—it made a lot
> of sense. But then my own kids didn't say the same
> things the children in his book said. So I never could
> respond the way he said I should."

Another mother saw the importance of having a theory —a "method-plan" she called it:

> "In Dr. _____'s book he tells you exactly the specific conversation, but he doesn't give you a method-plan. You know, a plan of action. . . . You finish reading the book and it really made a lot of sense, but where do you go? How do you use it?"

I think these parents felt that they were not given a model that would enable them to understand the principle from which a particular communication skill was derived. And so they could not apply the skill in new, often changing situations in their own families, because the situations were never identical to those the author used in his book. They could not generalize from the *specific* situation in the book to *similar* (but different) situations in their homes.

When I use the term "model" or P.E.T. "theory," I am not referring to someone's pet notion that has little or no basis in fact. In any science, a theoretical model is a blueprint or set of guidelines that helps people understand and explain a lot of very different events or happenings. P.E.T. is based on such a blueprint—a theory of interpersonal relationships that helps explain a lot (though of course not everything) of what goes on between two persons in a relationship. We now know better which elements of that model parents find most difficult to comprehend. Also, we have developed better ways to teach parents this basic theory. Unless they grasp these fundamentals, they are at a loss to know which skills to use in which situations.

The P.E.T. theory is not a blueprint of effective parent-child relationships alone, but a general theory that applies to all human relationships—husband-wife, boss-subordinate, teacher-student, counselor-client or friend-friend. At first, this surprises parents because, for reasons not clear to me, most parents see the parent-child relationship as very different from other kinds of relationships. In the eyes of parents, children are not people.

Most parents firmly believe that if they make a critical remark that puts down an adult, that person will be hurt and the relationship damaged. Do the same to a child, and they believe somehow the child won't be hurt, nor will the put-down do damage to the relationship. In fact, most parents even argue that children need criticism and put-downs and so it is the duty of a good parent to give kids a generous dosage of such messages—"for their own good."

Parents who strongly hold to the value of never using force in human relationships not only use physical punishment with their children but argue that it's good for them!

Also, parents are universally bilingual—they use one language for people and another for children. Should a friend drop and break one of their dishes, most parents would never want the friend to feel embarrassed or guilty, so their message would be some variation of, "Oh, don't worry about that dish—accidents will happen." Let their eight-year-old drop that dish and we hear another language—such as "Damn it, my good dish is broken—why do you have to be so clumsy? Can't you ever be careful?"

It's not been easy for parents to accept that children are people too, and that what happens in parent-child relationships can therefore be explained by the same principles that apply to all other human relationships. Nevertheless, to make any significant changes in their patterns of parenting, the parents we have worked with have had to make some rather drastic changes in their own theories about parenthood and about children:

1. They must stop seeing their children as a unique species and begin to perceive them as persons.

2. They must begin to accept that how their children behave is largely determined by what goes on in the parent-child relationship.

3. They must begin to understand some basic principles (fundamentals) about all interpersonal relationships.

This is why I think it is necessary in this first chapter to summarize the basic principles of the P.E.T. theory of human relationships. Parents who have read the first P.E.T. book or taken the P.E.T. course may feel they can skip this chapter, but in my judgment they will profit from this review, not only because we have made some recent additions and refinements but also because they may want to recheck their present understanding of the theory. Parents totally unfamiliar with the P.E.T. model would be well advised to read the first P.E.T. book in order to get a full treatment of the basic theory. For without comprehending the theory they will lack the judgment to know when to use the P.E.T. skills described and illustrated in subsequent chapters.

THE INCONSISTENCY PRINCIPLE

One of the most commonly held beliefs about parenthood is that a parent must be consistent. If today you're unaccepting of a certain kind of behavior of your child, tomorrow you had better not feel accepting—or else you'll be inconsistent. That's bad, parents have been told. Also, if you "permit" some particular behavior on Monday, it is supposed to be harmful to the youngster when on Friday the very same behavior is driving you crazy and you find it intolerable.

This myth is exploded very early in the P.E.T. course, to the relief of parents who've been struggling to live by it, suffering guilt and remorse when they failed. P.E.T. teaches that some behaviors are acceptable some days because of the way the parent feels, but at other times the same things will not be acceptable, because the parent feels different. A mother of two aggressive children tells how she responds differently to her kids' frequent fighting:

> "Whether or not I'll allow them to fight around me depends on my mood. I mean, there are some times when I'm doing something like reading the paper

when I don't care if they're fighting around me or
whatever. But there are other times when I don't
want them to play around me. They feel it—it's like
a short wave. And then they'll go somewhere else."

A father, who is a physician, talked about his inconsistency in relation to his patients at the office:

"There are days when my acceptance level is very
good and I can sit and listen—even for an hour,
though my waiting room is crowded. . . . But there
are other times when my acceptance is just not there.
. . . And I can say to a patient, 'Hey, I'm picking up
that you need to talk or share something, but I can't
listen today.' And I tell them why I can't. And I say,
'Any other time' or 'Come back and make another
appointment.' I've never had a patient get mad at me.
To me it's been a revelation! Before P.E.T. when I
had something else to do and it irritated me that they
were wanting to unload, I would look at my watch or
let them know somehow I wasn't interested. . . . Then
they'd be angry, and I was being very dishonest with
them."

This doctor's reference to his "acceptance level" is a
concept derived directly from the P.E.T. model. It helps
parents understand how they inevitably will be inconsistent. In P.E.T. classes we first ask parents to
visualize a rectangle or window in front of them,
through which they see all the behaviors of their child:

```
┌─────────────────┐
│                 │
│                 │
│                 │
│                 │
│                 │
│                 │
│     ALL THE     │
│    BEHAVIORS    │
│     OF THE      │
│     CHILD       │
│                 │
│                 │
└─────────────────┘
```

Then we show how every parent's rectangle contains two different kinds of behavior: acceptable and unacceptable.

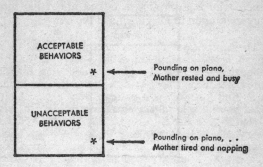

When a parent is feeling rested and is busy doing something interesting and satisfying, her three-year-old daughter's pounding on the piano might be quite acceptable to her. Yet the same behavior would be unacceptable if Mother is tired and trying to take a nap. Furthermore, there are days when a parent's Area of Acceptance is very large—everything is going great for him and almost nothing perturbs him. His rectangle would look like this:

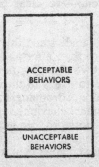

If, at another time, that father is upset or worried—
everything seems to be going wrong—his rectangle
might very well look like this:

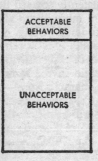

On such a day, almost everything his child might do
would feel unacceptable to him. These movements of
the dividing line (or "level of acceptance") are frequent and inevitable with most parents—and it's understandable and normal that they'll feel different from
the way they feel at other times.

> "I have those moments when I feel ineffective and a
> failure. I realize these moments come when I'm tired
> and feeling low myself. Then I'm great at finding
> everything wrong—everything out of place, jobs not
> done."

When parents understand this changing rectangle,
they tend to accept that, after all, they're only human
beings with their own changing moods. Then they can
become more able to live with their fluctuating feelings
toward their children, dropping the heavy burden of
guilt their inconsistent behavior had produced.

Two other factors produce fluctuations in parents'
attitudes and behavior. First, parents inevitably find
one child more acceptable than another, simply be-

cause of the differences in their personalities and characteristics. Secondly, parents find their attitudes toward certain behaviors changing as a result of the environment in which the behavior occurs.

Why will parents who have more than one child feel and act inconsistently toward them? Because some children, face it, are more acceptable than others—for many reasons. A toddler (Child A) may be very aggressive, highly mobile, and extremely curious, getting into everything and causing all kinds of havoc in the home. The other child in the family (Child B) might have very different characteristics—quiet, cautious, and careful. The parent's typical behavior rectangles for these two opposites will be markedly different.

Some children I've known have had such charm and appeal to me that I usually accepted almost anything they ever did. I've encountered other kids whose particular characteristics produced a lot of behaviors I found unacceptable.

How does the environment produce inconsistency in parental attitudes? Take rowdy horseplay. Outside in the yard, it may be quite acceptable to Dad—in fact, even enjoyable. In the living room, most of the same behaviors will be unacceptable.

CHILD A   CHILD B

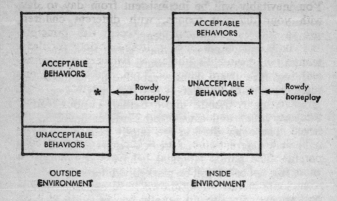

OUTSIDE ENVIRONMENT   INSIDE ENVIRONMENT

The table manners of your fourteen-year-old son may be acceptable to you at home, but unacceptable and embarrassing to you in a public restaurant.

All parents, influenced by the three factors—their own mood, the child, and the environment—will be continually experiencing inconsistency of attitude and behavior toward their children. Within each parent's rectangle, the line dividing the Area of Acceptable Behaviors and the Area of Unacceptable Behaviors consequently fluctuates as a result of the interaction of the three factors:

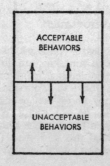

There you have it—the principle of inconsistency. You inevitably will be inconsistent from day to day, with your different moods, with different children, and in different environments. Accept this principle, and you'll eliminate a lot of guilt and anxiety. You're a human being, and it's human to experience inconsistent feelings toward your children. Recognizing this can make parenthood a great deal less difficult.

One more application of the principle of inconsistency needs mentioning. There is another commonly believed notion that makes parenthood seem much more difficult than it need be. This is the stricture that both parents must always feel and act the same toward a youngster's behavior—they must present a "united front." Apart from creating a lot of arguments or fights between parents, this notion can be the cause of a lot of guilt and resentment, as this mother reported:

> "My husband believes that negotiating with children is a weakness, like sending the children to bed because you're uncomfortable with them there. . . . P.E.T. was kind of an eye-opener which I had been looking for. In particular, the idea that husband and wife don't have to agree. When I read that page, I was sold. Oh, the guilt I had when I couldn't go along with him. . . . The idea that I had a right to disagree was fantastic. . . . It's still very threatening to him, but I feel very secure now. . . . When I first disagreed, it was scary, like I was standing up against the authority, which I had let him be for so long."

Another parent talked about her experience in trying to live by the united-front rule:

> "We've always heard you must have a united front, you know, or else your kids are going to be weird or unbalanced or something. And our instructor kept saying you don't have to. Your kids don't buy it anyway because they know two people can't always believe exactly alike on everything. With our son, Mike, I had always tried to maintain a united front. It was always 'Your Dad this and your Dad that, and you have to do whatever your Dad says.' But then I didn't

really feel like I had the freedom to help Mike solve any of his problems when his father was out of town a lot, because I had to make sure first it was OK with Dad. . . . I felt everything had to be cleared with his Dad."

To eliminate or reduce these kinds of conflicts that so easily erode marriage relationships, P.E.T. teaches parents to begin relating to their kids independently rather than trying to engineer a united front. Each parent becomes free to take his or her separate stance in response to a particular behavior of the youngster, as illustrated by these rectangles:

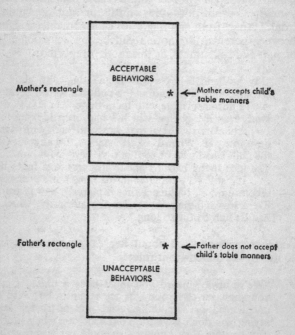

In this case, Mother should let Father deal with the youngster's table manners; after all, *he* is the one bothered by them. She shouldn't fall into the trap of acting as his agent. To do so, she would have to be untrue to her own real feelings—be dishonest, if you will. Not only will she be troubled by that (because of feelings of resentment or subservience), but there is the additional risk that the child will perceive Mother's dishonesty (or phoniness) and lose respect for her. Some of the intricacies of this united front problem are illustrated in this excerpt from a mother's interview in which she describes how she and her husband recognized their inconsistency and solved the problem of table manners in their family:

M: P.E.T. changed me as a human being in general. . . . The change was dramatic in the way I related to the kids. In fact, that's why my husband later took P.E.T.—he saw how my relationship changed with the kids. Two months later he was in the class.

I: How did it change?

M: Oh, I was a lot more relaxed. He saw a change in the communication—really beautiful communication. Another thing, he saw that I was letting him own his own problems.

I: Such as what?

M: Oh, an example would be table manners. I didn't care about the kids' table manners—that wasn't my problem. I didn't care how they got the food into them. But he was raised with a very strict uncle who had a real hang-up about table manners. And I found myself correcting the kids at the table because of his discomfort at what they were doing.

I: So you were going to have a united front.

M: I just took on his responsibility. . . . So when I got to that part of the course, I thought, "What am I doing, why am I nagging at them for something that doesn't even bother me, when it's really his problem . . . ?" I had previously thought he was easygoing and I was uptight, but then I discovered he owned a lot of the problems, not me. After that, I didn't have to be on the kids as much. And I found out I wasn't so bad after all. I'd felt I was the "heavy" in the family. So it relieved me of the pressure, and also caused him to come to grips with things that bothered him. . . . I also saw that when the kids were alone with me, they didn't do the things they did when he was there—to just hook him in. . . .

I: So how did you problem-solve it?

M: Well, it turned out that my husband was really concerned about the kids' table manners when we would go out to a restaurant. He didn't want them to eat with their hands and whatever. So we came to an agreement that if he would lay off the kids at home, we would have one night a week eating in the dining room with a table-cloth and candles, and the kids would have their best manners and learn how Daddy wants them to eat out in public. It could be relaxed the rest of the time and still they could get the training he wanted them to have.

I: How did that work out?

M: Great. Besides it was fun. You know, having the tablecloth and candles makes anybody shape up a little bit.

THE PRINCIPLE OF PROBLEM OWNERSHIP

A core concept in the P.E.T. model is the "principle of problem ownership." Its importance cannot be overstated, because we have learned from our interviews with parents that mistakes in using the P.E.T. skills quite often are the result of parents' confusion about this principle.

The concept of ownership of problems found its place in P.E.T. because so many parents fall into the trap of assuming responsibility for solving problems their children own, rather than encouraging them to solve their problems themselves. In the interviews we heard many statements like these:

"You know, they used to come to me with all their problems, like 'I lost a dime down a manhole cover, what do I do now?' You know, I had to solve *everything* for them, because this was the image I'd set up. Mom was the great solver of problems, until she got so frustrated that she didn't want to. And I didn't know how to get out of it. I didn't know how to say, 'Just leave me alone, I'm tired, I've got a headache. Get out of here, solve your own problem.' They didn't know how to."

"The biggest thing that happened to me in taking P.E.T. was to sort out who owns the problem. It was absolutely the most meaningful thing. It just blew my mind that Frankie had problems and I didn't have to own them. . . . And I'd been owning them for years."

"Before P.E.T., I wouldn't let her have her own problems to solve. I would try to help her in some way. But I think she's growing in her ability to handle her own problems. . . . It makes me feel good to see her solving her own little relationship problems. . . . I'm somewhat amazed, because I see her as having a lot more capability in that area than I had at her age, or even much older. I feel like I'm helping her to grow, and she has exhibited a lot of growth that I never had. . . . The P.E.T. approach allows me to give her her own problems with a minimum of my putting in my solutions. . . . My realizing she owns her problem kind of frees me to step back and not impose my solutions which don't really fit the situation as well as the ones she is able to come up with herself."

When parents understand the principle of problem ownership, it can have a profound effect in bringing about a change in their behavior toward their children. In the P.E.T. course parents are first introduced to this concept by means of the same rectangle we use to differentiate "acceptable" and "unacceptable" behaviors. However, a third area must be added, as in the right-hand rectangle below:

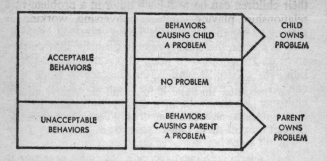

Beginning with the bottom part of the rectangle on the right, these behaviors, you will remember, are the ones unacceptable to the parent because they interfere with the parent's right or prevent the parent getting his or her needs met. Examples: child being noisy when parents are talking, child dawdling when parent is in a hurry, child drawing on wallpaper, child leaving toys or clothes in living room, child making scratches on table, and so on. Such behaviors signal that the PARENT OWNS THE PROBLEM, and it's up to the parent to try to modify the behavior that is causing him or her a problem.

In the top part of the rectangle we show behaviors of the child that signal that he or she owns a problem —the child's needs are not being met, the child is unhappy or frustrated or in trouble. Examples: child upset at not having anyone to play with, child rejected by one of his friends, child finding her homework too difficult, child angry at his teacher, teen-ager unhappy with being overweight. These are problems children experience in their own lives, independent and outside of their parents' lives. In such situations the CHILD OWNS THE PROBLEM.

The middle area of the rectangle represents behaviors of the child which are causing neither the parent nor the child a problem. These are the delightful times in parent-child relationships when parents and their children can be with each other in a problem-free relationship, playing together, conversing, working or sharing an experience. This is the NO PROBLEM AREA.

It's when the child owns the problem that parents so often are tempted to jump in, assume the responsibility for solving it, and blame themselves when they can't. P.E.T. offers parents an alternative to help their children: let the child own his problem and find his own solution. Somewhat oversimplified, this new approach is made up of these elements:

1. All children inevitably will encounter problems in their lives—all shapes and kinds.

2. Kids have unbelievable and mostly untapped potential for finding good solutions to their problems.

3. If parents hand them prepackaged solutions, children remain dependent and fail to develop their own problem-solving skills. They'll keep coming to their parents every time they encounter a new problem.

4. When parents take over (or "own") their children's problems, and therefore assume full responsibility for coming up with good solutions, it becomes not only a terrible burden but an impossible task. No one has the infinite wisdom always to generate good solutions for other people's personal problems.

5. When a parent can accept that he or she does not own the child's problem, he then is in a much better position to be a "facilitator" or "catalyst" or "helping agent," *helping the child work through the problem-solving process on his own.*

6. Kids do need help with certain kinds of problems, but in the long run the kind of help that is most effective is, paradoxically, a form of "nonhelp." More accurately, it's a new way of helping that leaves the responsibility with the child for searching for and finding his or her own solutions. In P.E.T. we call these the "Helping Skills."

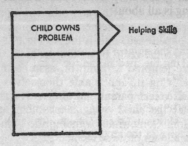

When the child's behavior causes the parent a
problem (behavior we have previously located in the
bottom third of the rectangle), a different set of skills
must be used. These are skills that will be effective in
bringing about some change in the unacceptable behavior of the child. When a child is interfering with a
parent's rights or is doing something that prevents the
parent from meeting his or her needs, the *parent owns
the problem* and hence will want to use skills that will
be *helpful to self*. In P.E.T. we call these "Confrontation Skills."

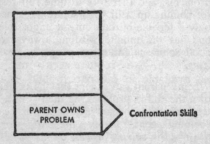

When the *parent* owns the problem, this calls for
a posture that will communicate to the child, "Hey,
I've got a problem and I need *your* help"—quite a
different posture than when the child owns a problem
and the parent wants to communicate, "It seems like
you have a problem; do you need *my* help?"

We can graphically show what Parent Effectiveness Training is all about:

1. We teach parents skills that will be effective in reducing the number of problems owned by the child (making the area in the top third of the rectangle smaller).

2. We also teach parents quite different skills that will be effective in reducing the number of problems their kids cause them (making the area in the bottom third of the rectangle smaller).

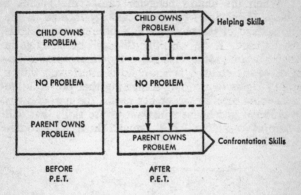

The successful application of these two sets of skills enlarges the No-Problem area—making much more time available in the parent-child relationship, when neither has a problem and both can get their needs satisfied and enjoy their life together.

In Chapters III, IV, and V, I'll focus exclusively on the Helping Skills, identifying the difficulties parents most frequently encounter, offering parents suggestions and guidelines for overcoming or avoiding these difficulties, and presenting case illustrations of the rewards and benefits they can expect when they employ these skills effectively with their children. In Chapters VI, VII, and VIII, I'll do the same for the Confrontation Skills.

III

NEW INSIGHTS FOR HELPING CHILDREN WITH THEIR PROBLEMS

It certainly hasn't been easy to get parents to change the way they typically talk to their children when the *child owns the problem*. Their habits are ingrained and often firmly fixed. Most parents, confronted with a situation where a child is experiencing a problem, respond the same way their own parents did. And because they have not had a chance to learn a better way, parents keep making the same mistakes *their* parents made.

Those whose own parents preached and moralized tend to preach and moralize with their own youngsters. A mother whose parents relied heavily on lecturing and inundating the child with facts is very likely to respond the same way in trying to help her own child with a problem. Children accustomed to reassurance and sympathy will become reassuring and sympathizing parents. Those whose parents always jumped in to give their own advice and solutions to problems find themselves doing the same thing when they become parents.

P.E.T. requires parents to *unlearn* most of their habits of talking to kids when they encounter problems in their lives. More accurately, *parents have to learn to stop talking and start listening.* But it turns out that many parents don't know the difference between listening and talking! We have made advances in showing parents the difference.

It's a rare parent who has never been told by now how essential it is to listen to children. In books and magazine articles, from the platform or the television tube, authorities seldom fail to hand out this hackneyed advice as part of their prescription for effective parenting.

Almost as consistently as this dictum is preached, parents feel convinced that in practice they really do listen to their children. "Of course I listen to my children," most parents admit. Few parents nowadays accept the old notion that "children should be seen and not heard." So it comes as quite a surprise when parents find out early in the P.E.T. course that while they've been buying the concept of listening *in the abstract,* they haven't been effective listeners *in concrete situations* where it is sorely needed by their children.

In P.E.T. parents first learn that there is a great difference between *listening* to kids and *talking* to them. One mother expressed it this way:

> "What bothers me is that you may never know your child is having a problem—they can carry it around for days. And to think I've missed the opportunity to help them because I closed the door. . . . I've always spent a lot of time talking with them—*I think I did a lot of the talking.* . . . Our son is the one we've had the hardest time getting close to. I just couldn't reach him. He's kind of quiet and I just would try to think of *things to say to him,* because I felt I'm his mother and should be communicating with him more."

Parents reveal this confusion between listening and talking in excerpts such as these, taken from our interviews:

"When this problem came up, I had no idea what I would do. In the past I've been just scared to death I'd have to face something like that and I wouldn't know *what to say*."

"Before P.E.T. I probed more. If my child had a problem I would have said, 'Well, what's the matter now? Why are you upset?' You can tell right away, the minute someone walks in the room, if they're upset over something. And I'd always be right there *questioning*."

With few exceptions, parents enrolled in P.E.T. have demonstrated that their typical response to a child who shares a problem has been not to listen but to talk—*they feel they must say something to the child,* send some kind of a message to him, tell him something.

In P.E.T. we've always felt our first task was to help parents become acutely aware of how they typically respond verbally when their children share their problems with them. Sometimes the method we employ has created puzzlement and, not infrequently, a good deal of resistance. Recently we have learned how to reduce some of this puzzlement and resistance. In this chapter I will offer parents some new insights and list some clearer guidelines for becoming a more effective listener.

WHEN PARENTS USE THE TWELVE ROADBLOCKS TO COMMUNICATION

In the first class session, P.E.T. instructors do an exercise with parents in which the instructor successively plays the role of each of several children who announce they're experiencing a problem. Parents in the class are asked to write down word for word exactly how they would respond to each of these children. Their responses are then collected and analyzed. Well over 90 percent of their responses fall into one or more of twelve basic categories. We call them the Twelve Roadblocks to Communication.

Take a fourteen-year-old boy who tells his parent about the problem he is having with his homework and school:

> "I just can't get down to doing my homework. I hate it. And I hate school. It's boring. They teach you nothing important to your life—just a bunch of junk. When I'm old enough, I'm going to quit school. You don't need schooling to get ahead in this world."

Here are some of the typical responses parents make to the youngster in this classroom exercise. In the right hand column I show the Roadblock into which each response falls:

Response	Type of Roadblock
"No son of mine is going to quit school—I won't allow it."	ORDERING, DIRECTING, DEMANDING
"Quit school and you'll get no financial help from me."	WARNING, THREATENING
"Learning is the most rewarding experience anyone can have."	MORALIZING, PREACHING
"Why don't you make a schedule for yourself to do your homework?"	ADVISING, GIVING SOLUTIONS
"A college graduate earns over 50 percent more than a high school graduate."	LECTURING, TEACHING, GIVING FACTS
"You're being shortsighted and your thinking shows immaturity."	JUDGING, BLAMING, CRITICIZING
"You've always been a good student, with lots of potential."	PRAISING, BUTTERING UP
"You're talking like a 'hippy.'"	NAME-CALLING, RIDICULING
"You don't like school because you're afraid to put out the effort."	INTERPRETING, ANALYZING
"I know how you feel, but school will be better your senior year."	REASSURING, SYMPATHIZING
"What would you do without an education? How would you make a living?"	PROBING, QUESTIONING, INTERROGATING

"No problems at the dinner ta- WITHDRAWING, DIVERTING,
ble! How's basketball these DISTRACTING
days?"

This exercise proves that the typical posture of
parents, when confronted with a child "owning" a
problem, is to *say something*—give an order, warn,
moralize, advise, teach a lesson, criticize, name-call,
diagnose, praise, reassure, interrogate, or divert. When
parents use such responses, the communication between parent and child can be diagrammed this way:

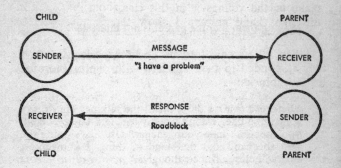

These typical responses are called Roadblocks because they so frequently block further communication
from the child. They also can have destructive effects
on the child's self-esteem, as well as on the parent-
child relationship itself. The Twelve Roadblocks carry
a high risk of having one or more of these effects on
children:

Making them stop talking.

Making them defensive.

Making them argue, counterattack.

Making them feel inadequate, inferior.

Making them resentful, angry.

Making them feel guilty or bad.

Making them feel unaccepted as they are.

Making them feel not trusted to solve their own problem.

Making them feel they are not understood.

Making them feel their feelings are not justified.

Making them feel interrupted, cut off.

Making them feel frustrated.

Making them feel put on the witness stand and cross-examined.

Making them feel the parent is not interested.

Several parents told us about experiences when they responded to their children with one or more of the Roadblocks:

"Before, I think I did a lot of the talking. They'd say something like, 'I don't like my teacher.' I'd say, 'Well, you shouldn't hate your teacher.' Or, 'She's doing the best she can,' and that kind of thing. I know now, that will close off their thoughts."

"I took many trips to the doctor or the dentist with the kids, and all the way they used to complain. They didn't want a shot or they hated the doctor. Trying to make them feel better, I'd deny their feelings by saying, 'Oh, you're not really scared to go,' and such. But that was wrong, I sure know that now. . . . If someone tells them they shouldn't feel that way, it makes them feel they're wrong—that something is wrong with them for feeling scared. Well, it doesn't give them a good feeling about themselves."

"When Timmy started nursery school, he'd come home with nothing to say about the morning's events. I'd question him directly, and he wouldn't respond. . . . Then I began to notice that he rarely answered any of my direct questions. It was very frustrating to a schoolteacher Mom like me to have a child who wouldn't speak up when questioned. . . . One of the first things I discovered was that my habit of questioning Timmy directly put him in a very vulnerable position. He hated to be wrong, so, rather than answer a question in a wrong way, he wouldn't answer at all. I listened to myself for a week and heard the stridency in my voice. It was a humbling revelation. The strict objectivity and prosecutor's pose which worked well in the classroom were overwhelming to my tiny five-year-old. His only defense was silence. Then I began to find that I could get answers by gentler means. If I'd be patient and listen carefully, I would eventually hear him mention something about his day at school. . . . Little by little be began to open up and let me have a glimpse of his inner self."

All three of these parents discovered for themselves an important principle in human relations: when someone is troubled inside, it's seldom helpful to probe, moralize, teach or reassure. More than likely, such messages, as well as any of the other Roadblocks, will stifle problem-solving.

NEW INSIGHTS ABOUT THE TWELVE ROADBLOCKS

Experience has shown us the kinds of difficulties parents have with the Roadblocks. Some come away from P.E.T. thinking they should never again ask a question, give information, offer solutions, give an order, or joke with their kids. Others find it almost impossible to understand why certain of the Roadblocks can be inhibiting—questioning, for example. Still others cling to the mistaken idea that anyone who has a problem always wants to be given a solution.

When the Roadblocks Are Not Roadblocks

We had not always made it clear to parents that the Roadblocks do not *inevitably* block communication or put down the child or damage the relationship. Perhaps in our zeal to influence parents to stop sending Roadblocks when children own problems, we instructors unwittingly projected a purist position: that parents must forthwith eliminate from their speech all the twelve categories of response we call Roadblocks.

Nothing could be farther from the truth. In the first place, it would be impossible! None of us is perfect. Even in situations where the Roadblocks do have a high probability of blocking communication or hurting the relationship, all parents will occasionally slip and send a Roadblock. I know I do. On hearing my daughter complain about some problem she is having at school or with a friend, I sometimes catch myself puffing up with admiration of my own wisdom, blurting out some piece of advice or gratuitously offering a solution to her problem. Fortunately, she seldom accepts my solution on these occasions, and our relationship does not seem to suffer perceptibly from my intrusions.

I'm sure other parents, with the best of intentions, also still send Roadblocks occasionally—and without dire consequences. The key word is "occasionally." If parents can learn to avoid the Roadblocks in *most* situations when their children have problems in their own lives, an occasional lapse will not be harmful to the relationship.

We did not stress enough in early P.E.T. classes that many times the Roadblocks are not felt by a child as blocking communications. These are the times when neither the child nor the parent has a problem—when the child's behavior is not giving him a problem nor is it giving the parent a problem. You'll recall that we locate such behaviors in the No-Problem area of the rectangular window:

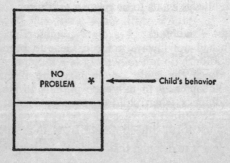

At those times when neither owns a problem, parents can send almost any kind of message to their kids without worrying about blocking communication or damaging the relationship. See how many Roadblocks you can spot in the following parent-child interaction:

> *Situation:* Dad and nine-year-old Karl are building a playhouse in the backyard.
>
> D: Hand me the hammer. Hurry!
>
> K: OK. It's here on the ground.
>
> D: If you keep taking my tools, we're not going to get this finished before dark.
>
> K: We need two hammers, so I can nail the bottom while you're nailing the roof.
>
> D: Hey, why don't you go ask Mr. Silas next door if we could borrow his?
>
> K: That's a good idea. I'll be back.
>
> D: Good boy!

In this situation Dad sent an Order, a Warning, a Solution, and a Positive Evaluation. Yet there is no evidence at all that their relationship is anything but pleasant and enjoyable. Now try to identify the Roadblocks in this second incident.

> *Situation:* A father and his sixteen-year-old daughter, Laurie, a budding local tennis champ, are discussing the relative proficiency of two professionals, Chris Evert and Billie Jean King.
>
> F: Billie Jean is the best, no doubt about it.
>
> L: I disagree.
>
> F: You're crazy, that's what!
>
> L: Chris beat her the last three times.
>
> F: Now, you're distorting the facts, young lady. Billie Jean had a two-year lay-off. You conveniently forgot to mention that.

L: So what? She said herself she was back in form.

F: You're biased toward Chris because she's closer to your own age. Right?

L: I am not! I just think she's the superior player.

F: How many times has Chris won at Wimbledon? Answer me that!

L: Yeah, but today there are many more top women players, so there's more competition.

F: Excuses, excuses! Your argument doesn't hold water. Hey, are you sure you're not influenced by that romance between Chris and your heartthrob, Jimmy Connors?

L: Oh, Dad! Course I'm not.

F: When you get good enough to beat your old man, I'll accept your judgment.

L: Bet you a quarter I beat you Saturday!

F: OK, cocky, you're on!

In this argument, Laurie's father used the following Roadblocks, some more than once: Name-calling, Negative Evaluation, Interpreting (Diagnosing), Interrogating, and Giving Facts. Did they appear to damage this relationship? Not at all, because father and daughter are operating in the No-Problem area; so were the father and son building the playhouse together.

At such times, parents and their children have fun together—kidding each other, competing in games, arguing, working at a common task. These are the times when most, if not all, of the Roadblocks seldom come across as roadblocks to communication. Parents (and kids, too) can safely give directions, teach, warn, give advice, affectionately call each other names, ask questions, joke, and even preach to each other.

But now a note of precaution. At any time when parents and children are interacting without a problem in their relationship, things can happen to move the relationship quickly out of the No-Problem area. Something said by the parent may hurt the child's feelings or put the child down; or the child might do something that gives the parent a problem. Suppose, in the situation where Dad and his son are happily building a playhouse, the son suddenly says, "Gee, Dad, you won't let me do anything—you're doing all the fun stuff." Or when father and daughter are arguing about who is the better woman tennis player, suppose the daughter stubbornly keeps up her barrage even after her father says, "I simply must stop discussing this because I have only fifteen minutes to finish the speech I have to give tonight."

In the first case, the father should switch immediately and listen to his son's feelings; in the second, Dad needs to send his own feelings. The principle: *Be alert to pick up clues that announce that the relationship is no longer in the No-Problem area, and stop sending Roadblocks.*

What's Wrong with Asking Questions?

We've learned that many parents resist the proposition that interrogating or questioning can be a Roadblock. It's a common belief that if you want someone to talk about a problem, you ask him questions. Consequently, it has not been easy to influence parents to give up this form of response. They say, "Physicians use questions, lawyers use questions, teachers use questions—and don't they get people to talk?" The answer, of course, is yes. But much deeper analysis is needed.

In the first place, questions can be threatening and shut off further communication as in the following exchange:

CHILD: I'm mad at Ross and I don't like to play with him because he always starts crying and wants to go home.

PARENT: What do you do to him that makes him cry?

CHILD: I don't do anything! (*Silence*)

Note that the parent's question contains an assumption: the child is at fault because he "must be doing something" that causes his friend to cry. No wonder he gets defensive and denies the accusation. When questioned, children often get angry, too.

In the following conversation the parent's question seems natural enough, but it also produces angry defensiveness:

> CHILD: I'm not hungry tonight. I just don't feel like eating.
>
> PARENT: What did you eat after school?
>
> CHILD: Nothing much. That's got nothing to do with it! (*Silence*)

Here again, the parent's question points the finger of blame at the child. Result: no more communication.

Questions have another inhibiting effect on communication; they tend to limit the child's next response, greatly narrow his options, or reduce his area of freedom. Take this brief interaction between a mother and daughter:

> D: I'm so miserable at school! All my friends can talk to boys, but I can't. I stand there like a dummy and can't think of anything to say.
>
> M: What do the other girls talk about?

By that seemingly appropriate question the mother unwittingly, yet quite predictably, has greatly restricted her daughter's communication. In effect, the question "programs" the daughter's next message. It tells her, "I don't want to hear anything else but what the other girls talk to the boys about," or "This is what I want you to talk about next—nothing else."

The problem here is that the youngster may feel like talking about some other facet of her problem —perhaps her feelings of inadequacy, her jealousy, her fear of being evaluated, her unsightly complexion, her feeling unattractive, or that she so desperately wants dates with boys that she becomes nervous and anxious. However relevant any one of these feelings might be to her problem, the daughter has to put it aside to respond to her mother's restricting question.

Not threatening or inhibiting are "open-ended" questions. They seldom inhibit communications. Examples:

"Do you want to talk about it?"

"What are your feelings about this?"

"Have you some thoughts about this?"

"What are your best guesses about what is going on?"

Someone once made a remark to me that wonderfully described why probing questions so often disrupt or inhibit people's communication: "Ask people questions when they have a problem and you'll get an answer, but nothing more."

Don't Kids Need Information?

Roadblock Number 5, "Lecturing, Teaching, Giving Facts," has always given parents some trouble. They don't understand why we classify giving facts and information as a roadblock or barrier to communications between child and parent. "When kids have problems," they assert, "naturally, they need information and want it." Or we often hear parents claim, "After all, parents do have more facts and information than youngsters."

Apparently we have not always dealt with this problem adequately enough in P.E.T. to clarify the confusions this issue so frequently generates in parents' minds. Perhaps I can now.

First, remember that what we call Roadblocks are the twelve typical verbal responses parents make *when the child owns a problem*—when the child is troubled, frustrated, afraid, perplexed, unhappy, or otherwise unfulfilled. At such times, giving facts and information *can* cut off further communication, produce resistance, and impede the child's problem-solving. There are many reasons why, at such times, giving facts and information *may* produce unfavorable results:

1. Kids (and people in general) are not ready to assimilate logic, facts, or information if they're in an emotional state and need to ventilate their feelings.

2. Often, kids already know the facts we so wisely offer them and resist being told what they already know.

3. Parents often come out with facts and information before they know what the real problem is. Hence, their facts are irrelevant and inappropriate.

4. Teaching and lecturing often makes youngsters feel that they're being patronized. The message they hear is some variation of "You're uninformed, but I am informed; I am smarter than you." Seldom do people respond warmly to that message.

5. Giving facts to a child who is experiencing a problem draws the parent into the problem-solving process as a participant. The message: "You can't solve your problem without my help." Often this is not welcome or it prevents the child assuming full responsibility to solve the problem himself and become more independent.

For all these reasons, trained professional helping agents (counselors, therapists) are extremely cautious about "teaching" people concerning personal problems. Other ways of responding are far less risky, and, in the long run, more effective. Competent helping agents rely more on *listening*.

But in some situations it can be helpful to give a child information—teach, if you will. While it's difficult to define these situations precisely, here are some guidelines:

1. When you're reasonably certain your information is relevant to the child's real problem.

2. When you're certain the child could not get access to the facts himself.

3. When you sense the child's readiness for your teaching—that is, he is "buying" you as a consultant.

4. When you're confident of the validity of your own facts.

I think that giving information or facts might be appropriate and/or helpful when a child says:

"I'm having trouble understanding the directions for assembling this bicycle. Can you understand that paragraph?"

"I don't think I want to put a Band-Aid on my knee, 'cause it might stick to the scab. Is there some way of not having it stick?"

"Since we moved I haven't been able to find my skateboard. I've looked all over."

I think that giving facts or information would almost always be ineffective and block further communication when a child says:

"I hate doing this math. It's just too hard for me or else I'm too dumb."

"I don't know how many kids to invite to my birthday party. I'm only sure of four of my friends that I definitely want to come. It's a big problem."

"I just can't lose weight. It seems impossible. No matter how little I eat, I still stay the same weight."

One final word about giving facts and information. You'll recall the section, "When the Roadblocks Are Not Roadblocks." The principal thesis was that when there is *no problem in the relationship,* most of the Roadblocks are not felt by children as blocking communication. Information-giving and teaching, being no exception, can be used by parents with little risk of hurting the relationship with their children, *as long as the behavior of the child remains in the No-Problem area*. That's the key point for parents to remember.

ADVANCES IN TEACHING PARENTS LISTENING SKILLS

Teaching parents the skills that will increase their effectiveness in helping children with the multitude of problems they encounter in life takes time. While most parents have little difficulty acquiring an intellectual understanding of the new skills, some must undergo a basic change in their attitudes before accepting the validity of the new skills sufficiently to begin putting them into practice at home. Strong resistance to the new skills is not uncommon. Now our experience in P.E.T. classes has provided us with more understanding of the various reasons for parents' resistance. So we have developed improved methods of teaching the helping skills.

I'll describe these advances in detail, but first I want to review the specific helping skills of P.E.T.

The Four Basic Listening Skills

From the earliest beginning of P.E.T. my objective was to teach parents all that I knew from my own professional training about being an effective counselor or helping agent. I wanted to "give away" to parents the very skills I employed as a professional counselor and therapist. They had worked for me— that I knew. Almost without exception, the youngsters I counseled responded positively to the communication skills I used.

Youngsters of all ages gradually opened up to me and talked freely and honestly about their feelings and their problems, commenting often that never before had they been able to talk to their parents that way. The particular way I talked to these youngsters often (but not always) resulted in their finding constructive solutions to their problems—without my giving them information, advice, or solutions. Whatever I did in these counseling sessions also fostered deep and loving relationships between the kids and me. To most of these young people I became someone very special in their lives. Some brought me little gifts at Christmas time; some brought their friends to meet me; almost all looked forward to their next session with me; and most hated to leave at the end of each fifty-minute session. If I could teach parents these potent communication skills, I thought at the time, parents should be able to produce the same outcomes as I. This was the challenge. Which is why we teach the following four listening skills in P.E.T.

Passive Listening (*Silence*)

A child will find it difficult to talk to you about what is bothering him or her if you are doing most of the talking. "Silence is golden" certainly applies to effective counseling because passive listening is a strong nonverbal message that conveys to the youngster:

I want to hear what you're feeling.

I accept your feelings.

I trust you to decide what you want to share with me.

You're in charge here—it is your problem.

Effective counselors stay silent a large percent of the time they spend with their clients. Passive listening encourages youngsters to share their feelings and often to get into deeper and more basic problems than the one initially presented. On the other hand, silence is not enough. When youngsters share a problem, they want something more than silent listening!

Acknowledgment Responses

While silence avoids the Communication Road-blocks that so often tell the child his messages are unacceptable, it does not for sure prove to the child that you're *really* paying attention. Therefore, it helps, especially at pauses, to use nonverbal and verbal cues to indicate that you're actually well tuned in. We call these cues "acknowledgment responses." Nodding, leaning forward, smiling, frowning, and other body movements, used appropriately, let the child know that you really hear. Verbal cues like "Uh-huh," "Oh," "I see" —what counselors humorously call "empathic grunting"—also tell a child that you're still attentive, that you're interested, that it's acceptable for him or her to go on and share more. Effective counselors use a lot of these acknowledgment responses as a natural expression of their interest and attentiveness.

Door Openers or Invitations

Occasionally, children need additional encouragement to talk about their feelings and problems, especially at the beginning of a session. Consequently, effective counselors frequently start with door openers or invitations to talk, such as:

Would you like to talk about it?

I'm interested in your thinking about that.

Sounds like you have some feelings about that.

Do you want to say more about that?

Notice that these responses are open-ended; they leave the door wide open for a child to talk about any aspect of a problem. The child is given a lot of freedom to decide just what it is he wants to share. And, of course, they convey no evaluation or judgment of what the child has been communicating previously.

Active Listening

The professional counselor's most effective skill, *by far,* is a type of verbal response which contains no actual message of the *counselor,* but only mirrors or feeds back the *child's* previous message. It is called Active Listening. It differs from Passive Listening in that the receiver, by feeding back what he hears, actively demonstrates that he truly understood the sender and also heard the words. He proves this to the sender by actually "feeding back" the meaning of the sender's message, in his own fresh words, of course. Here are some examples of parents' Active Listening responses to typical messages of troubled children:

1. c: I'm too dumb to learn arithmetic. I'll never be able to do that stuff.
    p: You feel you're not smart enough, so you doubt you'll ever get it.
    c: Yeah.

2. c: I don't want to go to bed in that dark room with all the ghosts.
    p: You think there are ghosts in your bedroom and that scares you a lot.

3. c: What do they do with people when they die?
    c: It sure does.

    p: You've been thinking about people dying and wondering where they go.
    c: Yeah. You never see them again do you?

4. c: I don't want to go to Bobby's birthday party tomorrow.
    p: Sounds like you and Bobby have had a problem maybe.
    c: I hate him, that's what. He's not fair.
    p: You really hate him because you feel he's been unfair somehow.
    c: Yeah. He never plays what I want to play.

5. c: (*Crying*) I fell down on the sidewalk and scraped my knee. Oh, it's bleeding a lot! Look at it!
    p: You're really scared seeing all that blood.

In each situation the parent responded to the child's message with Active Listening. Obviously, Active Listening is *not* silence (Passive Listening). And certainly it's entirely different from each of the twelve Roadblocks, because the parent is not sending a message *of his own*. The parent's response is simply a *feedback of the child's message*.

Because Active Listening is a new way of responding for most parents, we have found they need an understanding of what it *looks like*, not just the way it sounds. In P.E.T. we diagram Active Listening and encourage parents to retain this graphic representation in their minds.

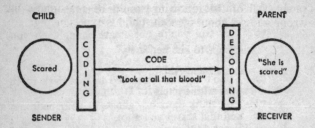

This is what ordinary person-to-person communication looks like. A *Sender* talking to a *Receiver*—in this case a child (with a problem) talking to a parent. The child has fallen down, scraped her knee, sees all the blood, and is scared. The child's fear, however, is a complex set of physiological and mental processes going on inside the child, where it always will remain—private and unobservable. To communicate to the parent how she feels, the child must select a code (symbol) that she hopes will represent (symbolize) what is going on inside her "bag of skin" (her organism). We call this selection act the "Coding Process." The code the child selects is what gets sent (transmitted or communicated) to the parent—certainly *not* the child's inner feelings.

Now, the parent, on hearing the code ("Look at all that blood!") must try to guess or infer what the child's particular code represents. So the parent engages in the "Decoding Process." The outcome of that process (in this case, an accurate decoding) emerges in the mind of the parent (completely inside the parent's bag of skin) as, "She is scared."

There you have the anatomy of the communication process. Looks simple, doesn't it?

Although this picture of person-to-person communication does remove a lot of its mystery or complexity, the process does not always work out so neatly. For one thing, the receiver's decoding process is *always* a guess or an inference—one never really knows for sure what's being experienced inside the sender. In our example, the parent might well have decoded inaccurately. All of the following would be reasonable but wrong guesses about what the child is experiencing:

"She wants me to kiss her knee."

"She wants a Band-Aid."

"She's angry with herself for falling."

"She needs a doctor."

"She's in terrible pain."

In our illustration, each of these inferences (decodings) would have been inaccurate; the child was experiencing only *fear*.

Your next question most likely is, "But how does the receiver know whether his or her decoding was accurate or inaccurate?" My answer: Most parents as receivers never do try to find out, but there is a very simple way they can. The method is Active Listening, and here's how it looks in our diagram:

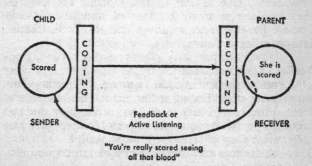

Active Listening is nothing more than the Receiver verbalizing a "feedback" of the results of his decoding process. It communicates to the Sender, "This is what I think you're feeling—am I right or wrong?"

Usually, if the Receiver is right, the Sender will then say something that confirms the accuracy of the feedback—like, "Yeah, I *am* scared" or "I'll say I am" or "Right!" or "I'm scared I'll lose all my blood" or "I'm afraid it won't ever stop." If the Receiver is *wrong* (has decoded inaccurately), as with, "You're in terrible pain," the Sender usually corrects the Receiver with a message like, "No, it doesn't hurt bad" or "No, I'm just scared" or "You don't understand." By feeding back—Active Listening—the Receiver has a sure way of checking on the accuracy of his *understanding of the sender's message*.

Before, you had a picture in your mind of the *usual* "communication process." Now you have a picture of the process of *effective communication:* the Receiver understands what the Sender means and, equally important, the Sender knows it!

Why We Teach Parents Active Listening

Because parents are so accustomed to warning, moralizing, teaching, questioning, judging, praising and reassuring, it's only natural that they wonder why they need to change their habits of talking to kids and to devote a lot of time practicing this strange, new way of responding. Our answer to this remains the same— they will derive many unexpected and often unbelievable benefits from acquiring skill in Active Listening—benefits to themselves, as well as to their kids.

Feelings Get Dissipated

People think they can get rid of feelings by suppressing or forgetting them. Actually, troublesome feelings are more likely to go away when they are expressed openly. Parents can help children express exactly what they're feeling by using Active Listening. Then the feelings often seem to disappear into thin air.

Feelings Become Friendly

"Feelings are friendly" is an expression we use in our classes to help parents accept that feelings are not "bad." By Active Listening the parent accepts the feelings, and this helps the child accept them, too. He learns from his parents' response that feelings *are* friendly, not bad or scary.

A Deeper Feeling of Caring

Being heard and understood by another person feels so good that it invariably makes the sender have warm feelings toward the listener. Children, particularly, respond this way. Also, the listener begins to feel warmer and closer to the sender. Listening empathically to another makes one understand that person and appreciate his uniqueness. The listener *becomes that person* momentarily when he puts himself in the other's shoes. Listening then produces feeling of caring and loving.

Children Will Start Listening to You

When someone listens to your point of view, it becomes easier for you to listen to his. Therefore, children will listen to their parents' messages if their parents first have heard them out. When kids don't listen to parents, it is often because the parents have not been good listeners themselves.

Children Will Become More Responsible

We know that talking out a problem helps you think it through. Active Listening is an effective method for facilitating talking, and it helps another find solutions to his problems. People need listening when they have a problem, and kids are people, too.

Active Listening will help a child think for himself and discover his own solutions. Messages of advice, logic, instruction, and the like convey lack of confidence in the child. Parents will see their children becoming more self-directing, self-responsible and independent.

You Will Learn to Trust Your Child

You will acquire more *trust* in the child's capacity to handle his problems and work through them. By watching your child solve his own problems, without your solutions, you will learn to trust his capacity as his own problem-solver.

You Will Become More Accepting

You will learn to accept his feelings, no matter how different they may be from what you think a child "should" feel. Acceptance, however, takes time to develop.

You Will Enjoy Being a Helper

So many parents have told us that Active Listening makes helping children much more enjoyable. Because they now have a tool that promotes the child's problem-solving and solution-finding, parents don't have to shoulder the burden of feeling that they always must provide the right solution. They can be counselors now, relieved of the full responsibility they felt in the past.

Your Child Will Be a Separate Person

You will be able to see your child as *someone separate* from you—a unique person no longer joined to you, a separate individual having been given by you his *own* life and his *own* identity. This "separateness" will enable you to "permit" the child to have his *own* feelings, his *own* way of perceiving things. Only by feeling "separateness" will you be able to be a helping agent for the child. You will be "with" him as he experiences his problems, but not joined to him.

You Won't Have to Be "Super-Parent"

Most parents labor under a common misperception that to be a "good parent" means you have to solve all your kids' problems, shape their behavior, call all the shots, be in charge, always be right, come up with all the answers, be totally responsible, and even assume all the blame for their failures—in short be Super-Parent! One mother spelled out her strong feelings about trying to be Super-Mother:

> "When I took the P.E.T. course I was able to give up being the controlling person. It's so much of a relief, you know, that you can give up the burden of owning everybody's problems, which I did. I was the 'problem-solver,' the super-mother of my whole shitty-assed world, I swear."

Other parents told us much the same story in different words:

> "You can saddle yourself with so many problems. If you're willing to take them on, people are willing to give them to you. . . . Now I accept the idea that you don't have to be perfect in every respect."

> "I used to have a very poor posture—physically. I stood like this, bent over. And I'm sure it's because of this sack I carried over my shoulder with everyone's problems in it. As I let go and let them own their school problems, work problems, car problems, I started to stand up straight. I really did. I've stood up straighter since. . . . I'd been trying to hang on, because that was my old behavior. The biggest thing I remember was that it was such a huge relief."

> "For me it was just the greatest savior to get the information that I didn't own the problems of everybody. It just opened the door for me to grow in all kinds of ways. Just a marvelous door opener."

> "I was a parent that was an overanxious, overprotective, preaching, moralizing, very heavy mother. I was just too much. I was bound to be a good mother, so I was going to help. Poor kids. I'm trying to change to a person who will really pull back and let them lead their own lives, but be there when they need me. That's not easy."

IV

BECOMING A LISTENING PARENT:
Problems and Solutions

Old habits are hard to break, and parents find it hard to resist the temptation to be interrogators, moralizers, and solution-givers. The new skill for some parents feels unnatural, and when they try it they often feel clumsy—like learning to cut meat left-handed when all your life you have held the knife in your right hand. Then, too, some children inexplicably won't open up and share their real feelings right away, which is discouraging to the parent who is so eager to see the new skill work. And then there are parents who try to use Active Listening at the wrong times—when they're too angry, too threatened by what they hear, or too strong in their own values and beliefs.

In this chapter, you will hear from parents who encountered such difficulties as they attempted to apply their newly learned listening skills in real situations at home. Whenever it seems clear why these parents ran into difficulty, I'll point this out and suggest how they might have avoided the problem.

ACTIVE LISTENING DOESN'T FEEL RIGHT AT FIRST

Some parents right at the start experienced difficulty with Active Listening. They felt stilted, self-conscious or phony; the idea of responding to their kids in a new way felt like a brand-new coat that didn't fit.

> "The Active Listening . . . I remember having a great deal of difficulty with it. I must have had a mental block. I couldn't do it. I couldn't really get into it. I think I was afraid of parroting or of my kids thinking I was trying to analyze them. . . . I was always a blank —just not hearing. . . . It seemed like everyone in class was Active Listening much better than I. I just felt I didn't have it in me."

A minister's wife, with a degree in Christian Education and the soft-spoken mother of two, said:

> "It was a mechanistic thing for me . . . it started as a gimmick. . . . And even if it felt like a gimmick I needed to try it. Then all of a sudden, the gimmick sort of went away and I wasn't aware of it being a gimmick. And then I was aware of the caring that really allowed it to be a real way of communicating."

A young father found it difficult at first because Active Listening seemed incongruent with his self-image; it was too passive a role:

> "For me it was very hard to Active Listen. I'm probably an example of the average young working father trying to get ahead, coming home tired. . . . You know, it was difficult because the average male has a concept of his role in the family as his being more of a domineering type. So it was hard for me to listen to some of their problems."

A mother told how unnatural Active Listening felt to her:

"I just remember that when I first started using it, I felt very strange. It sounded phony to me. . . . My kids seemed to open up fairly fast, but I just felt funny. . . . I guess it was because I never really listened to my kids before."

Other parents had similar reactions:

"I tried to Active Listen my twenty-four-year-old stepson last year when he was going through a broken love affair. I didn't think I was very effective. I felt awkward at it. . . . It sounded so dumb!"

"It was a very strange feeling. I remember sitting at the supper table. My husband, Jim, was very depressed about something at work and I tried Active Listening to him. . . . It first felt artificial, in some ways. And at the same time it felt good. And after a while, it didn't feel artificial anymore."

"I think I was very stilted at first . . . it was a new thing, you know. . . . Maybe I wasn't really feeling *with* him—just stilted at first. It's a new way of relating. . . . But there was enough success that I was encouraged, even though there were times when it was discouraging."

Plainly, Active Listening is a new way of talking —a new posture toward a person with a problem, a new way of responding to another human being. It's as different from the typical Roadblock responses as night from day. No wonder parents feel strange, phony, stilted, artificial, insincere, gimmicky. It's a rare parent who goes through this initial stage without Active Listening feeling unnatural.

I liken acquiring skill in Active Listening to learning any new behavioral skill—tennis, golf, dancing, or using chopsticks. The learner invariably feels clumsy and self-conscious. And with Active Listening, parents not only must learn a new verbal behavior, but unlearn old verbal habits. Fortunately, with sufficient practice and experience, most parents move through the initial stage into one in which the new skill comes to feel more natural.

At first, Active Listening *is* a "technique," employed quite consciously and deliberately—often mechanistically or without much accompanying feeling. Even so, as parents continue to use it, they begin to experience emerging feelings of caring and empathy ("feeling with him," as one mother put it). It's then that it begins to feel better, as expressed by the parents in the previous excerpts—"It was a new way of relating," "It didn't feel artificial anymore," "And then I was aware of caring which really allowed it to be a *real* way of communicating."

I have heard Active Listening criticized (mostly by professionals) as being a mechanistic technique that should not be taught to parents, because they will not have acquired the feelings of empathy and caring so necessary for being an effective helper (facilitator). The feelings must be taught first, so the critics argue. Our experience leads me to a contrary view: when parents learn the technique and use it continually, they begin to experience the requisite attitudes and feelings. The use of Active Listening, at first a mere mechanism, will in time make parents more genuinely accepting and caring of their children.

If this is a valid explanation of what happens, we can be far more optimistic than ever before about the feasibility of producing a society whose children will be brought up in a climate of acceptance, caring, and empathic understanding.

WHEN CHILDREN WON'T TALK

Confident in having learned how to Active Listen and with high expectations of using it successfully, many a parent finds that his or her child simply doesn't open up and freely communicate "as in the textbook examples we got in class."

"Sometimes, if I'm asking a question about what maybe happened at school, they really don't want to tell me. I'm ready to listen and there's nothing they want to say."

"She was sitting there all bunched up and sulking and I said, 'You don't look very happy.' She replied, 'Well, I'm not, and I don't want to talk to you.' And I said, 'You really don't want to talk to me,' and her reply was, 'No.' "

A father described this frustrating encounter with his twelve-year-old daughter, Kathy:

K: I hate you!

F: I believe you really do hate me right now.

K: I do! I don't know why I had to inherit all of your bad characteristics.

F: I know you're disappointed about that.

K: I don't want to talk with you.

Parents need not feel discouraged when, at one time or another, a child doesn't feel like talking or announces he won't talk. "You can lead a horse to water but you can't make him drink" contains a principle that is equally applicable to children's talking. There is no sure way to *make* kids talk. Certainly Active Listening won't. It is, however, the best skill I know for *facilitating* communication, provided the child feels a strong enough need to do so.

In fact, Active Listening is *not* always the best way to get a child to *start* talking. Simple door openers or invitations do a better job:

Would you like to tell me about your day at school?

Want to talk about what seems to be bothering you?

Would it help to talk about what has made you upset?

Once a child accepts your invitation to share his experience or feelings and begins talking, *then* Active Listening is the best way to let him know he's understood and his feelings are accepted. So Active Listening is an effective method for facilitating *further communication* from a child, after he's started to share a problem with you. Yet parents still need to be prepared for some children to stop communicating at any time.

Another important distinction needs to be made between Active Listening when it's the child who needs to talk versus using it when the *parent* has a need for the child to talk. In the latter situation, Active Listening is seldom effective, as in the first incident above when the mother seems to be revealing her own need to have her children talk about school. Recall her words:

> "Sometimes if I'm asking a question about what maybe happened at school, they really don't want to tell me."

Obviously, the mother wanted the children to talk more than they did. But children's willingness to talk to their parents depends on their developing a level of trust that what they reveal will be received without criticism, righteous indignation, put-downs, or threats. Sometimes that trust is not there at first, as this mother discovered:

> "She knew I was going to class to try and be a better parent, but somehow she didn't trust me, because I reverted to power and I still do. . . . It was sort of rough going there for a while, but I'd drop it when she clammed up and after a lapse of time I'd come back and tried to Active Listen to her. Then I felt she really did trust me. I mean I was sincere and I think she believed me then and gradually opened up. . . ."

Parents often forget that kids, too, have needs for privacy and at certain times don't want parents to know what's going on inside, as this mother reported after nine years of "practicing P.E.T.":

> "She'd come home from school and I'd be all happy to see her and I'd want to know what went on. But she's a very private person, and she'd say, 'Nothing.' And I would keep pecking at her, you know. . . . My husband feels very private about his feelings . . . and I used to climb the walls because he would keep so

much of himself inside and not share. So here's Leah coming home from kindergarten and it seemed innocent to ask her about school—how could she think of it as so private? My husband is much more open now, but Leah still has a tendency to be very private about her life. . . . Now I can see that she's just a very different person—that she doesn't relate the way I relate. . . . I think I just accepted the fact that I can't change her."

Kids are no different from adults—they sometimes don't feel like talking, they often resist probing interrogation, they won't talk unless they have trust that what they say will be accepted, and at times they want their privacy respected.

YOU HAVE TO BE IN THE MOOD TO LISTEN

Some parents get the erroneous idea in the P.E.T. course that they have an obligation, now that they've learned Active Listening, to make themselves available, no matter what, to listen every time their children have a problem. Only after they discover how many times they are not in the mood to listen do they adopt a more realistic expectation for Active Listening. They soon accept that you *can't* listen unless you feel like it. For one thing, parents run into the limitation of time, as revealed in these excerpts:

"I just may not have those five quiet minutes to Active Listen so they'll come up with their own solution. You know, I'm waiting for the doctor to call me back for something that's wrong with me, and I'm cooking in the meantime, and I'm expecting company in fifteen minutes. . . . You think, gee, I've got to Active Listen to this problem, but there's no time for it. And it's very frustrating . . . when the timing is wrong."

"He came in very angry yesterday from a big trip with his father. I told him he had to set the table, but he wasn't about to do that. He flounced about, saying he'd had a busy day, and he said, 'Nobody cares, just nobody cares!' And he walked out. And I had company and didn't have time to find out what was really bothering him. . . ."

Such situations are common in most homes, and they present parents with a difficult choice: do they meet their own needs or the child's? While each parent has to decide for himself what to do in each situation, some guidelines might be helpful:

1. Try to decide what to do on the basis of a quick assessment of who is hurting most—whose needs are strongest.

2. Try to figure out some way to do what you have to do and still listen to the youngster. ("I have to keep on getting dinner ready, but how about talking about it while I'm working?")

3. Set a time to talk later when you won't be busy. ("I'd like to listen to you but I just can't now. How about right after dinner?")

4. Acknowledge the child's feelings, then tell him how you feel. ("You're really angry and upset, and I wish I had time now to listen, but I'm so afraid I'm going to be late for my doctor's appointment.")

At times parents may not feel in the mood to use Active Listening—when they're uptight or worried about some problems of their own. To listen to another person empathically and accurately requires a very intense—really rapt—attention, and parents simply cannot respond with the necessary concentration if they're engrossed in their own feelings and problems.

One mother described a time when she simply couldn't listen to her daughter, Jan, because of resentment that had built up toward the youngster:

"I just didn't want to hear her, you know. Like I felt like a doormat—I resented her so much. I felt I had to give and give—and I wasn't getting anything in return. You know, I was bogged down myself and I didn't have any room for anyone else's problems."

A father describes when he isn't in the mood to listen:

> "I've learned to honor when you can't Active Listen. If things are in such an uproar, and I'm just so angry right now, you know, I can't really listen to anybody. Or just really upset in some way. Saying that I can't listen right now doesn't say I can't ever listen—just at some later time I might listen."

The key to one's ability to Active Listen effectively is probably contained in this analysis by a mother, a self-described "domestic engineer" with three children:

> "Active Listening has been a really useful tool with me—not only with my family but other places as well. If I feel loving toward other people, I do it naturally without even thinking about it. . . . But there are times when I really don't care how other people feel, and then I couldn't care less about using Active Listening."

The power of Active Listening to help children deal constructively with their feelings and problems is derived not from the *technique* (feeding back the child's message in your own words) but from the parents' attitudes of caring and acceptance sensed by the child. The technique is merely the vehicle for communicating those basic attitudes and feelings. When parents, for whatever reasons (lack of time, preoccupation with their own problems, anger or resentment), know they're not feeling acceptance and caring and therefore are not in the mood to understand a child's problems, it's far better not even to try Active Listening. If they do, children more than likely will not be encouraged to share their deeper feelings. In fact, these are the times when children clam up or say, "I don't want to talk to you."

I don't think children need parents who are *always* good Active Listeners; they do need parents who use Active Listening when they can genuinely feel understanding, accepting and caring.

Empathic listening is inviting someone else to drink from your cup. But if your cup is not relatively full, you will probably not feel good about sharing. Besides, the other person will be disappointed by the meagerness of what you offer.

"DON'T USE THAT ACTIVE LISTENING ON ME"

A number of parents we interviewed told about youngsters who at first strongly resisted Active Listening or even became irritated with their parents when they used it:

"I've tried mirror-talking [Active Listening] with Sarah. She's fourteen years old. And her reaction was, 'Don't you try that mirror-talk on me.' . . . My first attempt was absolutely disastrous. She just said, 'Don't do that to me.' "

"First time we used it with Pat, our sixteen-year-old— she must have been about twelve then—she didn't like it at all. She said, 'You're repeating everything I'm saying. You don't need to repeat it, I heard myself.' "

"With James, when he'd be complaining about something, I'd say, 'It sounds like you really don't like such and such.' And he'd say, 'Don't talk that way to me. I don't like that kind of talk.' "

What goes on here? Why does Active Listening, usually so effective in helping children vent their feelings and solve their problems, provoke such resistive responses from some youngsters? Our interviewers gave us some answers.

First, in most of the cases where parents ran into these initial reactions the children were older—in the teen years. This strongly suggests that these kids at first didn't like Active Listening because they had experienced so many years of receiving quite different kinds of messages from their parents. We get some clues to support this hypothesis in these excerpts:

"My children were fairly old, you know, teen-agers. They were kind of set in their ways. . . . And whenever I would say, 'You feel such and such,' it really bothered them. I could see a little red flag pop up and they would come back and say, 'You don't know how we feel.' "

"There are ways to ask questions, you know, and I guess they were used to my asking questions, so that wasn't as threatening as trying to use the Active Listening."

A father had this explanation for his kids' resistance:

"They could tell right away we were trying out things —mostly the Active Listening. When we tried to feed back what they're experiencing, they resented it. I think this is largely because they were already teenagers when we started it. And I think if we had done that when they were very young, from infancy on, we wouldn't have had that."

One effective way we have found to avoid the resistance of older kids to Active Listening is for parents to explain to the youngsters, before using the skill at home, exactly what their newly learned skill is all about. Some parents told us they showed their class workbooks to their kids, pointing out the list of Roadblocks, admitting how much the parents had used them in the past. This usually provokes a lot of good-natured discussion, as well as laughs from the kids. And after they know what Roadblocks are, youngsters better understand the Active Listening method and how it can be used.

Active Listening may sound strange to children for another reason. When they first try this new way of responding, some parents unconsciously get into the habit of prefacing all of their responses with the same phrases, such as:

"It sounds like . . ."

"You feel . . ."

"You're saying to me . . ."

"It seems like . . ."

Far less likely to produce resistance are short Active Listening responses that accurately reflect back only the child's feelings, as for example:

"You're afraid of thunder."

"Your knee really hurts."

"You're angry at your sister."

"You'd rather stay out and play."

"You don't like your soup too salty."

A simple rule that will help parents make their Active Listening responses more concise and direct is: *Begin with the child's feelings.*

OVERDOING ACTIVE LISTENING

Some parents discover that they try to listen too much, like this mother of four, speaking in her brightly colored office, cluttered with papers, books, and posters:

"I got so gung-ho that I Active Listened *everything.* I don't know why nobody said anything to me about about it. Finally, this girl said, 'You know, it's not even fun to talk to you, because you don't tell anybody about how you feel—you just listen. You use Active Listening all the time!' She didn't like it, she felt very uncomfortable. She felt like she was being psychoanalyzed. And I used Active Listening to be helpful—I wanted to be helpful—because I was 'big mother.' "

A father admitted to overdoing it when he said:

"Intellectually it was very easy for me to accept Active Listening—it was right on. But . . . becoming over-involved sometimes when there's no reason to Active Listen, I'd Active Listen someone to death. You don't necessarily have to Active Listen everything, which I tended to do just to work my skills."

A mother with four kids (all under five when she took P.E.T. three years ago) talked about her exhaustive use of Active Listening:

> M: I started out every morning. I said, 'I'm going to Active Listen today.' And by nine o'clock I was exhausted with Active Listening.
>
> I: Oh, really.
>
> M: Yeah, I really was. I ran it into the ground. I Active Listened when there was no point to it. I found it very tiring, because I was trying to think of it most of the time during the day. . . . I wasn't doing anything else—just barely doing the breakfast dishes and getting lunch.

Why do some parents grab on to this new skill with such fervor and then overuse it? Quite naturally some were trying to make up for lost time: "I'd been roadblocking my kids for so long—now I found a better way and I couldn't wait to try it out." Others failed to realize how much time and energy they could consume being a counselor for the people in their lives. Problems, especially with young children, can be inexhaustible.

For other parents, the reasons were more complicated. One mother, for example, came to an unusual insight that explained why she was overdoing it:

> "Using the skill, you know, you can be very dangerous. . . . It gave me more skill, more power to get stuff out of people. A lot of times I didn't give back. I was sort of a frustrated therapist. I wanted to be a shrink or something. So I just kept listening and listening and listening. I misused it. I just really misused it. . . . You know, I used it to manipulate other people."

Other parents eventually learned that they were using Active Listening every time their kids revealed a problem, no matter how superficial:

"I think one of the things you have to remember is that Active Listening is to be used when the emotions are running high. If you tend to practice it on things that are kind of casual, well, maybe they don't even need any response. . . . I think there's a tendency for people when they first learn Active Listening to come home and use it on things that are not really appropriate problems. I can see why it's frustrating. I can see my friends who have taken P.E.T. do that to me. I'll be saying something kind of casually and they will Active Listen. I know they're doing it and I don't really want to hear it then."

From the interviews with parents we have greatly expanded our understanding of what can happen when parents are given this important counseling tool. Certainly, it should not be used indiscriminately, and obviously not too frequently. Parents need some guidelines that might help them avoid the pitfalls experienced by those who did overuse Active Listening:

1. All problems kids experience are not serious enough to warrant a "counseling session." Your nine-year-old might say, "The peanut butter is so hard I can't spread it without breaking my bread." This hardly warrants an invitation for her to explore more deeply, as in "Would you like to talk about it?" or "You're really feeling frustrated."

2. Kids give clues when they're up against problems that are serious to them. Look for tears, withdrawing, pouting, strong anger or fear, radical shifts away from typical behavior (talkative child being unusually silent and thoughtful).

3. Before putting Active Listening to work, test the waters to determine if your youngster really wants a listener or sounding board. Try Passive Listening (silence) for a few minutes. Or send out a Door Opener such as, "Want to talk about it more?"

One mother of two teen-age girls, who also works as a volunteer with the youth in her church and has had additional crisis-oriented training in Listening, learned on her own when Active Listening worked best for her:

> "If you run into somebody who is really totally discouraged or has a tremendous burden or problem, it doesn't matter how simple or crude an Active Listening response is. They're not going to care what you're doing, because their need is so great to be listened to that the most elementary Active Listening response will bring results. . . . It's the difference between some superficial little problem and some really deep encompassing problem. With the latter they're not going to care how good you are at Active Listening as long as they feel it helps get their feelings in order. . . . When you really need Active Listening, you don't care how the other person accomplishes it."

LISTENING WITHOUT ACCEPTANCE WON'T WORK

It's a rather sure bet that Active Listening will turn out to be ineffective when it's used to change a behavior that is unacceptable to the parent. Parents forget that Active Listening should signal genuine *acceptance of a child*—a willingness to accept how the child sees his own world. If parents use Active Listening when they actually feel unacceptance, they reveal their lack of understanding of the fundamentals—the basic theory underlying P.E.T. This is the very point I underscored so heavily in Chapter II. I will say it again here: *Active Listening is inappropriate to change behavior of the child that is located in the bottom part of the Rectangle—the Area of Unacceptable Behavior.*

See if you can detect this mother's attitude of unacceptance toward her daughter, Dorla:

> "Dorla is a hard child to raise. . . . You know, with her anything is fine. She just doesn't care—she's pleased with anything—very happy-go-lucky girl. . . . We kind of try to Active Listen to her but she's hard to . . . you can't catch her. I mean she's very busy and wants to run out and play. We tried it. You can't start

a big Active Listening thing with her too much. The
main time she'll talk is at night in her bed, when we
tuck her in at night. You can sit on her bed and talk
to her forever then. But one time I found Active
Listening good with her is when she gets mad. She
gets real mad. . . . But I've gotten into the habit of
saying, 'You're really mad, Dorla.' And she said,
'Yeah, I'm mad.' I think it's good for her but it doesn't
go much further, and she seems to get better right
away now."

Here are clues why the mother feels her Active
Listening had only limited success with Dorla. She first
describes Dorla with faint praise—as a very happy-
go-lucky child sho is "pleased with anything"—"anything is fine" with Dorla. Could it be that the mother
doesn't really accept Dorla as she is? "She is a hard
child to raise," she confides. Perhaps the parent is in-
correctly using Active Listening to change Dorla, perhaps to make her more serious (less vulnerable, perhaps).

In this case, it seems to me that Active Listening
might have been employed inappropriately—as a technique for modifying the daughter's personality characteristics. Active Listening is a way of responding to
children when they confide to parents that they have a
problem. But it sounds as if Dorla really doesn't have
a problem—she's "happy-go-lucky" and "pleased with
everything." No wonder her mother can't "start a big
Active Listening thing with her." This may be a case
of *Mother owning a problem* (being dissatisfied with
or worried about Dorla's basic nature). Remember:
when a parent owns a problem, it is inappropriate
and ineffective to use Active Listening.

Here's another mother inappropriately using Active Listening. She offered the interviewer tea with
lemon and mint on a freshly polished silver tea set in
her immaculate, large home and related an incident
with her teen-age son:

"Our second son got into a great deal of trouble in
April. . . . And it had to do with some associates he

was with. It would be easy to point the finger at them and say it was their fault, but after all he *was* associating them—it was his choice of friends. . . . And we didn't like his friends. . . . One of the things that really was bugging us was that he would wear old ratty blue jeans to school. So, if he would ask where his blue jeans were, you know, I'd say, 'They really are your favorite pants, aren't they?' And he would say, 'Yeah, I like to wear them.' And I said, 'They make you feel good when you wear them.' And he would answer, 'Yeah, they make me feel I'm one of the gang.' "

This brief incident tells a lot. First, the mother admits she didn't like her son's friends—she felt unaccepting of his associating with them. With this underlying feeling, she was understandably "bugged" when her son wore "ratty old blue jeans" that made him feel "one of the gang." Now, let's put ourselves into this family situation when the boy asks his mother where his blue jeans are. Certainly that is no deep and serious problem! He merely wants to locate them. He only wants information, not a counselor. It's the mother who owns the problem—she doesn't want him to wear something that might cement further his identification with a group of boys she judges undesirable. Yet she employs Active Listening to get her son to talk about the problem *she owns:* "They really are your favorite pants, aren't they?" The boy never said anything about his blue jeans being his favorite pants. So why did the mother feed back? Obviously her true feeling is: "They're not my favorite pants for sure."

What should this mother have said? The P.E.T. theory, applied here, would require some message that would communicate to the boy that *mother* had a problem. (In Chapters VI and VII I'll demonstrate the skill of confronting children who cause parents a problem and I'll show what messages are most effective in influencing children to change their behavior.) The mother in this incident might more appropriately have told her son first where he could find his blue jeans and then confronted him with *her* problem:

> "I have a problem when you wear those jeans: I'm thinking it means you're associating with those boys I disapprove of and then I get afraid you're going to get in trouble again."

Whether or not such a message would influence the boy, nobody can predict, but at least it's an honest message that shows the mother's concern; it reflects her real feelings much better than the Active Listening.

The basic principle bears repeating: *Active Listening is a tool for communicating acceptance of a child with a problem, so that he is encouraged to talk about it and maybe find his own solution.*

ACTIVE LISTENING WITH A HIDDEN AGENDA

An additional cause for the failure of Active Listening in some families is that parents use Active Listening to bring about some preconceived outcome, usually unbeknownst to the child. In P.E.T. this is called "having a hidden agenda." One such hidden agenda that sometimes surfaces when parents employ Active Listening is their desire for the child to arrive at one particular solution valued by the parents. Their hope is that through Active Listening they will influence the child to come to the "right" decision. One mother described this incident:

> "It's raining and I want him to wear a jacket or a hood or whatever. And I said, 'It seems as if you don't want to cooperate' or 'It seems as though you want to go out and get wet and therefore miss school.' I don't get too far. I get ranting and raving and arguing from him. . . . He's negative and resistant and this is the way he's going to react to me."

And well he might react that way, when he hears the response his mother gave him. The clue to her hidden agenda is in the phrase, "You don't want to cooperate." That's tantamount to saying, "You don't want to do what I've already decided you should do."

Another incident reveals the parent's hidden agenda:

> "At dinnertime one evening my daughter was playing at the sandbox with four or five friends. I called her to come in for dinner. She began to whine and complain, saying she didn't want to come in. I tried Active Listening, saying, 'You really wish you could stay and play—you would like it better if you didn't have to come in.' She complained all the louder, saying she didn't want any supper and ending with, 'And I'm not coming in.' This brought a 'Get in here' command from me and she obeyed, crying all the while. *As I look back on this I can see it was really a loaded situation.*"

The mother's insight is correct—it *was* a loaded situation for the child. For mother was fixated on only one solution: her daughter has to come in and eat right now. With that hidden agenda it would be next to impossible for her Active Listening to come across to the child as empathic understanding and acceptance of her feelings.

Experience convinces me that Active Listening will never be an effective tool to subtly influence a child to accept a preconceived solution already chosen by the parent. To the child the feedback probably comes across as a sop, or an indirect way of inducing conformity and obedience.

Again, the principle needs reiterating here: *Active Listening is a tool to help a child find a solution to his or her problem, not a tool to get compliance to the parent's solution.*

Had this mother felt genuinely accepting, her Active Listening might have started a problem-solving process that could have gone something like this:

M: You really wish you could stay and play.

C: Yes, I hate to leave my friends, 'cause we're having so much fun.

M: You don't want to have to stop your fun with your friends.

C: That's right.

M: Can you think of some solution to this that you could accept?

C: Well, I could eat later. Or I might put my dinner on a paper plate and eat it at the sandbox.

No doubt other solutions might have been generated by the daughter. More important, the problem-solving process is taking place within the child. And that is what Active Listening is intended to do.

"WHAT IF YOU DON'T LIKE WHAT YOU HEAR?"

Because empathic listening is so effective in getting kids to express their real feelings, it's not surprising that they will sometimes say things their parents won't want to hear—such as:

"I don't like you."

"You love Jimmy more than me."

"I'm so unhappy—nobody likes me."

"I want to quit school."

"I cheated on the exam."

"Smoking grass is simply great."

"I got kicked off the baseball team."

"College is for the birds."

Some parents are unprepared for feelings like these, for a variety of reasons. They may have certain hopes and expectations for their children that they hate to see thwarted; they may have little trust in the ability of their youngsters to find constructive solutions to

serious problems; they may develop strong fears and
anxieties that their kids will get into legal troubles or
will do something that will damage their entire lives;
or they simply may find it hard to accept negative feelings of any kind, as with this father, a biology professor:

> "Well, the biggest problem for me all along has been
> dealing with negative feelings—accepting the kids'
> anger, unhappiness, disappointment. . . . It's left over
> from my parents who refused to admit that negative
> feelings existed. I grew up in a very happy family—
> superficially even more happy than it actually was.
> My parents just didn't like to admit there were nega-
> tive feelings. If we felt bad about something, we were
> supposed to go somewhere and when we felt better we
> could come back. . . . And so I'm no good at dealing
> with negative feelings myself."

The mother of five-year-old Laura tells how very hard
it was to accept her daughter's problem with kindergarten:

> "She kept talking about being sick or being too tired
> or she didn't want to get dressed in the morning. . . .
> Well, she was hysterical at the school thinking she'd
> have to stay—just determined she wouldn't. Crying
> so violently. . . . I just kept going back to 'Is there
> something in the classroom or something on the play-
> ground you don't like?' What came out was that she
> was lonely on the playground, she had to walk alone
> just watching the other kids. She'd ask some to play,
> but they were always playing with someone else. . . .
> I was so upset! I called Charles, my husband. He
> came home and talked to her, too. The main thing
> we wanted was for her to be happy at school. She had
> been at first. That's why this scene was so emotional.
> I think that's what's so hard for parents. The hardest
> thing about P.E.T. is that the child owns the problem.
> Because, it tears you apart. She was only five—five
> years old! And I thought, 'My gosh, she'll never like
> school if this keeps going on.'"

Perhaps even more frightening was this situation described by the mother of a teen-age youngster threatening to quit school and leave home:

> "She's saying, 'I hate school, I'm bored with school,' and 'I'm going to drop math or else I'll get an F.' Then later, 'I don't think I want to go to college, but I know you want me to go, and Dad wants me to go.' . . . I think she might have left home—at one point I worried because I thought she would split. She said, 'I can't wait to get out of this house—I can't wait to be on my own, 'cause this family drives me crazy.'"

At such critical times, some parents are sorely tempted to revert to their old ways of responding— sending Roadblocks:

> "It's really hard for me to listen to my daughter's feelings about being overweight, because I had the same problem. So it's hard for me to hear her clearly and empathize with her feelings. . . . She'll come in crying and my stomach turns because I went through the same trip—I still have to deal with the problem of being overweight. . . . I've become aware just in the last few months that I feel very resentful having to help her with that problem. . . . I Active Listen, but it doesn't work effectively. It becomes like a gimmick— a technique. Because I'm sitting there and my stomach is churning, and I want to say to her, 'Look, I don't like that part of you that doesn't have control over your overeating.' It's hard for me to be accepting. . . . I just can't do it. It's an impossibility for me."

Other parents find themselves throwing up their hands in defeat, not knowing what to do, as in this parent interview:

> "We're not really good enough at doing it to follow right through. I often find I'm stuck and I think, 'Oh, dear, where do I go from here?' I feel like I'm going in circles and I don't know where to go from there, so I have to drop the listening."

Some parents are more persistent—they hang in there somehow, perhaps not liking what they hear, yet determined to put Active Listening to its severest test. They just won't give up. Perhaps they have some source of inner faith in the Active Listening method; perhaps they stubbornly hate to give up. Whatever the reason, some parents (usually on their first attempts) found their persistence was eventually rewarded. I venture the guess that once parents stick it out and find that Active Listening really does work, they pass a critical stage in their learning, not unlike a novice skier who finally gets down to the bottom of a steep hill after a lot of falls en route.

Having taken P.E.T. twice, Lana's mother, who had described her initial fear that Lana would never like school again, managed somehow to keep going:

> "Oh, she then went on and said she was tired of cutting and pasting—her fingers hurt. This was where she always got her gold stars—for cutting and pasting. . . . And she said, 'Makes my fingers hurt.' And then she said, 'I don't like to sit all the time and do paperwork.' . . . That day she went to school. . . . It was like once she got it out she felt better about it. Even though the problem was still there, it was just like it was a relief, that she could get it out and that we told her we understood that she felt bad about going to school."

The more trust a parent develops in the capacity of children to cope with their problems constructively and find their own solutions, the more successful that parent will be in sticking with the Active Listening skill, even when he or she doesn't like what a child is revealing. I don't think we know how to give that trust to every parent. Some have it even before they learn about P.E.T. Others develop it after they try Active Listening and see it work. But some hang on to the notion that you can't trust kids. One articulate and opinionated mother of four (three teen-agers)—the same mother whose son wore "ratty blue jeans"—shared her lack of trust openly in this interview:

"I'll tell you, basically I don't agree with the P.E.T.
method of treating children like adults, because children
by definition are not adults. They do not have
the experience to enable them to always make wise
decisions concerning some things. Some decisions they
can make. On certain decisions you just absolutely
cannot let them make their own decisions, because it
isn't fair to them. They haven't had the experience to
know. I don't think a sixteen-year-old knows what
college could mean to him. I don't think a sixteen-
year-old girl in the moonlight can have any conception of what it would be like to bear an illegitimate
child. So I don't think she should be given the freedom of choice to be romantic and swept off her feet
at sixteen."

While this way of viewing children is not at all
uncommon with parents who have not been exposed to
P.E.T., it is rather rare with parents who have. What
can be said to such parents? Can they be helped to
develop more trust in the problem-solving capacities
of their children? Perhaps. At the very least, I can share
the learnings I have acquired from my own experience
and from the parents who told us what happened in
their families.

You'll Never Know Whether Kids Can Be Trusted Until You Trust Them.

If parents never try the Active Listening method,
they'll never know whether a child can solve his own
problem or handle his feelings constructively. When
parents respond to a child's problem with Roadblocks,
they deny that child the chance to work through his
problem and earn his parent's trust. Roadblocks tell
the child, "You really can't be trusted to solve your
problem." (You *must* do this, you *should* do this, you
darned well *better* do this, let me tell you *my solution*
or give you *my advice,* you need *my facts* and *my
wisdom,* there's something *wrong with you* even to have
this problem.)

The Roadblocks Will Prevent the Child Finding Out What the Real Problem Is.

In case after case, parents who relied on Active Listening watched their child move away from the *presenting problem* ("I'm not going to college," "I hate kindergarten" or "This family drives me crazy") and eventually focus down on the real or basic problem. Parents without trust quickly jump in and try to solve the presenting problem with orders, threats, advice, solutions, or moralizing, completely unaware of what the real problem might be.

There Is Plenty of Time to Share Your Knowledge and Wisdom, If It's Needed.

Children are painfully aware of their parents' greater experience and knowledge. In fact, most children greatly overestimate how knowledgeable and wise their parents are, in turn denigrating their own capabilities. Making one's knowledge and wisdom available to a child (or to another adult, for that matter) is a matter of timing. If you Active Listen right at the start, you may help the child discover the real problem. Then the child just might solve it without any of your knowledge and wisdom; or you might find the child only wanted to get his feelings off his chest and needs no solution; or if he gets stuck and can't find a solution, you can always ask if he would welcome ideas or suggestions. By waiting, you have greatly increased the likelihood that he'll be ready for your contributions, and you'll have practiced a principle of good teachers and effective consultants:

> People would much rather discover their own solutions; they're more ready to accept another's only after they have failed to find their own.

THE TEMPTATION TO USE ROADBLOCKS

Apart from the fact that it's hard to change old habits of responding, I think parents use the Roadblocks

for another reason. They're anxious to get rid of a
child's problem as quickly as they can. Either they
don't feel like taking the time to listen or they get very
uncomfortable hearing that their child has a problem
("Not another problem!"). Most of the Roadblocks
give people an illusory feeling that they have dispensed
with the problem. Unfortunately, the Roadblocks seldom get rid of problems. One mother put it this way:

> "It first felt very strange. Because it was easier to
> tell them what to do. Active Listening was tough, par-
> ticularly with a very young kid fooling around. A lot
> of times I really didn't want to listen to them you
> know, I just wanted to tell them what to do and have
> them get the hell out of my way. Because I was un-
> happy a large share of the time, you see, and I didn't
> want any more problems."

Another parent recognized her own impatience as a
barrier to listening:

> "It's easier to come up with a solution, and more
> expedient. It's so much easier to say, 'Why don't you
> just go do this?' They may say, 'Hey, that's a good
> idea!' and the problem is solved. It's over with, you
> know. . . . I may not have those five more quiet min-
> utes to Active Listen in such a way that they can come
> up with their own solution. . . . Yet when I look back
> on it that's what I should've done, because it helps the
> child grow up. I know for myself that when I had a
> problem I went to my mother or father or older sister
> and they said, 'This is what you should do.' And so at
> thirty-one years of age I am just now learning how to
> solve my own problems. And I still have trouble some-
> times. . . ."

Some parents try to get rid of problems by reassuring and sympathizing right away, as with, "Oh, I
don't think it will be that bad" or "You'll find a new
friend soon" or "Thunder can't hurt you." It's as if
they cannot tolerate their children feeling bad. They
want to hurry and get rid of the feeling—it hurts too
much to see the child troubled. But children's feelings

rarely go away when parents jump right in to reassure.

This does not mean that there is no place at all for reassurance. Reassurance can be helpful, but only sometimes and only *after the child knows his feelings* have been understood, as in the following incident reported by a parent whose daughter dreaded going to the dentist:

> "Sue just flew off the handle. She didn't want to have braces. Her friends had a dentist that gave him something—a spacer, I think—and he didn't have to have braces. I said, 'Maybe you'd like to go and talk to Tim's dentist and see if he feels your teeth are developing and he could do something so you wouldn't have to get braces.' She just flew off the handle, saying, 'I don't want to do that.' I went back to her room and said, 'You're really feeling uptight about seeing the dentist.' And she said, 'Yeah, I'm afraid that I'll have shots.' At that point I said, 'I had braces for two years and never had a shot—shots are usually given when you have your teeth pulled. Mike's had braces for a year and a half and he's never had a shot.' And so between the Active Listening and my consultation she was feeling so relieved by the time she got into bed."

This mother used enough Active Listening to communicate empathy and acceptance, which freed her daughter to express her fear of the shots (the real problem). Because the youngster appeared uninformed, the mother gave her facts that seemed very germane to the child's problem. It's important enough to emphasize again: only by helping your child get to the real problem will you come to know what facts might be appropriate.

SOME GUIDELINES FOR IMPROVING YOUR LISTENING SKILL

We learned a lot from our interviews about the difficulties parents experienced as they tried to put their newly acquired listening skill to work in the home.

When parents use Active Listening, the results are not always what they hope for, nor do they turn out like the textbook cases the parents had read in the P.E.T. book. Active Listening, while simple in theory, is not always easy in practice. So it should be useful to provide guidelines for parents who have difficulties with Active Listening and want to improve their skill.

1. *Know when to use Active Listening.*

Remember that Active Listening is only a technique so you can better communicate your acceptance and empathy. Use it when you're free enough of your problems to feel accepting and want to help your children with their problems.

2. *Know when not to use Active Listening.*

It won't work when you're feeling unaccepting of your children—when you own the problem. Nor will it work to influence them to change some behavior you don't accept. Don't try it if you don't have the time or aren't in the mood. Don't use it as a technique to manipulate your children to behave the way you want them to behave.

3. *Competence comes only with practice.*

Parents won't become competent at Active Listening without lots of practice. Practice with your spouse and friends, as well as with your children.

4. *Don't give up too quickly.*

It takes time for your children to realize you really *do* want to understand and you *are* accepting their problems and feelings. Remember, they've been accustomed to hearing you warn, preach, teach, advise, and interrogate.

5. *You'll never know the capabilities of your children unless you give them a chance to solve their own problems.*

Start, if you can, with the attitude that your children can solve their own problems without your direction or solution. You'll be surprised how your trust will grow.

6. *Accept that Active Listening at first will feel artificial.*

It undoubtedly feel more gimmicky to you than to your children. With practice, you'll feel more natural and less clumsy.

7. *Try using more of the other listening skills: passive listening, acknowledgment responses, and door openers.*

Every response of your child does not need feedback. Use Active Listening primarily when feelings are strong and the child's need for acceptance is apparent.

8. *When your children need information, give it.*

Just make sure you first know what the real problem is before you give information. Check with your children then to see if your information is wanted. Give your information briefly. And, of course, be prepared to have your ideas rejected—they might not be appropriate or helpful.

9. *Avoid pushing or imposing your Active Listening on your children.*

Listen for clues that tell you they don't want to talk or are through talking. Respect their need for privacy.

10. *Don't expect your children to arrive at your preferred solution.*

Remember, Active Listening is for helping children with *their* problems—a tool for helping them find *their own* solutions. Be prepared for times when no solution surfaces—your children might not even tell you how they later solved the problem. They will know, but you won't.

V

HOW FAMILIES CHANGE WHEN PARENTS BECOME EFFECTIVE LISTENERS

When parents begin to get more effective at using Active Listening in the home, they find it hard to believe that it works so well—in many different kinds of situations and with children of all ages. From initial skepticism in many cases, parents come to appreciate the amazing power of this simple way of communicating acceptance and understanding. "I wouldn't have believed it if I hadn't seen it happen with my own eyes," one parent remarked. Her statement represents the attitude that came through in so many of our interviews. Often parents reported incidents involving very brief encounters requiring only one or two Active Listening responses. Other families worked through longer incidents involving complex problems and deep feelings.

THE MAGIC OF "I HEAR YOU"

Active Listening, you'll recall, demonstrates to another person that you not only listened but you *heard*.

The effects of that message often make it seem something magical has happened. This was brought out clearly by a minister who told of this brief incident with his fifteen-year-old son, Arnold:

"When we first tried this [Active Listening], I happened to be the observer, and I thought it was so fantastic. . . . My wife had just said something to Arnold when we were sitting on the patio. And he just turned to Liz, my wife, and screamed loudly, 'You just bug the hell out of me.' The veins just stood out on his face—it was the first time I'd ever seen this side of my son, because you know being the P.K., Preacher's Kid, he was kind of the symbol of what all nice boys and girls should be. Now here he was screaming at about ten decibels of sound. And Liz just looked at him and said, 'I get under your skin, huh?' And if you could have watched the expression on his face! He was expecting her to jump back at him with an equally loud and bombastic and critical statement. And when it didn't come back . . . he went from about ten decibels down to a conversational tone and said, 'You sure do, Mom.' But the next statement was the significant one—he said, 'And I suppose I get under your skin, too.' I couldn't believe it! Something that could have been a holocaust for two hours, and perhaps noncommunication between them for a day, was solved in just a matter of minutes . . . just because one person dared to say, 'I hear you.' Not, 'You're wrong,' but, 'I hear you.' "

A similar incident was described by a mother, a clinical psychologist, in whose home relatives were visiting:

"The granddaughter—she's about two and a half—looked out the kitchen window and saw the swimming pool. She'd apparently just learned to swim, so she started jumping up and down excitedly, 'I want to go swimming, I want to go swimming.' There was no time for swimming and the weather wasn't right for it, so the child's mother and grandmother all started sending Roadblocks: 'No you can't go in now; we're not prepared for it; we've got to get back to the city; we'll find some place to swim tomorrow.' Anyway Margie just yelled all the louder. I was at the other end of the kitchen and wondered if I could get through to Margie. So I said, 'Hey, Margie, you really feel bad that you have to wait until tomorrow to go swimming, don't you.' She said, 'Yes.' And that cut it off like a knife. And let me tell you, her grandfather was so embarrassed he grabbed a pencil and piece of paper and said, 'What's the name of that book again [the P.E.T. text]?' (*Laughter*) It's so neat! She just needed to be heard. And you have to see it to believe it."

The value of one "I hear you"—as opposed to numerous suggested solutions—is apparent in this quick interchange:

"Our daughter has trouble getting to sleep at night, even though she's tired. She comes into our room several times, complaining that she's worried that if she doesn't get her sleep she won't do well on a test she's having the next day. We offer the suggestion that she lie in bed and rest and we reassure her that she doesn't really need so much sleep, and other such suggestions. Last night the same thing happened, but instead of offering solutions, I said, 'You're really having a problem getting to sleep.' She said, 'Yes,' and left our room and did not reappear."

A six-year-old came into the house with a bleeding knee from skating, crying loudly. Her mother tried Active Listening:

M: Come in and sit down.

C: I don't want to.

M: Hmm, bad knee, huh? How 'bout a Band-Aid?

C: I don't want one.

M: Well, then take off your skates.

C: No, I want to go out skating again.

M: You don't want me to do anything, right?

C: No, I only wanted you to know I got hurt.

M: You want me to see your cut and know you got
     hurt.

C: (*Very definitely*) Yes!

Immediately, the child turned and left to go back
skating.

Then there was the three-year-old frightened by
thunder during a storm:

> "She got very upset hearing this thunder and seeing
> the lightning—mainly the sound. She came crying to
> me, saying, 'I'm afraid—I don't like the thunder.' I
> started out with Roadblocks, saying 'It's just the clouds
> bumping into each other.' But she kept crying and
> saying, 'I don't want to hear it, I'm afraid.' I said, 'It
> won't hurt you, it's just a noise.' Still more crying.
> Then it came to me—Aha, Active Listening! We had
> the lesson the week before. So I said, 'You're worried
> about the thunder and you wish it'd stop 'cause it
> scares you.' Her expression changed immediately. All
> the worry went away, and she went trotting off with-
> out another word. That was the end of it! She just
> wanted me to understand how she felt. And that was
> the end of it. It was just a beautiful example—just
> trotted off, that was it!"

The same happened with Tommy, age two. His mother
described it this way:

> "He'd gotten to be a big crier about being hurt. In
> preschool he hangs out with other little kids that have
> a habit of coming in and saying, 'I got an Ow-wy, got
> an Ow-wy,' yelling and crying loudly, you know, wait-
> ing for those hugs and sympathy. Tommy was pick-
> ing this up. The next time he came in with one of
> those little Ow-wy's—and it wasn't severe—I said,
> 'Wow, it looks like that really hurts.' La-di-da, he
> just went off. That was it. And I've used that since on
> him."

What's the source of this seeming magic of Active
Listening? Something does happen inside a child when

he feels "I've been heard," but what is it? Because we can't see it, we can only hypothesize.

Perhaps the child needs to be "accepted" as a real person—a person who hurts, or, at other times, is scared, disappointed, sad, lonely. Or maybe children need only to be recognized or acknowledged or confirmed by another—much like when they're doing something *satisfying:* "Look, Ma, no hands!" or "Hey, Dad, I can stand on my head!" Perhaps they need it also when they tell us, "I'm scared of thunder" or "I cut my knee." In any event, we have found in Active Listening a consistently powerful tool for responding constructively to children with a momentary problem.

FEELINGS ARE TRANSITORY

Parents are often surprised how quickly a child's feelings go away when he is heard. This holds true even for very strong and deep feelings. Listen to Bobby, three and a half years old, who hated peas; his father, an early skeptic of Active Listening, tried it to prove it didn't work, and reported:

> "One time Bobby said he didn't like the peas. And instead of saying, 'Eat the peas, Bobby' or 'Shut up,' I said, 'Bobby, you just don't like the peas.' And he said, 'Oh, I guess I do.' I just couldn't believe it! But he ate the peas, yeah. It was unbelievable. . . . It was the first time I'd used it."

And here are Cathy and a friend who were crushed when Cathy's mother's guide dog punctured a ball they were playing with:

> "My daughter Cathy's friend had been given a little imitation football. But Franz, my guide dog, had a fixed notion that all balls are intended for amusement. So the first bounce and Franz leaped into the air and punctured it, leaving nothing but a limp rubber container. The little boy was heartbroken and wailing loudly. His parents jumped in with, 'Oh that's

all right, we'll get you another one tomorrow.' That didn't do a thing but make the yelling louder. I said, 'You're really upset that Franz would pop your ball, aren't you?' And he said, 'Yes.' And then he went off and found something else to play with. The promptness with which that satisfied both the kids!"

Parents who learn to listen with empathy and understanding to the remarkable flow of feelings that kids express cannot help but discover how transitory these feelings are. Most of us have been brought up to think otherwise. If someone says, "I hate you," we're crushed; we believe we've permanently lost a friend. In P.E.T., however, parents are taught to distinguish between a child's *feelings* and the *code* he selects to communicate those feelings. They are not the same.

When a child says, "I hate you," he's using those words as a code for expressing some feeling he is experiencing at the time—e.g., *angry* because you won't give him candy, or *frustrated* because you won't play with him, or *deprived* because you won't buy him an expensive toy. Here's where Active Listening is helpful; it gives parents a specific method for responding to the child's feelings, not his code. Our diagram of Active Listening may help clarify this point:

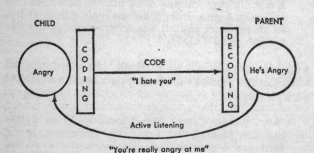

By *coding* the child selects a code for his verbal message. By *decoding* the parent makes an inference from the child's code: what is he feeling inside? By con-

sciously using Active Listening a parent trains himself
to respond to the child's feelings, *instead of the code*,
which so often is more jarring or threatening to parents than the feeling, but which is the real thing that
needs to be dealt with.

One mother and father of four (ages seven to
thirteen) seem to understand this process in this excerpt
from their interview:

MOTHER: And there were times when Chuck was
           little and was really mad at me. He said,
           "I hate you." And that just about killed
           me! I really felt my life was over as a
           mother. But now it wouldn't bother
           me. . . .

FATHER: Yeah, she used to come in and talk to
           me, completely deflated if he'd said some-
           thing like that. It would take all the wind
           out of her sails, with no place to go. . . .

MOTHER: I learned not to take what they say per-
           sonally as being against me, but instead
           to just realize how they're feeling. . . . Now
           they're getting a chance to express their
           feelings and to be heard . . . and a chance
           to know those feelings are OK.

HELPING KIDS ACCEPT REALITY
AND LIMITS

Life for kids confronts them with limits and re-
strictions. In fact, life can be cruel for kids. Active
Listening is a very effective tool for helping them accept
limits and adjust to the harsh realities of life. A father,
a biology professor who had grown up in a "happy
family," told us about the time when his nine-year-old
was helped to deal with his feelings of deprivation over
not being able to buy a new bicycle:

"He very much wanted a new bicycle—a dirt bike
like all the other kids around here. . . . He got the
idea he would trade his old bike in, so I helped him

polish it all up and he took it down to the store and he picked out this one he liked, and the guy told him his bike was in great shape and would give him thirty dollars for it. But the one he wanted was ninety-five dollars. He was just crushed when he came in, but he was holding it in, not saying anything about it. When he came home I said something like, 'Bob, you must be terribly disappointed about this; it's really hard to take when something like this happens.' And then he just broke down and cried about it. . . . Then he sort of moped around and didn't know what to do. I told him again that I understood how he felt and that somehow I knew he could deal with it, and when he felt like it to come out and help us dig in the garden. He came out a half-hour later, and he was just ecstatic all afternoon. He was so turned on. . . . Here he had suffered that crushing blow, but his feelings had been accepted and he probably realized he could deal with them. Somehow, it made him just feel real good about himself. . . . I think it's just great through the course to be more aware that it's OK to feel negative feelings; and it's a good thing to let them work it out themselves and just accept their feelings without pushing them out of it."

One mother told about using Active Listening with her three-and-a-half-year-old son, Tod, who was having problems following his father's death:

"Dealing with my own grief was task enough, but I had a high investment in helping my children deal positively and creatively with their father's death, too. . . . Tod's initial and repeated response was, 'I know Daddy died, but when will he come home?' Or he'd want details, asking, 'Is he dead on the bed?' or, 'Where did they put him?' or 'How did he get to God? In an ambulance or in a hospital airplane?' Two months after Frank's death we went to Florida . . . and I recall Tod crying and being upset our first night there. He awoke from a very restless sleep and gasped, 'Daddy's dead; he died.' It went like this:

M: You seem very upset.

T: Yes, I miss Daddy.

M: You're probably remembering the fun times we've had here.

T: Daddy took me swimming and we went to Disney World.

M: I guess it was kinda hard to come to Florida and to realize that Daddy wouldn't be here to have fun with us anymore.

T: Yes, I really miss him.

"After that, Tod's reaction was not always what I expected, nor even wanted to hear, but I learned the importance of respecting and accepting his feelings. I'm sure he was able to accept Frank's death with less anxiety and upset than I expected."

Parents learn in P.E.T. that they don't have to give in to all their kids' wishes or demands. Active Listening provides a tool for handling kids' pressure. In this dialogue between Alice and her mother, note how the mother started out using Roadblocks, to no avail:

A: Can I have a present because I'm sick?

M: No. We can't give you presents just because you aren't feeling well.

A: Well, Janey got a present when she was sick.

M: Well, Janey was really sick and was in the hospital. You're not that sick.

A: That isn't fair, that she gets a present and I don't!

M: Alice, we just can't get a present every time you don't feel good. We don't have the money to buy things all the time like that. You have other things at home to entertain you.

A: I want a present. It's not fair!

M: You really feel gypped when Janey gets a present and you don't when you're sick.

A: Yeah. (*Pause*) Can I have a present?

M: No.

The mother added, "And that was it! No more arguing, no going around in circles. All it took was for me to Active Listen once and she accepted the answer. . . . I don't think she felt like she lost, even when she didn't get what she wanted. She just wanted me to know her feelings."

Helping children understand and accept life's limits and life's blows through Active Listening undoubtedly gives many parents an alternative to *permissiveness*—giving in to children's demands and pressures to be given whatever they want, whenever they want it.

Even with infants, Active Listening may foster acceptance of what has to be—as in this incident, which I admit amazed me as much as the mother, especially in view of how young the child was:

"At this time she was probably about fourteen months —she's five years old now. Kay would take her nap in the afternoon, and of course she was in diapers, and and she'd have her bowel movement sometime during her nap. She'd wake up and her skin would be red and angry looking—very sore. When I changed her it hurt a lot, and yet it had to be changed. She'd kick and fight and scream at the top of her voice and wouldn't hold still for me. She was preverbal and so I couldn't really talk to her or reason with her. But one time I thought I'd try to reach her on a feeling level (in the book it says infants can sometimes be reached). So I just turned my attention up to her face rather than at the diaper and said, 'I know it hurts (very calm, very reassuringly), but this has to be done. We have to clean this up.' . . . And then she calmed down. She still kinda cried a little because it still hurt, but she wasn't fighting me and kicking, you know, trying to get away from me. . . . Well, I really felt amazed."

A fourth-grade teacher and mother related how she used Active Listening when her three-year-old son became angry because he couldn't have a piece of pie before dinner:

"He just started to whine and raise his voice . . . said I was a naughty girl and that he didn't like his brother, Clark. . . . And he said, 'I don't like this house.' I responded with, 'You're unhappy with this house right now, and you don't like your brother either.' So then he picked up his Snoopy and his Pooh, and said, 'I don't like these, and I don't want to play with them.' He was really hostile and angry. . . . And I just said, 'You're just unhappy with everything right now.' . . . Finally he took his toys and slammed them down. And I said, 'You're feeling like nothing is pleasing you right now.' He kept saying he didn't like me, didn't like the house, didn't like this and that. I said, 'You're just unhappy, nothing in this house is making you happy.' That lasted a couple of minutes, and then he just kinda wandered over and leaned against my leg and said, 'Mommy, I'll have my pie after dinner.' And that was it, you know. Instead of putting the clamp on his anger, I just used P.E.T. to allow him to dissipate it, and it went away just like water on the ground. . . . I was happy with my role in this interchange, because I didn't get upset . . . because I had a tool and I just let him get it all out."

As with this mother, Active Listening provides parents with a new way of responding to the angry and hostile feelings kids so often feel when they can't get everything they want everytime they want it. It gives parents "a tool," which they learn to use in lieu of the Roadblocks, and the result in most cases is that the child gets all his feelings out in the open. In time they usually dissipate.

Nothing can be more frightening to a child than the prospect of going to the dentist, where he is sure he'll suffer pain. In this incident, Active Listening seemed to help Phillip face the ordeal:

"Phillip had to get braces. One day on the way to the dentist he said he had a stomachache. The conversation then went something like this:

M: You're nervous about going to the dentist.

P: Yeah, I really don't want to go.

M: You really wish you didn't have to go now.

P: Yeah. I'm really scared about getting shots of Novocain. I wonder if I'm going to have to get a lot of Novocain shots from the orthodontist.

M: Oh, you're worried that he's going to be like the dentist and give you Novocain to have your braces put on.

P: Yeah.

M: Well, I don't think so. But it's kind of scary not knowing what to expect.

P: (*Looking relieved*) Yeah. It's scary not knowing what to expect. . . . I really hate pain. I'm really scared of pain. But I know I shouldn't be.

M: I wasn't aware of how you felt. Yeah, pain is fearful and most people are afraid of it; even boys and men are afraid of pain every bit as much as girls and women.

"Well, he went in and had his two-hour appointment. Every time we go to the orthodontist now he complains a little, but he's getting better each time, so he just kinda goes in though."

"I DIDN'T LIKE KIDS"

An unexpected effect of using Active Listening, at least for some parents, is that they get to like their children better. This probably comes about because Active Listening fosters greater understanding of another person—what's inside, what he's really like. And when we really understand others, it's difficult not to like them. A mother, speaking in her beach-town apartment, said:

"I could never relate to kids before. I used to shut them off. Not only my own, everybody's. I didn't like kids. It's probably because I didn't know how to relate to them—how to talk with them or listen to them."

Another mother told us what happened to her when she first tried Active Listening—how she found out her preschooler, Warren, "did have something to say, not like he's just a kid":

> "If he was starting to get in my way and under my feet, I'd just pick him up and put him on the counter. He was delighted that I was putting him right there with the dishes and talking to him and getting my dishes done. He was having a ball, bursting bubbles and talking to me. I kinda learned that he did have something to say—not like he's just a kid and what does he want to talk to me about, and do I have to go through all this baby stuff. . . . He'd explain to me what his pictures were that he drew, which gives me a big kick. . . . He explains everything he draws, what it is. Or else he talks about his two friends, Billy and Carl down the street. . . ."

This mother was finding Warren much more interesting —she was actually enjoying the conversation, much as she would with another adult. Her attitude is all the more remarkable, considering what she told us a few minutes earlier:

> "I was ready to take Warren to a psychologist, because I thought there was something wrong with him. No child could be this rotten and horrible! But it's not like that anymore. It really changed our whole lives, for all of us."

GETTING DOWN TO THE REAL PROBLEM

Rarely do kids start right out in a conversation to share what's really bothering them. They begin talking about something superficial or on the surface—what professional counselors call the "presenting problem." Not understanding this about kids, parents typically start sending Roadblocks, such as questioning, giving advice, teaching a lesson, moralizing or judging, which keep the child focusing on the presenting problem. As I pointed out previously, this prevents a youngster from progressing down to the deeper problem which is really bothering him.

To put it another way: untrained parents move in to help their children *before they even know what the real problem is*. They are so anxious to solve what they think the problem is that their anxiety interferes with the child's telling them what is really bothering him.

But when parents learn to Active Listen, they facilitate what we describe in P.E.T. as "moving from the presenting problem to the basic problem." This is working for the divorced mother of Mark, aged four, who got terribly angry at his brother.

> "Mark started having really bad nightmares the end of December, and got pretty bad asthma. The pediatrician put him on medication and said he'd have to run a lot of allergy tests. But the medicine didn't do much to clear it up. Sometime in February I had the P.E.T. course. I had Mark for the weekend and his breathing was terrible—really, really bad. Right before he went to bed, I sat in bed with him and started rapping, saying, 'Something really seems to be bothering you.' He'd had a scene with his brother who'd torn up some of Mark's projects. Mark screamed at him and got hysterical and ran into his room. I said, 'It seems to make you upset when you scream at Timmy.' He said, 'Yeah.' I said, 'It's OK to scream, don't worry about it.' And that didn't do a thing. So I went back to the Active Listening. He said, 'When I scream, my bones are going to break.' He pointed to his ribs . . . he started coughing from his asthma and said, 'Do you hear? It's breaking, it's breaking, and the house is breaking, too.' He was referring to the house where he lives with his father. And he started getting all choked up and his asthma was getting real bad. And I said, 'You think that the house is going to just break down.' And he told me he had a dream in which the house broke and everything was broken: 'And I was just there with my room and my toys—and Daddy wasn't there and my bones were broken.' So I took a wild stab and said, 'You're really sad because your family is broken.' And he just started crying and cry-

ing and I was holding him and letting him cry. And
when he was done crying, his breathing was like a
million times better. And he wanted to talk all about
why my husband and I left each other. But I said,
'The family is broken up and that is making you mad.'
He kept saying, 'Not mad, sad.' And I said, 'Yeah,
and you think everything is breaking up and you'll be
alone.' So I started telling him how it was decided
where he was going to live. . . . And he really liked
hearing that—he wanted to hear that two or three
times that night. I explained how Daddy and I both
wanted him, but if he lived with Daddy he'd have his
same room in a big house, but with me he'd have a
tiny room in my apartment. I acted out how my husband and I argued, 'I want to take Mark' and I said,
'No, I want to take Mark.' And then he got this big
smile—his breathing was clear. It was like a miracle!
Unbelievable . . . And I went over once or twice during the week and went through the story again with
him—the whole scene. He liked hearing it, and he
cried again. . . . It was really coming from inside of
him. And each time his asthma seemed to get better.
And there's not a sign of it now! There's nothing.
No coughing, no breathing problem, nothing. It's incredible!"

And incredible it often seems to me, too, when I
hear stories like this from parents, documenting the
amazing power of Active Listening. In the interviews,
parents described many such incidents, all of them too
numerous to summarize here.

There were many incidents involving children not
wanting to go to school—they developed stomachaches
and headaches, they threw tantrums, they cried, and
they hung desperately onto their mothers at the school
steps. Active Listening helped these parents find out
what the real problems were, as in this incident:

"In January she started not wanting to go to school.
So we discussed it at our P.E.T. class. We were at a
loss, to tell you the truth. . . . She'd wake up in the
morning and say she didn't feel good and she'd better
stay home 'cause the other kids might catch what she

had. . . . Then one morning it was a stiff neck. I told
her, 'OK, you get dressed and you go with me to the
school, and if you don't want to stay, I'll bring you
home.' . . . When it was time, the kids lined up to go
into the classroom, and I told Joan it was time for
her to go in, but she screamed, 'No,' and burst into
tears and ran back to the car. So I took her home,
but I was determined I was going to Active Listen.

". . . I said, 'Joan, it sounds like you really don't
like school—you're not happy there.' And she just
kept saying, 'I don't feel good, I don't feel good.' She
didn't really say what was bothering her at first—she
kept going round and round. And then all of a sudden she started talking about the fact that she never
got a candy bar at school! It turned out the teacher
was giving candy bars if a kid reached a particular
score—it had to do with the reading objectives. It'd
been going on for a couple of weeks. . . . This was
what triggered it. . . . It was supposed to be an incen-
tive but Joan was working as hard as she could—she
was the youngest in her class and with kids who
scored high on the test. But she had perception problems, so she and one or two others in the class were
the only ones who didn't know how to recognize the
alphabet. . . . She didn't feel like she was very valued
—she couldn't earn a candy bar."

Joan's parents promptly initiated talks with the
teacher and the school psychologist and Joan was
placed in another class. The mother concluded, "And
then it was beautiful, because she wasn't low on the
totem pole. . . . It was over in a month. . . . She likes
school and she's doing real well. It's really neat!"

This same mother describes how she used Active
Listening to help her four-year-old son get down to
the real problem:

"I was baby-sitting another child who had been a
real friend to Tim. But after a while Tim started to
become extremely antagonistic toward the child—
constantly fighting. I'd say such things as 'Mary
doesn't really like it when you call her names.' Or,
'It hurts when you hit Mary.' Or, 'I can't have you
hitting other children.' "

These Roadblocks failed to help Tim with his problem, which lasted for a couple of months. One day, after Tim pulled Mary's hair and his mother made him go to his room, Tim put on a real temper tantrum—"the biggest one I've ever seen," she reported. Finally she got him calmed down and said, "Just quit screaming and let's talk about it." The conversation then proceeded as follows:

M: Tim, you're really mad at me, aren't you?

T: No.

M: Tim, did Mary do something that made you mad?

T: No.

M: You don't like Mary.

T: No.

M: You think Mommy spends too much time with Mary.

T: Yes. You love Mary more than you love me!

M: You really think I like Mary more—that she's more important to me than you are—that I like Mary more than you, because sometimes I get mad at Tim and you don't see me getting mad at Mary as much.

T: Yes.

The mother then explained to Tim that he was very special to his daddy and her because he was their son, and his sister was very special to them because she was their daughter, and Mary was very special to *her* parents because she was *their* daughter. Tim then settled down and began naming all his special friends, saying they were very special to their mommy and daddy because they belonged to their parents, too.

Then the mother talked about the Active Listening she had used:

"I was aware I was trying to use Active Listening. I was never aware of listening for the child's feelings before we took P.E.T. I only listened to his words, not the message underneath. The most I've gotten out of P.E.T. is the Active Listening. . . . I was very aware I was trying to use Active Listening—trying not to blame, or say, 'You shouldn't hit Mary' or 'You're a bad boy.' "

DEVELOPING SELF-RESPONSIBLE KIDS

One of the most satisfying rewards parents derive from Active Listening is watching their children become more self-responsible. Empathic and accurate listening communicates to the child a number of attitudes:

I'm not going to take over your problem.

But I will help you find *your* solution.

I really have faith in your ability to handle this problem constructively.

You're not loved less for having problems—they're a normal part of each person's life.

These attitudes, it seems, exert a powerful influence on kids to assume responsibility for handling their own problems, rather than remain dependent on their parents. Parents often tell us that they're amazed to discover how capable and resourceful their kids are when given the chance (and the responsibility) to solve their problems in their own way. One mother, a graduate student in psychology who had taken P.E.T. early in her parenting career (when Alice was two), described this situation with Alice, now ten:

"Alice is a pretty well-behaved kid in school, but the teacher had been around to sections in the room where there were a lot of boys causing a lot of trouble. . . . She came home in tears the other day—just a flood that lasted for about fifteen minutes. 'It wasn't fair'; 'I hate my teacher'; 'He's terrible'; 'He doesn't listen to anybody.' Because he'd moved her one final time and she was really angry about it. She tried talking to him but he wouldn't listen. After she got all the anger out she calmed down. I said, 'If he won't listen, what ways can you think of that might get his attention . . . ?' She said, 'Well, I might write him a note.' So she sat down and wrote this note that said, 'I feel like you're punishing me by moving me around.' It just blew my mind because I didn't really realize she could do that. So she wrote this note saying it made her feel angry, it wasn't fair treatment for being good and she wanted to be given a choice of where she sat for a while and she realized how hard it was for him to listen to everybody with so many kids in the class. She took it in and, my God, that teacher read it, and he let her choose where she wanted to sit! I couldn't believe it!"

Another ten-year-old daughter also surprised her mother with her capacity for self-direction:

"I think she's growing in her ability to handle her own problems. Before, I wouldn't give her her own problems to solve. I'd try to help her in some way. She and her friend had been to a meeting and she was telling me all these terrible things about Barbara and what Barbara had done. 'Barbara called me a bad name and she hit her little sister and knocked her down.' I was only part-way responding, you know, not even trying to Active Listen, but not really responding verbally in my old way. And right in the middle of saying all these terrible things about Barbara, she walked over to the phone and called Barbara and said, 'Barbara, I'm sorry for what I did and want to apologize.' I was kind of amazed when she did that because here I thought it was all Barbara's fault, you know, blaming everything on her."

One mother reported this interaction with her son Jerry, eight years old:

J: Mom, what would happen if someone was playing in someone's yard and they broke their clothesline?

M: Sounds like you're worried, Jerry.

J: Yeah, I didn't know the person, I just ran away.

M: You're worried because you ran away?

J: No, I am scared! What can they do to me?

M: You're afraid what they might do to you for breaking their clothesline.

J: Not just me, Alan was there too, and we were playing on the clothesline next door to Teddy's house and it broke so we just ran away and now I'm afraid they'll find out it's broken.

M: Wow, sounds like you're really upset, Jerry!

J: Yeah, Mom, what should I do?

M: You'd really like it if I would tell you what to do.

J: Oh, I know you won't, it's my problem. . . . But, Mom, if you were me what would you do, Mom?

M: Well, Jerry, if I were you, I guess I'd have several choices. I could just forget it ever happened, and since you don't know them they'd probably never find out who did it. Or I could ask Dad to help me fix it. Or I could go and tell them I broke their clothesline and would be glad to try and fix it. Then again, I could ask Alan to help me fix it. There are many things I guess I could do, but at this point, Jerry, I'm not sure just what I would do.

J: Oh. (*Silence*)

"Jerry then went into the living room and began watching television. I just assumed he was going to forget about doing anything. A lot of time passed and Jerry got up and went outside. About fifteen minutes later Jerry came running in the door, very excited."

J: Oh, Mom, I decided to go over and tell those people that I broke their clothesline and that I was sorry it happened and that I could try and fix it. Well, Mom, the man was so nice he said,

"Oh that thing always breaks, don't worry about it, but thanks for telling me." Isn't he nice, Mom?

The mother added a postscript:

"When Bill came home, Jerry felt so good about himself he repeated the whole story to his dad. That was a very exciting moment for Jerry. He felt so good about himself and both Bill and I felt so good about him. He was able to make a decision on his own and one that had not been forced on him. There are so many changes that have taken place in the past two years since our family has been living P.E.T.! Our children have been the best advertisement and do the most P.R. work for P.E.T. because they're continually singing its praises."

This shows how parents can present alternative solutions to children, yet still keep responsibility with them for deciding which (if any) they will accept. First, Jerry's mother effectively used Active Listening to help him "define the problem" (Step I of the Problem-Solving Process). But then she chose to participate in Step II, "generating possible solutions." Then she backed out of the problem-solving, allowing Jerry to complete Steps III, IV, and V: "evaluating the solutions," "making a decision as to the best solution," and "implementing the solution." With young children, especially, there are times when it may be beneficial to offer some alternative solutions they might not think of themselves. Even so, usually it's better for a parent to wait and see if a child can come up with his own solutions first.

"THEY'LL GROW MUCH FASTER THAN YOU THINK"

Many parents reported amazement at how fast their children learned to solve their own problems, when given the chance. Before taking P.E.T., the parents we interviewed so consistently jumped in to take

full responsibility for their kids' problems that they
never found out just how much their children could do
for themselves. Even infants learned how to take care
of themselves and solve their own problems, as illustrated in these two incidents reported by the mother
of a twenty-two-month "baby" boy:

"He'd come over a lot and say, 'Want a drink of
water, I want drink.' Before, I'd get up and give him a
drink. Then I realized the kid can stand on the toilet
and get a drink himself. But I never thought of that
for children that young. So the next time he wanted
a drink, I said, 'I'm really tired. . . . I don't feel like
getting you another drink—I just don't want to get
up again.' He kind of looked at me with his little baby
face, and I said, 'There's a cup in the bathroom on the
sink.' And he went into the bathroom, and by himself
he climbed up on the toilet and got himself a drink.
And he's been doing it ever since. Now he'll go to
the refrigerator and take an apple instead of begging
me. It's kinda like he feels a need and then sees first
if he can solve it himself. . . . It saves a lot . . . and
he's self-confident about things like that now—very
proud of himself. . . . It helps him grow—not so dependent on other people. It's super. It's super!

"Like going potty. He came over and told me he
needed a diaper change. And I said, 'You know I
just don't like doing that anymore. . . . You're too
big and you could go potty like Christa can go potty.
. . . She's potty-trained, so have her show you what
to do.' Now this is the honest truth: the other day I
go into the bathroom and there's Christa with her
baby talk talking to Jimmy, who's propped up there
on the toilet—this little kid on this monstrous toilet.
Propped way on the edge and holding on. Christa is
holding his hands for him, babbling to him, 'Go potty,
go potty.' Well, you know, I think he and Christa
are going to solve this by themselves. I'm not going
to step in at all. I had a terrible time potty-training
my older kid, so I'm just not going to step in with
my M&M rewards, or whatever. . . . I'm finding a
lot of freedom in this new way. . . . They grow much
faster than I ever gave them credit for . . . grow much
faster than you think they will."

A parent told how she was able to transfer responsibility from herself to her two youngsters. Result: both daughter and son learned how to use the sewing machine!

> "When Bob was about thirteen, he wanted me to sew something. I said I wasn't willing to sew all his stuff for him, and he said, 'Can you teach me how to use the sewing machine?' So I did. Then Frances wanted to learn. She was so young I was more hesitant about her, but I taught her how to wind the bobbin and how to regulate the stitches and all that business. So they learned to use it. Bob learned to patch his pants himself with these wild patches; Frances made doll clothes on it. I'm totally released from all that process. . . . The sex-role stereotype things are what we've done away with. . . . I've also taught all my kids how to bake cookies and cakes."

The P.E.T. skills influenced parents to have much greater respect for the potentialities of their children, and with this came a new way of seeing their children:

> "I think parents never have the feeling that children are capable people. You know, we just think of them as *children*, and the concept of children equals inability to deal with life."

How the rewards from this new helping posture accrue to parents as well as the children is illustrated in this interview:

> "When she'd come in with a conflict she was having with some other child in the neighborhood, I decided I would just stay out of the problem and by Active Listening to her and not sending any of my solutions I kinda freed her to solve it in her own way. And it was amazing to me that she was capable of solving these problems, and coming up with such beautiful solutions."

One parent, after first interfering, finally decided to bite her tongue and put full responsibility on her son for solving a conflict in which he and his friend, Michele, had become engaged in a bitter battle of spitting on each other. Michele's parents also got heavily involved trying to get the problem resolved. Mike and Michele eventually worked through the conflict alone and resumed their friendship. That night, Mike shared his feelings with his mother. She reported:

> "After Mike told me about how the problem got resolved, he said, 'You know, Mom, it wasn't your problem or her parents' problem. It was a problem between Michele and me. You don't ever see adults running around asking a little kid to solve their problems.' And I said, 'No, you don't.' So he says, 'Then why should adults come around and try to get into our problems?' And I said, 'That's kind of confusing, isn't it?' And he said, 'Yeah. It wasn't the adults' problem, it was Michele's and my problem and if everyone had left us alone, we could have figured it out.' And I said, 'Wow!' "

Another parent talked about what happened when she gave solutions to solve her son's problems:

> "I think the reason he got so angry with me is that he always heard me giving an answer or a prescription, 'Well, do this and this.' And then, if it went wrong, he could blame me. But if it went right, he'd never get any credit for it. . . . People would like to have thought a good solution was their idea, but if it goes badly they can blame you. . . . I didn't think he really wanted to launch out on his own and make his own decisions. When I look back on it now . . . those kids are making tremendous progress—many more decisions on their own than they've ever made, just in the last couple of months."

A father talks about how much relief he experienced when he stopped feeling responsible for solving his kids' problems:

> "It's just a strain to constantly have to be responsible for somebody else's behavior, or feel that you are.

Now we don't have to feel that way anymore, and it's really neat. . . . I don't have to solve everybody's problems, because I can't. I make mistakes. Now I don't have to feel I have to be omniscient and take care of everything. I tried, but I was a miserable failure. . . . I feel now I've taken the weight of the whole world off my back."

When parents constantly jump in to solve their kids' problems, they're fostering dependency which leads to even more demands from the child. As one mother put it, she became a "slave" to her child:

"Things are nice with Alan. I don't feel I'm his slave anymore. I've always felt pretty tied to preschoolers. I think I used to like having them depend on me—it made me feel important. After a lot of years, though, it also gets to be a bore and a drag. I'm finding a lot of freedom in this other way of doing it—letting them grow faster, faster than I ever gave them credit for. Before I rationalized by saying he's only a baby. Now that he can do all these things on his own, he doesn't have his slave anymore. He seems to like it."

The temptation to be Super-Parent and take over the ownership of a child's problem is understandable since children often seduce or pressure their parents to give them answers or tell them what they should do. A mother told us how her eleven-year-old son tried to transfer responsibility to his parents for solving a serious problem that had him paralyzed with indecision:

"He signed up for football, and as he got into it he found out it really wasn't his thing. But he wasn't willing to admit that, initially. After he went through the physical exam and got his uniform, he started getting stomachaches right at four-thirty, just before football practice. Or he'd get a hangnail or the toe would hurt or he twisted his ankle in bed. . . . He managed to get on the team and that was important to him, but there was this unwillingness to really say, 'I really don't want to do this.' But I want to tell you it was really damned hard, because he kept wanting to put the problem on me or he'd put it on my husband. There were times when we felt like telling him to quit the whole thing—it was really hard to remain separate as he was struggling through all this. And we could feel what he was going through. At such times I really got tensed up, but my husband would say, 'Let's hold off and just listen.' It took him two months, but he finally decided he'd take the responsibility for himself. It was really tough. But he walked up to that coach and told him that he felt he needed to quit. It was like a whole burden had dropped off the shoulders of this little eleven-year-old. Even though he kept wanting us to decide for him to quit, we refused, and I'm really so grateful that we did."

A similar incident occurred in another family. This one was about a child's ambivalence toward judo lessons:

"Ken, who was about eight, was taking judo lessons. A week or two after the course started he got very upset about it. He didn't like the instructor and all the physical requirements he had to go through. He was in a quandary about whether or not to stay in, and he came to me and asked me whether or not he should quit judo. Of all our children, he was the one for whom I had made the most decisions. So this was par for the course for him to come to me and ask, 'Should I quit or not quit?' But before I decided for him, which would have been my normal pattern— you know, to tell him he started it and should see it through—I said, 'You really have mixed feelings about whether to go on with judo.' I started to Active Listen, but he just couldn't mobilize himself to decide —he was so unaccustomed to making his own decisions. . . . I said, 'You're unhappy with judo.' And he said, 'I don't like the instructor—he pushes us around and he's mean to us, and I don't know how to tell him. . . . And I'm also afraid that you and Daddy will be upset if I stop.' He got very impatient with me, demanding that I tell him what to do. 'Why can't you just tell me what to do and I'll do it? . . .' I was afraid of abandoning him, but I did not decide for him. It was scary, but I refused to decide for him. . . . A week later, when judo came up again, he decided himself that he wanted to stop. As soon as he realized

that I didn't have a hidden agenda for him to stay
with the lessons, then he quit himself—he made his
own decision."

You can see the struggle parents go through when
they try to hand over the reins of their children's lives
in the face of strong demands from their kids that their
parents keep hold of the reins. P.E.T. apparently provides parents with the courage and the skills they need
to break out of this "parent trap."

PARENTS GET NEW INSIGHTS ABOUT THEMSELVES

When parents begin using Active Listening, they
often hear feelings and ideas from their children that
cause the parents to gain new insights about themselves and how their behavior has been detrimental to
their children. In the following dramatic incident, a
dentist father learns how his high expectations had
been making his oldest daughter feel bad about herself:

"My twelve-year-old felt very compulsive in school—
if she didn't get 100 percent in all her courses, she'd
be a failure. If she came home and told us she got
only 89 percent, before I'd have said, 'Well, too bad,
maybe next time you'll be able to be a little sharper
and study harder.' Before the last parent-teacher conference, Sally was extremely upset because she had
dropped two percentage points in English. . . . And
I said, 'You know, it sounds like you're a little upset.'
And she replied, 'You're going to be very disappointed. . . . I didn't work hard all quarter.' And I
managed to say, 'That must be kind of a letdown for
you.' And that went on for almost a half-hour. She
was in tears, almost expecting me to get mad. And I
just said, 'You're really going to do what you want to
do; I just hope you satisfy yourself; no matter what
your grades are, I like you.' She was sobbing and
I was holding her and she finally said she liked me,
too. . . . In the half-hour we talked I found out she
didn't like a certain teacher, and I found out why she

didn't like him. I found out what girlfriends she was having an argument with—I mean we covered everything. It just blossomed into a real discussion in which I didn't really have a feedback [Active Listen] very much—just every once in a while to let her know I was listening. . . . She was so emotionally drained, that's why she started crying and I sat and held her for a while, telling her I didn't expect fantastic results in school, because no matter what, I liked her. And that's basically what P.E.T. has done for me. Because the way it was when she first started school, we really expected her to be superhuman and an achiever. And if she didn't perform, I think we made her feel we didn't like her. . . . As a parent, I was a classic—'thou shalt perform,' 'thou shalt never make a mistake,' 'I demand that you perform perfectly because I can't accept anything else.' And it's really been great since."

"I'D BE BETTER OFF DEAD"

None of the stories submitted by our sample of parents more clearly illustrated the dramatic effects of Active Listening than this account of a mother's first experience using Active Listening at home with her eight-year-old son, who felt his life was rotten and "he'd be better off dead."

"My story is simple in the telling. The ending is so obvious in retrospect that I still have trouble believing that I never saw what was happening—what I was causing to happen—before Parent Effectiveness Training and Active Listening.

"While I was enrolled in the course, my oldest child, a boy then eight years old, began to make frequent remarks to the effect that his life was really rotten, that he'd be better off dead—really 'heavy' statements that filled me with deep concern. I have had one clear and unwavering goal in raising my children, and that has been that they should feel positive about themselves and be able to wake up in the morning feeling that they really loved being alive; had I been primarily concerned with some other aspect of their growth—intellectual abilities, getting them to behave 'properly,' anything else—this development might not have hit me as hard as it did. But it was the case that my oldest child, and only son, appeared to be feeling exactly the opposite of what I had so greatly hoped, and sincerely endeavored, to have him feel.

"When the P.E.T. instructors introduced the list of 'Roadblocks,' I laughed with everyone else; it was so easy to hear myself using every one of those 'stoppers,' and to see right away which were my 'favorites.' I learned about Active Listening and dutifully practiced my skills with fellow class members. But, I didn't put 'two and two together'; the solution was right in front of me, and I didn't see it. I never did see it until after I'd done it.

"A few weeks later my son walked dejectedly into the kitchen while I was preparing dinner and dropped another of his depressing pronouncements. I was not very adept at Active Listening at that point; my few previous attempts at using it at home had sounded ridiculous, but I decided to give it a try. He'd say something like, 'Boy, I sure don't like my life very much,' and I'd feel the wheels churning madly inside my head, trying to transform those words into a feeling statement that I could feed back to him; then I'd say something which struck me as totally unsuitable and unimaginative such as, 'Sounds like you're really feeling down.' He didn't seem to notice my incompetence; he let go with another 'Nobody cares about me,' and another 'You and Daddy are always doing things with Jennifer and Rebecca (sisters),' and another. I was thinking, 'This is the most depressed kid I've ever seen,' and about how if his words were tangible things, we'd have had garbage strewn all over the kitchen, and I was feeling guilty sometimes and then angry and then frustrated, but I continued to say, 'Hmmm,' and 'You're pretty sad about that,' and 'You think we like them better than you.' It all sounded pretty contrived to me, and I didn't think we had much chance of arriving at one of those Hollywood endings in the P.E.T. book. He wasn't saying any of the 'working-toward-solution' things the children in the book say; he just continued to dredge up more and more distressing situations. The child went back to things that happened when he was about three years old!

"Forty-five minutes later I said that I wanted very much to continue what we were doing but that I was becoming concerned dinner was going to be late and that perhaps we could set a time to get back together again. He said that was OK, that he was finished, and he *hopped* down from the stool where he'd been sitting and went outside *whistling!* I was dumbfounded. Then it hit me; I'd never allowed that child to have a bad day! There had always been some explanation for an unhappy moment, something we could do to make it better, and he'd held on to every one of them! I had never extended him the simple sympathy from one human being to another that would have enabled him to let them go.

"That was a year ago; there has been no recurrence of apparent depression. There have been unpleasant or discouraging incidents. Never do I explain them away or offer solutions; I mutter my Active Listening responses as best I can. Life is not all glorious and rosy; all problems aren't immediately dissolvable; some days everything seems to go wrong, and that's all right. It took me eight weeks and cost me sixty-five dollars to figure that out and to discover the disastrous consequences of trying to make it be otherwise for my children—not a very high price, considering. . . ."

VI

NEW INSIGHTS TO HELP PARENTS GET THEIR NEEDS MET

It's one thing to become a competent listener when your kids have problems in their lives, but quite another to become effective at getting your own needs met as a parent. Children give parents problems, in hundreds of ways. Living with a child inevitably means that certain behaviors will be unacceptable to you at certain times, because they interfere with what you want to do, prevent you from enjoying life, or make you feel frustrated or plain angry.

Many parents are not assertive enough with kids, and their permissiveness fosters the kind of children who run all over them. Others try to be assertive, but the methods they use are so hostile and aggressive that the relationship with their children gets fractured and their kids' self-esteem damaged.

The P.E.T. model explicitly sanctions parents to be assertive when their children's behavior causes them problems, but it also offers specific skills, new to most parents, that will help them assert themselves much more effectively and constructively.

We have found that it's not easy for some parents to make this change. Permissive parents have often become locked into that posture because their own parents were strict and authoritarian with them, and they see only one alternative to what they hated in their own parents: to become lenient and permissive parents. Other parents are under the misapprehension that a good parent is one who must "sacrifice for the good of the child." These parents often feel that getting their own needs met would be an act of selfishness. Still other parents avoid direct confrontation with their children because of the fear their children won't like them. Some parents, undoubtedly influenced by their experience with their own parents, are actually afraid of conflict. It's true that standing up for your own rights in a relationship may provoke a conflict, so it's understandable that parents who have had bad experiences with family conflicts may prefer permissiveness to assertiveness.

In this chapter I'll report what we have learned from parents about the difficulties they encounter in trying to use I-messages, and I'll offer specific suggestions or guidelines for overcoming these difficulties or, more hopefully, some ways of avoiding them.

But first, you may want a brief summary of how the P.E.T. model deals with behavior that causes parents a problem. (For a complete description see the P.E.T. text book.)

YOU-MESSAGES VERSUS I-MESSAGES

In Chapter II, you'll recall, we identified the bottom part of the Behavior Rectangle as the area into which we place behaviors unacceptable to the parent. That area represents times when the *parent owns the problem*. And the skills for dealing with such situations are "Confrontation Skills."

Our experience in working with a quarter of a million parents has provided us with the opportunity to find out how parents typically confront kids when they engage in unacceptable behavior. P.E.T. instructors present a number of such situations to all the parents in the class and ask them to write down how they would confront a youngster. Almost without exception, their messages fall into one of the Communication Roadblocks—the same twelve described in Chapter III:

1. Ordering, Directing, Commanding
   "You go to your room."
   "You stop making so much noise."

2. Warning, Admonishing, Threatening
   "If you don't stop, you'll get a spanking."
   "Mother will get angry if you don't get from under my feet."

3. Moralizing, Preaching
   "Don't ever interrupt a person when he's talking!"
   "Always say thank you."

4. Advising, Giving Suggestions or Solutions
   "Why don't you go play with your friends?"
   "Can't you put your clothes away?"

5. Teaching, Instructing
   "It's not good manners to use your knife that way."
   "Books are for reading, not throwing."

6. Judging, Criticizing, Blaming
   "You're being very careless."
   "You're being a bad boy."

7. Praising, Buttering Up
   "You're usually very nice to your friends."
   "It's not like you to be so inconsiderate."

8. Name-Calling, Ridiculing, Shaming
   "You're a busybody."
   "Shame on you for being so naughty."

9. Interpreting, Diagnosing, Psychoanalyzing
   "You are just a little jealous of your brother."
   "You always want to bother me when I'm tired."

10. Reassuring, Sympathizing, Supporting
    "Don't worry about my feelings."

"I'm not really bothered by the noise."
"I can understand why you hit baby brother."
"Oh, it's all right."

11. Probing, Interrogating
"Why did you do such a thing?"
"Do you realize what you've done?"
"Why do you have to have the radio on so loud?"
"Who taught you that?"

12. Diverting, Distracting, Humoring
"Wouldn't you rather read than watch that junk on TV?"
"Look how nice it is for playing outside."
"I'm so glad we have such nice, quiet children."
"Aren't you afraid you'll break your eardrums?"

Take another look at the Twelve Roadblocks. Each contains a heavy load of "You," some less obviously than others:

You stop that.

You shouldn't do that.

Don't *you* ever ...

If *you* don't stop that, then ...

Why don't *you* do this?

You are naughty.

You are acting like a baby.

You want attention.

Why don't *you* be good?

You should know better.

Hence, early in the development of the P.E.T. course we began to call such messages *You-messages*.

The impact of You-messages on children is predictable. With a high degree of probability they produce one or more of these effects:

1. Children resist changing when they're commanded to do something, or threatened if they do not.

2. Children turn off parents who moralize and preach or lecture and instruct.

3. You-messages communicate "I don't trust you to find a way to help me."

4. You-messages deny children a chance to initiate behavior out of consideration for the parent's needs.

5. Children feel guilty after being put down with evaluations or name-calling.

6. Critical, blaming messages reduce children's self-esteem.

7. Children feel rejected and even unloved when they hear messages that communicate how "bad" they are—or "stupid" or "inconsiderate" or "thoughtless."

8. You-messages cause reactive behavior, boomerangs that put down the parent. "You're *always* tired!" "You don't always pick up *your* clothes!" "You're a big grouch!" "Nothing ever pleases you!"

Far less likely to produce these effects are messages that inform a child how his behavior (unacceptable to you) is making you feel and what the consequences of that behavior are on your life:

"I cannot nap with a lot of noise in the house."

"I sure get discouraged when my clean kitchen gets dirtied up right away."

"When I have to talk on the phone, I get upset when there's so much noise that I can't hear."

For readers who may need a review, and those not familiar with the P.E.T. model, I want to reintroduce the diagram of the communication process to nail down the contrast between You-messages and I-messages.

When a child's behavior is unacceptable to a par-

ent because in some tangible way it interferes with the
parent's enjoyment of life or his right to satisfy his own
needs, the parent clearly "owns" the problem. The parent is upset, disappointed, tired, worried, harassed, bur-
dened, etc. And to let the child know what's inside him,
the parent must select a suitable code.

For the parent who wants to rest but his four-year-
old child wants to keep playing, the diagram would
look like this:

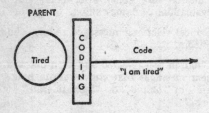

But if this parent selects a code that is "you"-
oriented, he would not be coding his "feeling tired"
accurately:

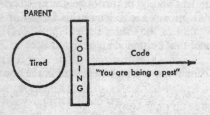

That is a very poor code for the parent's tired
feeling. A code that is clear and accurate would always
be an "I-message": "I am tired," "I don't feel up to
playing," "I want to rest." This communicates the feeling the parent is experiencing. A "You-message" code
does not send the feeling. It refers much more to the
child than to the parent. A "You-message" is child-
oriented, not parent-oriented.

Consider these messages from the point of view of what the child hears:

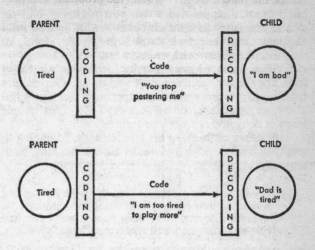

The first message is decoded by the child as an *evaluation* of him; the second is a *statement of fact* about the parent. "You-messages" are poor codes for communicating what a *parent* is feeling, because they will most often be decoded by the child in terms of either what *he* should do (from sending a solution) or how "bad" *he* is (from sending blame or evaluation).

From the experiences of P.E.T. instructors in the classroom and from our in-depth interviews with parents after the course, we have learned what difficulties parents have when they begin to apply I-messages at home. We have also added important additions and modifications to our concept of assertiveness and how to help parents achieve greater effectiveness by becoming more assertive.

"WHAT ARE MY REAL FEELINGS?"

When parents send You-messages, they needn't identify how they feel as a consequence of a child's unacceptable behavior. It's just a matter of blurting out a command, a threat, a put-down, or other you-oriented message: "You stop it," "You're going to get a spanking," "You're acting like a two-year-old," etc. Not so, when parents try to send an I-message. Now they need to know how they feel. "Am I angry, or afraid, or worried, or embarrassed, or just what?"

Most parents have difficulty identifying what they feel. They're not accustomed to doing so. Our culture teaches, as we grow up, that expressing feelings is impolite, or immature, or ego-centered. So most people learn to deny and repress true feelings.

A father of three, in his late twenties, beginning to work himself through the ranks of the banking business, says:

> "I try to pick the right emotion, the right feeling, but it was all so new to me—identifying my emotions. So sitting there trying to identify how I really felt and giving an I-message was a problem with me."

Eight years after taking P.E.T., this mother talks from her suburban home about her difficulty getting in touch with her feelings:

> "I think P.E.T. started me in getting in touch with my feelings—how I really feel. That can't be taught, but by using and giving I-messages you have to get in touch with your feelings. I can remember how difficult it was for me when our instructor would have us practice. . . . I'd give things out of my head, but they weren't real feelings—just thoughts. It's been hard for me and I'm still working on it. It's one of the biggest things P.E.T. did for me—not just in the relationship with my child but also with my friends and my husband—getting in touch with myself."

One mother used I-messages to confront her physician who had refused to tell her enough about her illness. But to get up enough courage, she resorted to writing out her feelings before the appointment:

"One of the hardest things for me to do is talk to someone who has more psychological size [stature or prestige] than I do. I was under the care of a physician who assumed I didn't need to know what was wrong with me. Here I was taking more drugs and just accepting what he said. But after taking the P.E.T. class I decided to organize all my feelings and all the effects his behavior had on me, just so he couldn't miss exactly what it was doing to me. . . . I wrote it all down, and went in and told him. . . . He tried to hedge again, so I said, 'I'm not willing to go on like this— I have to know more.' I never would have had the nerve to say that to a doctor before. So he said, 'Well, all right,' and he explained it. It really helped me."

Another mother, a journalism student with a four-year-old girl, points out the difference between being verbal and really knowing her feelings:

"Another thing is trying to get in touch with your own feelings, trying to verbalize it. I'm a verbal person, you know, I write. And my husband is extremely verbal, but as far as the area of emotions, it's incredible how inarticulate we are. Because feelings weren't talked about in my family, and not in his either. . . . The biggest change in me, attributable to the course, is being able to express my feelings. Because I didn't know the vehicle—I knew the way my parents ventilated their feelings was detrimental, so I didn't have a good model to model myself after. It gave me a vehicle to express my needs, you know, when I really felt something."

How to identify real feelings and find the courage to express them is hardly taught "in three easy lessons," but we have developed some teaching aids that may make it easier for parents "to get in touch with themselves."

1. Make a list. See how many different feelings you can write down on a sheet of paper. A list of twenty different feelings is a pretty fair performance. Ask your spouse to do the same. Then add to each other's lists.

You'll be surprised how many feelings you're aware of experiencing.

2. Write down, in a column, ten frequent behaviors of your child that are usually unacceptable to you. Think of each of these as behaviors that will deprive you of something you need or want. In a second column, after each of the behaviors, write the words, "I'm afraid"—ten times, of course. Finally, in a third column, write the words that will appropriately complete the sentence, as in this example:

Behavior	Feeling	Completion
Bobby runs wildly through the living room	I'm afraid	. . . he will knock over the lamps and break them.

Did you find that "I'm afraid" turned out to be a pretty accurate feeling to express how most of the unacceptable behaviors made you feel? My guess is that you did. This simple exercise usually convinces parents that a very large percentage of children's behaviors that causes them a problem are those that generate a fear of something—usually a fear that you're going to be deprived, going to lose something, or suffer because some need of yours will not get satisfied.

This is not to suggest that "I'm afraid" is the only feeling you'll ever have when your child's behavior is unacceptable to you, but it may convince you that fear is a very common reaction when you, the parent, own the problem. It makes sense when you remember that the bottom part of the Behavior Rectangle is the area where you place behaviors of your child that result in *your not getting your own needs met*. Naturally, you'll be afraid—who wouldn't?

3. Don't spend lots of time trying to find the most accurate or elegant words to define your feeling—such as "I feel mildly anxious" or "I'm chagrined" or "I'm painfully disappointed." Usually these are not your basic feelings at all, and anyway your child may not even know what they mean. My experience tells me parents

seldom have more than a few basic feelings: if a child's behavior causes you actual physical pain, "That hurts me" will suffice very well; if what he does threatens to deprive you, "I'm afraid . . ." will do; if he keeps badgering you to do something you don't feel like doing, "I'm feeling too tired (or too busy)," will get your message across clearly enough.

Parents have some special problems with *anger*. In our interviews we heard statements such as these:

> "I had to stop using the catch-all *anger*. Like, 'I'm angry' or 'I'm mad.' I used that too much at the beginning. But how often is someone angry? You really feel anger only two percent of the time."

> "I-messages are harder for me, because I tend to give an I-message that is disguised You-message—such as, 'I'm really mad and you shouldn't have done such and such.' Really, that's just saying, 'You did this, so I'm mad.' I tend to use 'mad' a lot, instead of trying to find the feeling underneath it."

Both of these parents recognized that their I-messages turned into expressions of anger far more often then seemed appropriate. Their explanation for this was that they were not in touch with "the feeling underneath," what I earlier called "basic feeling." From the experience of parents, we have learned something about anger that seems important: when parents express anger toward children, they often do not communicate their basic feeling. Behind most anger there exists another feeling.

For example, a ten-year-old, Tim, is pushing his baby sister dangerously fast in his wagon. Mother confronts Tim with "I'm very angry at you for pushing her too fast because she could have been hurt badly." Actually, the mother's first feeling was probably "fear," and the accurate I-message would have been something like, "I get scared when I see you push the baby so fast, 'cause she might fall and get hurt badly."

Anger is generated by a parent after experiencing

an earlier feeling. I am now convinced that an angry I-message feels like a blaming You-message to a child, so he'll feel put down and guilty, exactly as he feels with other You-messages.

Why do parents send angry I-messages? I think they consciously and deliberately want to punish children or teach them a lesson in hopes they won't ever again engage in the behavior that gave the parent the basic (or primary) feeling—such as fear, embarrassment, hurt, disappointment. If this is so, then parents manufacture their anger—they assume an angry *posture,* they *act* angry, they play *a role* of being angry, they *turn on* their own anger. This is not to say that their anger isn't real, because everyone knows how anger feels—you shake, you boil inside, your voice quavers. But these physiological concomitants come after you've put on the act of being angry.

How can parents stop getting angry? I think it's relatively easy to stop. Hold up a mirror to yourself and ask, "What am I really feeling? What is my primary feeling? What is my child's behavior making me feel? Is it fear, hurt, embarrassment, disappointment?" By getting in touch with your real feeling, and communicating it, in most cases you will accomplish your purpose of getting the child to modify his behavior. Then there'll be no need to "act" angry.

THE IMPORTANCE OF SENDING A COMPLETE I-MESSAGE

When I-messages fail to influence a child to modify behavior that is causing the parent a problem, it is often because the parent has sent one or more *incomplete* I-messages. One parent reported how Sue, four and a half years old, makes her brother Frank, six and a half, very upset by staring at him until he cries and screams:

> M: I'm very upset with the way you were carrying on —staring at Frank. I'm unhappy with your actions.

What's lacking in that I-message? Apart from the mother expressing her feelings too vaguely ("upset" and "unhappy"), there is a far more serious flaw in her I-message—she didn't tell Sue exactly how her behavior had a *tangible effect* on Mother. Sue's probable reaction to this message would be to wonder why Mother is upset and unhappy. How does her behavior tangibly affect her parent?

We've learned that an effective I-message needs three parts. This mother's I-message had only two:

Unacceptable Behavior	Feeling
When you stare at Frank	I get upset and unhappy.

A complete I-message contains: (1) a description of the unacceptable behavior, (2) the feeling experienced by the parent, and (3) the tangible, concrete effect on the parent (or the consequences). Mother's I-message should have sounded something like this:

Unacceptable Behavior	Feeling	Tangible Effect
When you stare at Frank	I get upset and unhappy	Because his crying and screaming interferes with what I am doing.

We can only guess, of course, what the actual, tangible effect was on this mother. It could have been that she can't stand the injustice of Sue's behavior or she doesn't have time to deal with Frank when he comes to her with his problem.

Take this incident of a parent trying to get her four-year-old son, Bill, to try on his new outfit for size:

M: Bill, we need to try this on so I know if it fits.

B: No, I don't want to!

M: Well, Bill, I can't get the outfit for you unless we try it on and see if it fits.

B: No, I don't want to try it on.

M: Let's go back into the dressing room and we'll try it on real quick. (Mother picks Bill up and carries him to the dressing room.) Bill, please will you try this on?

B: No.

M: Well, can I just hold it up to you to see if it really fits?

B: No, I don't want to.

M: Bill, I'm really angry! I need to try this on so we know if it fits. The lady out there is waiting for us.

The final outcome: the mother gave up and bought the next bigger size, hoping it would fit.

Now let's construct a hypothetical three-part I-message that might have had a better chance of modifying Bill's behavior:

Unacceptable Behavior	Feeling	Tangible Effect
When you won't try on this new outfit	I'm afraid to buy it	Because if it doesn't fit I'll have to drive downtown again to exchange it.

This complete I-message tells Bill the whole story—not only *what he is doing* that is giving Mother a problem, but also *what she is feeling about it,* and, equally important, *why the behavior will cause her a problem.*

Remember, the whole purpose of sending I-messages is to influence children to change whatever they are doing at the time. Usually it's not enough to describe the behavior you find unacceptable and tell them you're upset about it—or angry, or frustrated. *They need to know why.*

Put yourself in the child's shoes. You're doing something to get some need of yours met (or to avoid something that's unpleasant to you). Now, just because your parent says, in effect, "I'm upset with what you're doing," are you very motivated to change your behavior? Probably not. Because you have to hear a very good reason to change.

This is why parents need to be very explicit about the "tangible and concrete effect" of a child's behavior on *them*. Failure to communicate this to the child leaves him with no good reason to change, as this mother is beginning to realize:

> "This is what gripes me about children. You have to explain constantly why, why, why. If you tell them, 'Please don't do that,' that's not enough for them. . . . I have a reason I don't want a child to do such and such, and I wouldn't be telling him 'Don't do this,' if I didn't have a reason, right? But evidently they want to hear the reason, right?"

Sometimes failure to give reasons can make a child feel hurt and rejected, because if children are not told why the parent finds their behavior unacceptable, they may come up with a reason of their own. This occurred in one family, as recalled by the mother:

> "Once when Kirk had climbed out of bed after being put to rest for the night, Karl, my husband, told him, 'I'm not happy to see you—at all!' A few minutes later I found Kirk standing in the dark kitchen weeping beside the refrigerator. When I asked him what was wrong, he sobbed, 'Daddy didn't want to see me.' . . . Kirk had heard a personal rejection of himself."

We could expect an entirely different outcome if Dad had sent a complete three-part I-message—such as:

> "Kirk, when you get out of bed after you've been tucked in, I start to worry, because I'm afraid it's going to prevent me from doing my reading (or doing my work, or having time alone to talk with Mommy, or whatever)."

In addition to giving children a specific reason why the parent finds their behavior unacceptable, thereby increasing the chances they will be motivated to change, the complete three-part I-message has a significant effect on the parents. We discovered that when parents try to communicate the "tangible effect" portion of the I-message, they often realize there is no tangible effect at all! A mother explained this phenomenon:

> "I found I-messages most valuable in helping me see how arbitrary I am with my kids. When I try to send all three parts and I get to the part that explains what effect the behavior has on me, it would make me think, 'Well, I have no good reason!' If I say, 'I can't stand it when you're making so much noise around the house,' when I got to the 'because,' well, it would make me think I'm really not annoyed by it. I'd ask myself, 'Why am I annoyed about it?' So I've gotten into the habit now that if I can't think of any effect it has on me, I just say to the kid, 'Forget I ever said anything,' because it seemed I was being so arbitrary. . . . It's neat, you know, discovering that I couldn't even find a reason about half the time."

The clue to why this mother felt her discovery was "neat" was revealed when later she explained:

> "I was always very much into controlling kids. I thought that was a smooth way to run a bunch of kids —have everything controlled. But looking at it now, I say, 'Wow, how can I do that?' It caused me *more* work, not less, because I was concerned about every little thing they were doing. . . . Now I step back most of the time and say, 'So what?' "

She then reported a specific incident to illustrate how she applied her new attitude:

> "Caroline plays a lot with water in the bathroom. I'd be ready to send her an I-message that would tell her the effect on me: 'I don't want to have to clean it up.' Then I think: wait a minute, why do I assume I have to clean up myself? That's ridiculous. So instead I say to her, 'If you want to play with water in the bathroom, would you be willing to clean it up?' And she replies, 'Yeah.' And that's that—the kid cleans it up

herself. It's a whole different way, a whole different thing. Can you tell I like P.E.T.?" (*Laughter*)

Ten years ago, I would not have predicted that by teaching parents to send a complete three-part I-message we would be helping them discover *they did not even need to send an I-message.* By convincing parents they should explain to their kids when they found a particular behavior unacceptable, we inadvertently gave them a method which in many cases made the unacceptable behavior acceptable!

WHEN KIDS IGNORE YOUR I-MESSAGE

That I-messages do not inevitably influence kids to change their behavior, we have always known. However, we have not known all the reasons why they sometimes don't work. We know many more reasons now, largely because of our interviews with parents. Many of these parents encountered problems and failures—some temporary, some not.

> "Oh, I-messages! Sometimes they don't work when the kids don't want them to work, or they don't want to listen, and they want to do what they want to do, and they don't care what your feelings are or what you have to do."

> "I've felt a lot of times when I've sent I-messages to the kids, they don't care enough to do it, and it just doesn't get done. . . . For instance, I don't like to have their dirty dishes sitting in the sink when they very well could put them in the dishwasher. But it's no problem to them to see them in the sink. . . . They don't care enough about it, that's all."

> "Karen will just come out and say, 'But I really don't want to put my toys away.' "

The notion that I-messages should work every time is a gross misinterpretation or lack of understanding of the P.E.T. model. An I-message is simply the best way I know to inform someone that his or her behavior is causing you a problem. It also minimizes making the other person feel guilty, put-down, and resentful. But an I-message never guarantees you that the other person will immediately, or willingly, modify his or her behavior out of consideration for your needs. Human relationships are not that simple, nor human beings that predictable.

But we have identified factors that do influence the success or failure of I-messages. The first, which I've already dealt with, is the structure of the I-message itself, particularly whether it communicates the tangible and concrete effect of the child's behavior on the parent. Others are:

1. Whether the child feels the parent generally listens when he or she owns the problem.

2. The strength (or congruence) of the message.

3. How the parent responds to the child's resistance to the parent's I-message.

4. Whether the I-message sends a solution.

5. How much the parents resort to the use of power and authority.

Each of these factors needs further explanation.

Do You Listen When the Child Owns Problems?

I-messages won't work in families where parents tend not to listen when their children have problems. It's as simple as this: if you want your kids to listen to you (when *you* have a problem), they must feel that you generally listen to them (when *they* have a problem). Mutuality, no less. If you rub my back, I'll rub yours. Trade-offs, if you will.

Some parents complete the P.E.T. class certain they have a new weapon, and a more effective one, that will make their kids stop doing what has been giving the parents problems. They go home and start hurling I-messages right and left, and then wonder why they don't work.

I-messages must be seen as direct appeals for help: "The noise is keeping me from enjoying this TV show and I'd really hoped to enjoy it." Messages like this ask the child if he would be willing to help you. Now, if a child has problems and is accustomed to such responses as commanding, threatening, moralizing, judging, interpreting, and the other Roadblocks, it's unlikely that he or she is going to be in a mood to help you when you need help. This may explain why in P.E.T. we teach Active Listening first. We want parents to become effective listeners before they start to confront and expect their children to listen to them.

How Strong Are Your I-Messages?

I-messages don't work for some parents because the message somehow is too weak to get through to a child. There's an old joke about the man who sold a mule to his friend for a high price, claiming the mule was exceptionally well trained and obedient. Some weeks later his friend brought the mule back, complaining that the animal would not respond to any of his commands. Picking up a big club, the previous owner smacked the mule across his head and said "Gittyup." The mule started walking immediately. "I'm sorry," said the man, handing over the club, "I forget to tell you that you've got to get his attention first."

For I-messages to work, in some situations, you have to get the child's attention first. Not by giving him a blow on the head, of course, but by sending an I-message that is strong enough to have an impact. Some parents have difficulty making their I-messages match the intensity of their feelings. They "undershoot" by sending a weak I-message. Result: the child doesn't respond. A mother, wife of an army chaplain and mother of three, talked about her tendency to undershoot:

"I was especially having trouble with undershooting I-messages. My instructor encouraged me to be more assertive, but I thought at the time that if I were, I'd damage my children or my husband. If I came on too

strong, I'd trod on their rights somehow. Practicing in
class helped me try [stronger I-messages] and find they
weren't going to."

Another parent worried that I-messages might make
her child feel guilty:

"What I was learning about I-messages made me feel
they could possibly or hypothetically create a lot of
guilt in a kid. The I-messages were capable of making
you have strong feelings of omnipotence and you'd
create guilt or unhappy feelings."

Are the concerns of these parents justified? I think
not, unless parents go to the other extreme and "overshoot"—send I-messages that are full of strong anger
that blasts the child like a firecracker exploding in his
face. (Remember what I said about anger being a
punishing You-message.)

The most effective I-message obviously is one that
truly matches the feelings being experienced by the
parent—neither an undershoot nor an overshoot. If
your child's leaving his clothes out makes you feel
only irritated, say "I feel irritated" rather than "I'm so
mad." But if your six-year-old leaves a sharp knife on
the floor close to the baby and when you saw it you
got scared as hell, don't say, "I get a little worried . . ."
Instead, send a message that more closely matches your
blood pressure, such as "When I saw the knife, I was
scared to death, because the baby might have cut herself badly and that would really make me feel sad."

Parents often ask, "But won't such messages make
the child feel guilty?" A legitimate question. But I have
come to see that there are two different kinds of guilt.
One is a lot like, "I'm sorry for what I've done because
it hurt (or could have hurt) another person." This type
of guilt seems to be the natural consequence of a particular behavior. There are behaviors which in a sense
should produce guilt—and it's logical for the child to
feel sorry. Suppose I injure someone by driving when
intoxicated. I sincerely hope I would feel sorry—yes,
guilty.

But, typically, parents' messages produce a second type of guilt in a child, more like, "I'm bad, evil, or sinful." These are the You-messages which convey heavy judgment and strong put-downs, such as, "You bad, bad boy," "You're driving me to an early grave," "You should have known better," "I hope your own kids treat you like you're treating me," "I hope God punishes you for what you've done," and hundreds more in this vein. The effects of these guilt-producing messages can truly be destructive to children, often for a long time afterward. A good I-message will rarely produce this second type of guilt, because it tells the child only how his behavior makes you feel, not how you judge him for having behaved as he did. A distinction of great significance for the child.

The Importance of Shifting Gears

We have learned that no matter how good an I-message might be, no one likes to hear one. Who wants to find out that his or her behavior is unacceptable to another? It's not comfortable to learn that you've caused a loved person a problem. So even the best of I-messages frequently provoke defensive responses from the receiver. This is particularly true with youngsters, most of whom would much prefer doing what they want to do and getting their own needs met without opposition from their parents, as this mother well knows:

> "They want to do what they want to do and they don't care what your feelings are about what you're doing or what you have to do. . . . You know, they don't care—they've got their own thing to do."

No wonder parents find their I-messages provoking such responses as:

> "I don't want to."

> "It's not bothering you."

> "I don't care. I want to do it anyway."

> "The TV is not on *that* loud."

"I didn't make the mess, Susan did."

"I don't care if you're embarrassed."

Send an I-message to a child and invariably you cause
him to have a problem now. Your I-message interrupts
whatever he is doing at the moment to get his needs
met. So the child has to deal with your I-message
somehow.

In P.E.T. we stress how important it is for parents
to listen sensitively to the resistance their I-messages
provoke. We call this "Shifting Gears"—changing from
the confronting stance to listening posture. Observe
how the parent does this in the following incident:

> M: It's very cold outside, and when you go out with-
>   out your coat there's a chance you might get sick
>   and we'll end up going to Dr. Brown and spending
>   a lot of money.
>
> C: No! I won't get sick.
>
> M: You don't think you're going to get sick.
>
> C: No.

Immediately after this interaction, so the mother reported, her son went to the closet and got his coat.

Shifting gears doesn't always produce such immediate results, but in many cases it seems to help kids
when their parent acknowledges their reaction to an I-
message. There is a paradox here—it's as if *children
find it easier to change if they feel a parent understands
how hard it is.*

This use of Active Listening is distinctly different
from employing the skill as a helping agent when the
child owns the problem. When you shift gears into
Active Listening following an I-message, your purpose
is solely to reduce the child's defensiveness to your attempts to get your own needs met—very different from
wanting to help the child!

Solution-Messages Are Not I-Messages

Some parents think they are sending I-messages when in fact they are telling their kids exactly what they must do to relieve the parent of the problem their unacceptable behavior is causing. The message is variously worded but comes across as an order, or at least a very strong suggestion or solution.

Such solution-messages usually produce resistance (rather than a desire) to change. People don't like to be told what to do. And kids, let me say it again, are people too, believe it or not!

One mother talked about her habit of sending solution-messages:

> "Now that I'm thinking about I-messages, I realize I don't give them. I let the kids know my feelings and *what I want them to do,* but it's not really in the form of an I-message. Such as, 'I want you to wear this, because I don't like you to wear what you have on in church.' . . . The other day I had all the kids come in, because the table was all covered with their homework papers. I just said, 'I want you to go in and clean up the table.' "

Far less chance of causing resistance would be a message like this: "When the table is covered with papers, I can't set the table for dinner and I don't feel like cleaning it off myself." This I-message not only reduces the chance of getting resistence; it puts responsibility on the youngsters for initiating behavior that would help Mother with her problem. It gives the kids a chance to win some Brownie points, so to speak. A solution-message takes away that opportunity because the parent is *telling* them exactly what they should do.

Resorting to Power and Authority

When an I-message does not produce the desired results, there is always the temptation to resort to parental power. Some parents succumb to that temptation, as illustrated by the mother of five-year-old Carey:

> "And with I-messages, he doesn't care. He puts up a lot of defenses. I said, 'Carey, I really can't hear the TV when you're jumping up and down and screaming in the living room. It really makes it hard to hear the TV.' He says, 'Oh,' and continues what he's doing. Until I say, 'Carey, get out of the room.' And then he'll scoot."

While Mother's command made Carey scoot, it could have a long-range effect of teaching the youngster that he need not change his behavior when he hears an I-message—only when Mother gets mad enough to order him to change.

Several parents admitted to using physical force —pushing the child away or pulling the child by the arm—when I-messages failed. These were parents who were also experiencing a general lack of success with I-messages. Not surprising, because using power after an I-message fails is tantamount to saying to the child, "I have a problem and would like for you to help, but if you don't, I'm going to make you!" Not the kind of message that fosters in kids the desire to be considerate of their parents' needs, is it?

SOME GUIDELINES FOR PARENTS ABOUT I-MESSAGES

1. Parents' effectiveness with I-messages depends on the quality of the total parent-child relationship. If you do a lot of listening to your children when they own problems, you'll increase the probability of their responding constructively to your messages when you own the problem. The desire to help must be mutual— it cannot be one-way, at least not for long.

2. Practice getting in touch with your real feelings. If your I-messages are usually angry, you probably don't know the real feelings you're experiencing when your kids give you problems. Ask yourself,

"What do I fear?" because a good deal of the time behavior that you find unacceptable is in some way threatening the loss of something you need.

3. Don't expect kids to change their behavior if you don't tell them the tangible and concrete effects of that behavior. Give them the real reasons, because they must be convinced there is a good and logical reason why they should modify their behavior. Why else would they be expected to change? Remember, a good I-message has three components.

4. Don't expect that every I-message will work. *You* certainly don't always feel like changing every time you are confronted by a friend or spouse, either.

5. Don't think of your kids as fragile and easily hurt. If your I-message is not a disguised You-message, you can make it as strong as you feel and not worry about causing permanent damage to your child's psyche.

6. If the first I-message doesn't work, try a second that is stronger and more congruent with how you feel when you're ignored.

7. Listen carefully to the defensiveness you'll usually provoke when you confront your children, and shift into Active Listening. You may then want to send another I-message.

8. Tell your kids why they're causing you a problem, not what they should do to solve it. Give them a chance to be a helper for you.

9. An I-message is a nonpower method for getting what you need, so don't contaminate this powerful skill with follow-up commands, physical force, or threats of punishment.

VII

HOW I-MESSAGES BENEFIT PARENTS AND IMPROVE FAMILY LIFE

When parents start putting I-messages to work in their families, they are rewarded in a variety of ways. Not only do the I-messages bring about changes in the behavior of their children; they foster changes in the parents, too. Some get more courage to tackle complex problems; others begin to accept that their needs are also important. Parents report standing up for their own rights more frequently, as well as gaining better understanding of what goes on in the minds and hearts of their children. Many parents experienced that their use of I-messages greatly reduced nagging and hassling. Others told us they became more open and honest, not only with their children but with spouses and friends.

Many parents were also surprised to discover how often their kids demonstrate a willingness to help, once they're told that their parents are hurting. And parents were amazed at the ability of their children to find creative and appropriate solutions after learning they had been causing their parents a problem.

In this chapter, parents speak for themselves about the benefits of I-messages and describe how they were richly rewarded by their new-found assertiveness.

AN EASY-TO-LEARN TOOL

Our interviews brought us strong evidence that learning to use effective I-messages is easier for most parents than learning the Active Listening skill. One parent attributed this to the three-part formula (Behavior, Feeling, Tangible Effect):

> "It does give you a tool—it's very basic. The I-message is like a clause. You fill in the blanks. It's so specific that you can *do* it. I don't have to start thinking, I just automatically do it, because the three parts of the message are laid out so clearly. So whenever I'm in a situation, I can start out with 'When' and all of a sudden the message comes out."

Another parent had a similar explanation:

> "The I-message was the easiest thing in the P.E.T. course to apply. The instructor taught it to us by using the three parts. . . . It was much easier for me to put that kind of a sentence together than it is to Active Listen. I-messages seem to be easy to assemble, just by thinking of those three parts."

I-messages gave one mother more courage to step in and deal with problems:

> "I feel it's given me some sort of a tool to have courage to step in and deal with situations that I feel are wrong, even though I don't always do it right. At least I can now attempt it."

"IT REALLY WORKS!"

Perhaps another reason why so many parents found I-messages easy to learn is that they had early and immediate experiences when a single I-message produced startling results. These early successes undoubtedly encouraged parents to keep on using I-messages in subsequent situations.

Here's what happened to the mother of two-and-a-half-year-old Kay, who wouldn't go to sleep:

> "One night I was very tired and Kay was cranky. She wouldn't go to sleep, and she was just crying and wouldn't lie down. She was in there almost hysterical. I went through the whole list. I started out just talking to her, 'Come on, Kay, it's bedtime, now go to sleep. Come on, it's late now, just go to sleep, nothing to worry about.' Her crying kept going and my hostility level really started rising. 'Yes, you're going to bed right now; no, you are not going to play!' My tone got louder, and then I just spanked her and said, 'You *will* go to bed, now—I've had enough of this!' That didn't do it. She was still crying. I was desperate, wondering: what do I do now? Then I thought, let's try P.E.T. So I went in and sat down on the bed with her and held her a bit—but I didn't take her out of the bed. I said, 'Daddy and I don't get much time together, and I spend most of the day with you. I would like to spend a little time with Daddy. We need to relax at night and talk to one another. Sometimes we like to go to bed early, too. But we can't go to bed if you're crying.' She said, 'OK Mommy.' That was it. I couldn't believe it! While she didn't instantly go to sleep, there was no more crying, no more tantrums."

A father reminds his wife about her successful I-message:

> "One night you announced that dinner was ready, and nobody came. So you gave a very good I-message, 'I'm so frustrated, I've spend all this time preparing a nice dinner and it bothers me so much because the food is going to get cold.' It came across and I thought it really sounded so natural and it seemed to get action— it was interesting to watch the kids. They saw the logic of her concern and did come. I remember wishing I could give I-messages like that. She uses them more often than she realizes."

While still in the P.E.T. class, a mother had this very successful experience with I-messages:

"Soon after we started the P.E.T. class and had begun to work at the 'I statement,' I had opportunity to alter what had become an impossible, if somewhat expected, situation. With five small children and many errands and commitments, usually *for* the children, I found a constant uproar in the car very disconcerting. One especially difficult time happened to be in transporting our nine-year-old to choir practice, at our church several miles from our home, through a business district and several school areas, in late-afternoon traffic. Like most mothers, I often resorted to yelling, name-calling, etc., which obviously only added to the confusion. That red-letter day, I decided to express my *real* feelings, without shouting. I pulled over to the side of the street, stopped the car, and removed the keys. We sat there!!!—the children momentarily speechless, then questioning. I explained calmly, 'I'm terrified of driving just now! All the noise and movement makes me so nervous I'm afraid to drive. I'm really afraid we'll have an accident, so I'm going to wait for some calm to drive.' Needless to say, the calm arrived rapidly and remained through that trip. Now when the children get *too* rowdy for me to drive safely, I pull over and stop and the magic remains. I've made another 'nonverbal I-statement.' Even our baby knows what I'm saying!!!"

A problem common to many families was handled successfully with this mother's good I-message:

"The I-message is very effective. I know it is. It'll stop a kid in his tracks. I've watched that, because very often I'll give orders which are blatantly ignored. But if I give a three-part I-message, it generally will make sense. For example, I gave out one like this, 'I don't want to find dishes in the sink when I come in to prepare dinner, because then I have to do them myself and it makes me get behind in my dinner preparation. Then I get very angry.' The next day the dishes were put in the dishwasher, but it lasted only for the next two days."

This parent had to send another I-message when the kids forgot after two days, but that's not unusual, especially with younger children; they just forget easily.

THE YOU-MESSAGES GET HEARD

After learning I-messages, parents become very conscious of using You-messages. This increased self-awareness was reported by a number of parents:

> INTERVIEWER: How about your first attempts at an I-message?
>
> PARENT: Oh, well, they were more I-You-messages such as, "I don't like cleaning the counter, so you clean it up." (*Laugh*)

The same parent described this incident:

"My son is learning to drive. We were going up to the cabin and he was driving very fast, and I said, 'You're going too fast, you're going too fast.' Well, of course he became very defensive, saying, 'No, I'm not.' And then I thought 'Oh, oh, that was wrong!' So as we drove on, I said, 'I feel very nervous when we're going fast, and I'm afraid we might have an accident or another car might run into us.' He slowed up—it made sense to him why I was nervous."

A father became much more sensitively aware of the negative feelings produced by You-messages when his daughter sent him some:

"I'd just taken an exam and I was going over it, not feeling very happy about the results. Well, I passed the exam over to my daughter, Jan. She sat there and looked at it, and said, 'You shouldn't have gotten number two wrong' and 'You shouldn't have gotten number six wrong.' Every time she said 'You' it was just like I'd been kicked in the stomach. I felt like sliding under the table, and I was hurt, followed by a second emotion—anger. I was ready to say, 'Damn it!' and slam my fist on the table and walk out of the

room, but I said, 'Hon, there's something wrong here.
Every time you speak I feel like I'm getting kicked in
the stomach.' My wife was so surprised, she looked
up from the paper and said, 'Really.' Then we
analyzed the situation and discovered something we
had known before—that You-messages are judgmental
and it was as if she was standing above me and talking
down to me, knocking me."

Later this father talked about becoming aware of how
his You-messages were creating anxiety in his eleven-
year-old daughter, Margie:

"Margie has a hard time getting to the school bus
and remembering to take her lunch. So this one day
I got up in the morning and was coming on her like
an ogre. 'Do this, do this, do this, you do this, you do
this, you've got five minutes.' Push, push, push—just
raising the anxiety level in this little child until she
was so distracted she missed the bus. So I said one
day to myself, 'Now, wait a minute—I'm just driving
myself up a tree and driving her up the wall.' So I
decided to change. . . . I've actually sat at the table
with my son and sent You-messages like, 'You're
going to upset your milk now, if you aren't careful.'
He'd upset it! The anxiety level gets to the point where
it's built in and I just talk him right into a failure."

So parents in P.E.T. not only learn a new skill,
the I-message, but also become much more aware of
when they revert back to You-messages. Some unlearn-
ing of old habits obviously must accompany the learning of the new way of communicating.

"KIDS ACTUALLY WANT TO HELP"

To those accustomed to seeing their children resist
or ignore parental commands, threats, and other forms
of influence, it comes as a surprise to see how differently kids respond to a good I-message. In front of their
eyes, parents see their children respond as if they really
care about their parents' needs and feelings. A father

and mother talked about such a change in their young son, Jack:

> F: I was talking with a friend last night, and Jack was beating on a can in the other room. I couldn't hear, just could not hear. There was no door I could close, so I asked my friend to wait and went back and said, "I'm very upset and angry, because I really want to talk with Dick and you're beating on the can right now and I can't hear him." And he stopped. You know, he said, "OK.". . . Later I went back after the conversation and told him I was finished talking on the phone and so he could beat the can now.
>
> I: How did that make you feel?
>
> F: It's great!
>
> M: Well, it feels like he has a sense of respect for us, too. . . . He'll stop and that makes me feel good, feel that he loves me and respects me.

Another parent recalled sending a good I-message to her twelve-year-old daughter, Cathy, about her need to have the house in order when the mother returned from teaching at night:

> "A long moment passed after my I-message and she didn't say anything, which was quite different for her. Then finally she said, 'I didn't know you *needed* me to do that.' "

Like Cathy, kids are not often told what their parents *need*. Instead, they get told what they must do, or should do, or better do.

The power of I-messages is derived from the fact that a good three-part I-message is an admission on the part of the sender that he has a problem, plus an implicit *appeal for help* with that problem. In all human relationships, this kind of message carries a lot of weight—most people are usually willing to listen when a friend confides he has a problem. But if that friend

sends blaming messages and then adds "musts,"
"shoulds," or "oughts," most people bristle in defense
and resist in defiance. Nobody likes to be told what to
do, and that includes youngsters of all ages. In the following incident, note carefully the response of this
seven-year-old to his father's I-message:

> "My son, seven years old at the time, had developed
> the habit of sliding on his rump down the carpeted
> stairs. I had used power messages—everything, in-
> cluding spanking. In my need to stop the behavior, I
> had forgotten all about I-messages. One day, when he
> slid down the steps again I remembered and said,
> 'Mark, when you slide down the steps on your rear, I
> get very aggravated because I'm afraid the carpet will
> get torn loose from the steps and then the hall area will
> look like a mess.' Mark turned to me and said simply,
> 'I didn't know you felt that way.' He has never slid
> down the steps since that day."

Reading another incident written by a grandmother, I
found myself with tears in my eyes when I came to the
response of the child:

> "When our grandson, eleven years old, was visiting us
> recently and attended church with myself and my
> husband, we sat in a front pew. He repeatedly
> stretched his arms over his head, much to my concern
> that he was distracting those behind us. So I wrote
> him this message. 'When I see your arms stretched over
> your head, I think you disturb others behind us and it
> makes me feel embarrassed.' He wrote back, 'I'm
> sorry, Grandma,' and then stretched his arms *in front*
> of himself instead of over his head. Later, he was mak-
> ing drawings on the church paper and he wrote me a
> note, 'Am I embarrassing you, Grandma when I write
> on the paper?' Upon which, I wrote back, 'Of course
> not, and I'm so happy to have you sitting in church
> with us.' "

It now is clear to me that we grossly underestimated the desire and willingness of children to please.
They actually do want to help their parents. They do

want to contribute to making their parents' lives more pleasant. And they feel good when they can. Parents have underestimated children's desire to help, because so seldom do their messages communicate that they need help. And seldom do those messages leave it up to a child to behave in ways that would help.

THE INGENIOUS SOLUTIONS KIDS FIND

When parents send good I-messages that do not include solutions—such as you must do this, you should do this, why don't you do this—it permits youngsters to think up their own solutions for helping solve the parents' problems. And those solutions are often surprisingly creative and ingenious; often their parents would never have thought of them. Even two- and three-year-olds are capable of unusual solutions, as in this incident with a mother and three-year-old Mark, whose many fears kept him from going to sleep. So he'd often come into his parents' bedroom and wake them up:

> "He had expressed fears of certain objects in his room. He loves monsters in the daytime but at night gets frightened. Even a drawing of monsters or a paper skeleton we had at Halloween. He used to come in and get in our bed. We said, 'Mark, you know we'd appreciate it if you could stay in bed because we really need our sleep; when you come in and wake us up, then we're very tired the next day and get crabby.' The first ten times he didn't respond, but eventually he did. He'd get up and play his record player. Then we told him his record player also woke us up. . . . He was so cute—he just turned the machine on so he could hear that hum. And that was enough to comfort him. Most of the time we couldn't hear the hum."

A father told us about another ingenious solution that emerged out of a problem involving his son's ruining his newly planted grass:

"I came home and found Gary's street hockey net
sitting just off the edge of the driveway, right in the
middle of some new grass I had planted. There were
numerous footprints in the grass, which had just
sprouted. I sent him a strong I-message about how
sick I was to see the new grass messed up because I
didn't want to take the time and trouble to replant it.
He grunted an acknowledgment and went on about
his business—watching TV. A few days later I came
home to find a hockey game in process, with four or
five neighborhood boys and my son. The net was on
the driveway this time and I noticed the boys were
leaping across the new grass rather than stepping on it.
I commented on this and one of the boys popped up
with, 'It's a penalty shot for every footprint.' I never
did find out how this solution came about, but it
worked great, and it was one I never would have
thought of myself."

Kids are so creative in coming up with solutions
because they have such strong needs to do what *they*
want to do. You can almost see their little heads working to find a solution that will take care of the parent's
needs and still not stop them from doing their thing.
Perhaps this is what motivated Tim in this brief incident:

"A young mother in our P.E.T. class had polished the
stereo cabinet in preparation for company. Her two
little boys (ages seven and four) wanted to play their
records that afternoon, but she was worried about
fingerprints. She resisted saying, 'Ask me to put the
records on' and instead sent an I-message: 'When you
open up the lid, I'm concerned there'll be fingerprints
and I'll have to clean it again before company comes.'
Her seven-year-old came up with his own creative
solution: he carefully stretched down his pullover
sleeves over his hands and opened the stereo without
leaving fingerprints."

It warrants repeating: we tend to underestimate
kids' capacities when they're given a chance to use
them!

"IT FEELS GOOD TO BE HONEST"

When parents begin to send I-messages, not only do they notice changes in their children; they experience a significant change in themselves. The different words I've heard used to describe this change all seem to mean greater *honesty:*

> "I don't have to pretend anymore that I'm in the mood for playing with my preschooler."

> "I'm not wishy-washy anymore."

> "I'm much more congruent."

> "I'm more up-front."

> "I-messages allow me to be open and honest with others."

Apparently, the old idea, "You become what you do," applies here, too. By using a new form of communication, parents begin to feel *inside themselves* the very honesty their I-messages communicate to *others.* The I-message skill provides parents with the vehicle for getting in touch with their real feelings; You-messages are entirely other-oriented.

Our interviews gave us evidence that not only does P.E.T. provide assertive-training but also honesty-training, as this mother reports:

> "It seems to me that before P.E.T. I had to play certain roles—be a certain way. I don't think I have to be that way anymore. I'm free to be me. And to risk that I'll still be loved and accepted, and if not, well, that's all right. . . . And it's freed my husband to be more open, more willing to talk about things and not hold feelings in. . . . The whole thing about sending an honest I-message about how you feel . . . I feel now it's OK for me to say, 'I don't have time for it or I can't do it right now.' "

Another parent, this one a father, tells how he has changed:

> "It's been a lot better, because I feel both of us have gotten away from making promises we can't keep. And that's been a real relief. . . . If it's no, we'll tell them, 'No, maybe tomorrow, but right now I have something that's more pressing for me.' "

One mother talked about how she and her husband were brought up to repress their real feelings:

> "It's been one of our biggest difficulties—accepting negative feelings, which were not accepted in either of our families. I mean, we were all supposed to be happy and interested in things, and doing things. Feeling bored or feeling depressed was just a bad way to be. I think it was really great that through the course I became more aware that it's OK to feel that way."

Another parent felt "liberated" by the I-message concept:

> "I think it's liberating . . . for me to be able to express myself and not feel guilty for being self-centered or something like that. I think it helps to have the freedom to convey those messages to my children. I never used to say, 'You know I feel like such and such.' "

I-messages also have a cathartic effect; they help parents get their feelings out instead of keeping them bottled up inside, as expressed by this parent:

> "With an I-message you don't bottle up your feelings. You've expressed what you feel and you know someone else has heard you. Whether they do anything about it or not, things don't seem to be as big anymore."

When parents discover an alternative to You-messages, which are usually blaming or put-down messages, they find it much easier to be honest with others. This happens because the I-message is nonblaming and nonpunitive—less likely to be hurtful to the other person or damaging to the relationship. Obviously it's safer to say, "I'm too tired to clean up the living room again" than "You're thoughtless and inconsiderate." A mother makes this point in the following excerpt:

> "I used to give out my feelings, but I would camouflage them to protect myself. . . . I would always worry how the other person felt—how it would affect them. And now I guess I'm putting the emphasis on myself. . . . I have a lot of resentment built up because I don't share myself. But the formula for stating the I-message [the three parts] helps me state a negative feeling in a positive way, without hurting the other person."

So we learned from P.E.T. graduates that not only do I-messages influence kids to modify their behavior —they also have a profound effect on the parents. They begin to accept their own feelings—even negatives ones; they find it easier to share those feelings honestly; and they acquire greater freedom to be themselves in their relationship with others. Such outcomes, most professionals have always believed, could be expected only from intensive psychotherapy—certainly not from a twenty-four-hour parent education course.

HOW PARENTS DEAL WITH THEIR ANGER

Just about every parent gets angry at children from time to time. But some parents give the impression that anger is the only emotion they are capable of experiencing, because their confronting messages almost always are expressed as anger. You'll recall that we teach parents that anger is usually a *secondary* feeling, following on the heels of a *primary* feeling, which could be fear, hurt, embarrassment, and so on. And if parents will only get in touch with their primary feeling, they need not "become" angry.

Does this work out in practice? Do P.E.T. parents find themselves getting angry less frequently? Our study showed that some do, but it also revealed that others continue to send angry messages.

In the following excerpt, a mother, wife of an army physician living on a California army base with their three children, describes how she successfully used the P.E.T. model:

"Tony rode his bike to the Saturday afternoon matinee and he was to be home by five-thirty. In the meantime it had started to rain. So I waited. By five-thirty it was pitch dark and pouring rain and it got to be six and he wasn't home. I was really furious, but I also was very much afraid that something horrendous had happened to him. What was I going to do? Finally he he came home about six-fifteen and the first thing I said to him was, 'Wow, I was really worried! Did something happen?' And he said, 'Oh, no, Mom. We were just up at school waiting for the rain to stop, and when we decided it wasn't going to stop, we decided to come on home.' . . . Previous to P.E.T. I would have been just plain angry. Whether or not I would have realized I was afraid, I don't know, but I'd never have expressed that I was afraid of something happening to him. I'd have just said, 'Where were you, young man?' and 'Next Saturday you will not go to the movies again!' "

Another parent changed her way of dealing with anger:

"I would get angry at my husband and he'd say, 'What's the matter?' And I'd say, 'Oh, nothing.' But one thing I learned in P.E.T. that helped was that anger was a cover-up for a deeper emotion such as frustration or fear. . . . After I took P.E.T. I learned to look for the feeling that the anger was covering up and try and figure out where the anger was coming from. It was usually that all day long I had continual interruptions—telephone, kids had an accident—and I'm just frustrated in reaching my main goal for that day."

Other parents found it more difficult to stop sending angry messages, as in this incident involving another teen-ager coming home late from a movie:

"When the car door slammed at ten minutes after one, my first feeling was, 'I'm relieved that he's home.' But we hadn't slept and by the time he got to the bedroom we were madder than hornets. We just really told him—how inconsiderate he was and how he should have called and how he'd worried us. He said, 'Well, I'm sorry,' and just turned on his heel and went downstairs. Then we heard his door slam. My husband called out, 'Good night' and he slammed the door again. I lay there awake 'cause I was so mad at him. So I know, we just blew it. But the fact that we knew we had blown it was a great plus, because the next morning we encouraged him to talk about the movie, and we didn't say anything about the night before. We didn't bring it up and hound him again with it."

Other parents' angry messages brought results with no evidence of resistance or resentment:

"I was moping around and the children were running in and out, and I decided this is really stupid. So I just told them, 'I feel terribly angry and impatient right now and I don't feel like talking and giving everybody juice, and I feel like being all by myself.' They just looked at me and said, 'OK, we're going to play upstairs.' It seemed so simple—this was just great!"

While this mother did give *some* reasons (wanting to be by herself), it is clear that anger does not invariably provoke door slamming or damaged egos. And often an anger message will produce results. In fact, getting angry and expressing it is probably far healthier for parents than keeping it bottled up inside and feeling resentful or hateful toward youngsters.

Even if a parent's I-message comes out first as an angry message, it's not too late to shift to the primary feeling. At least that will let the child know you had a reason to be angry.

But if you're hearing yourself sending angry messages day after day, it is very likely you are not in touch with what's really bothering you. And you might ask yourself:

"What am I feeling deep inside?"

"What needs of mine are unmet?"

"Why am I not a happier person?"

"What's really eating me?"

You may find out you're not angry at what the kids are doing, but rather at what you're not doing—for yourself!

VIII

NEW APPLICATIONS FOR I-MESSAGES

In P.E.T. classes, as well as from data obtained from P.E.T. graduates, we have acquired some new ideas and insights about using I-messages in families. Although initially we taught it solely as a verbal method for influencing kids to change unacceptable behavior, the I-message concept has been greatly expanded. We now know I-messages can be used even with infants and toddlers who are too young to understand the spoken word. Also, we found an important use for the I-message in communicating feelings of appreciation and gratitude when kids' behavior has been unusually acceptable to their parents.

Finally, my own thinking about I-messages has been greatly expanded through discussions with Linda Adams, a consultant we employed to design a new course, Effectiveness Training for Women. She introduced me to the concept of the assertive I-want or I-need message to prevent unacceptable behaviors in the future.

In this chapter I'll explain and illustrate these new insights and new applications.

157

I-MESSAGES WITH INFANTS AND TODDLERS

Because an I-message is verbal, it's understand-able why most parents who read the first P.E.T. book or took the P.E.T. course limited their I-messages to children old enough to understand verbal I-messages.

We know better now. True, preverbal children present a special problem because they cannot under-stand the usual I-message. Nevertheless, it's quite easy to modify unacceptable behaviors of such children, provided the right approaches are used. Parents can choose from three different methods.

1. The Guessing Game

Barbara, six months old, starts to cry loudly in the middle of the night. Her parents are awakened from the sleep they need and naturally find this behavior un-acceptable. But how can they get Barbara to stop cry-ing? Quite simply, they start guessing. Finding the cause of her crying so that they can remedy the prob-lem is something like a puzzle:

> Maybe she's wet and cold. We'll check first on that. No, she's still dry. Well, could it be we didn't burp her enough and she's feeling uncomfortable with gas? Let's pick her up and start the burping process. Bad guess again—Barbara won't burp. Wonder if she's hungry. There's still some milk in her bottle, but it got pushed down to the end of the crib. We'll act on that hypothesis next. Success! Barbara sucks for a few minutes and then gets sleepy. They put her back into her crib gently and she falls asleep. Her parents can go back to bed now and get their own needs met.

Parents have to use this trial-and-error method very frequently with infants when they whine inces-santly, when they're restless and pestering, when they can't get to sleep, when they throw their food on the floor. The guessing game works effectively because when infants do things that are unacceptable to their parents, there's a reason for it—usually a very logical reason. When parents start using the guessing game, they stop resorting to punishment.

Sometimes parents find the guessing game easy, other times more difficult. The cliché "If at first you don't succeed, try, try again" is the soundest advice I know. Parents can get quite good at the game, because they get to know their offspring better and better. Parents have told me that they eventually learned to tell the difference between a wet-cry, a hungry-cry, and a gas-cry.

The guessing game is a kind of I-message. The parent, finding some particular behavior unacceptable (like crying in the middle of the night), takes action, as opposed to sending a verbal I-message. The action is in essence a nonverbal I-message: when the baby cries you pick her up and do something, as if to say, "I cannot stand your crying anymore!" Now, instead of leaving responsibility with the baby to initiate a change in her crying behavior, you, the parent, must take the initiative. Obviously, the baby cannot go get her bottle. Nor is she capable of saying, "I'll quit my crying, if you get my bottle." So the parent has to perform this function *for* the child. So the guessing game is a special kind of I-message *in which the parent provides the solution*.

2. Let's Make a Trade

Unacceptable behaviors of infants and toddlers can also be changed by trading: substituting unacceptable behavior with another behavior that is acceptable to the parent.

Laura, your curious one-year-old, has found a pair of your new nylons, which she finds enjoyable to touch and tug on. You find this unacceptable because you're afraid she'll snag or destroy them. You go to your drawer and pull out an old pair that is already snagged and beyond being wearable. You place this pair in her hands and gently take away the new pair. Laura, not knowing the difference, finds the damaged pair equally enjoyable to touch and tug. Her needs are met, but so are yours.

Dave is jumping up and down on the couch and Mother fears he'll knock the lamp off the end table. Mother gently but firmly removes Dave from the couch and proceeds to jump up and down with him on the pillows, which she removed from the couch and put on the floor.

Shirley, age eighteen months, starts to get up on her dad's lap on the very night he is dressed in his freshly cleaned light-colored suit. Dad notices that Shirley's hands are covered with jam mixed with equal parts of peanut butter. Dad gently restrains Shirley, but then immediately goes to the bathroom, gets a wet wash-cloth, and wipes her hands clean. Then Dad picks Shirley up and puts her on his lap.

Trading, too, is a special type of I-message. Non-verbally, the parent first communicates, "When you have jam on your hands I don't want you on my lap." Then, by washing Shirley's hands clean and putting her on his lap, Dad communicates nonverbally, "When your hands are clean I want you on my lap."

When parents start thinking in terms of trading to get rid of unacceptable behavior, they won't think about using their power—slapping, hitting, pushing, or other forms of punishment.

3. "I'll Show You How I Feel"

With kids too young to understand a message which tells them how you feel, you can try *showing* them. Again, this is a type of nonverbal I-message, as illustrated in the following incidents:

While Dad is carrying little Tony in the supermarket, he starts to kick Dad in the stomach, laughing with each kick. Dad immediately puts Tony down on his feet and continues walking. (Message: "It hurts me when I get kicked in the stomach; so I don't like to carry you.")

Judy stalls and pokes getting into the car when Mother is in a terrible hurry. Mother puts her hand on Judy's rump and gently but firmly guides her onto the front seat. (Message: "I need you to get in right now because I'm in a hurry.")

The key to this method is to avoid any behavior that will be punishing or painful to the child. After all, you only want him to know how you're feeling. Slapping, hitting, thumping, pushing, jerking, yelling, pinching—all these methods inevitably communicate to the youngster that he's bad, he's wrong, his needs don't count, he's done something criminal, and he deserves to be punished.

A NEW CONCEPT: THE APPRECIATIVE I-MESSAGE

In my first P.E.T. book and in the P.E.T. classes, I-messages were presented almost solely as an effective method for confronting children when their behavior was *unacceptable*. Many parents have been puzzled by this limited use of the I-message, and have asked perceptively, "Why can't you use the I-message to communicate your positive or appreciative feelings when your kid's behavior is *acceptable?*" Experience has influenced me, as well as many of the P.E.T. instructors, to consider seriously just how this idea can be fitted into the P.E.T. model.

I've always been ambivalent about sending messages that contained positive evaluations, largely because of my conviction that praising kids is so often manipulative and at times even destructive to the parent-child relationship. My argument went like this:

Praising kids is often motivated by an intent of the parents to get them to do what the parents have already decided is *best for them to do*. Or conversely, parents praise with the hope that the child will *not do* what they think he should not do, but instead will repeat the "good" behavior that's been rewarded by the parents' praise.

Psychologists have proven beyond any doubt, in literally thousands of experiments with humans and animals, that giving a reward just after certain behavior has occurred will "reinforce" that behavior—that is, increase the chances that the behavior will occur again. So rewards do work. Each of us goes through life repeating behaviors that in the past brought us some kind of reward. It's logical. We do things, again and again, because in the past they have somehow given us what we needed or wanted—we have been *rewarded*.

Praise, of course, is one kind of reward. At least that's what most people believe. So why not make a systematic effort to praise kids for "good" behavior? Why not also punish kids for "bad" behavior since we also have proof that punishment extinguishes behavior —reduces the probability of its being repeated. But punishment is not what I'm examining here (later I'll have much to say about that).

No idea is more entrenched in parent-child relations than the notion that kids should be praised for "good" behavior. To many parents it is tantamount to heresy to question this principle. Certainly most books and articles about parenthood recommend it, and in schools, as everybody knows, praise and other rewards are central to almost all theories of pedagogy—not only to reinforce what teachers consider proper behavior in the classroom but also to reinforce good study habits and giving right answers to questions.

However, pitfalls lie in the path of parents who use praise (and other forms of reward) as a way of shaping their children's behavior. First, to be effective, praise must be felt by the child as a reward. In many cases, this does not happen. If a parent praises a child for some activity the parent judged "good" but the child did not, the praise is often rejected or denied by the child:

> Jimmy has drawn a picture of his grandfather's farm-house. Daddy says, "That's a very fine picture, son." Jimmy is terribly displeased with his efforts and replies, "I think it's lousy." Daddy comes back with, "Well, it's not—it's a good picture."

The potential effects of this transaction: Jimmy thinks his father's judgment is bad or he begins to question his own judgment—most likely the latter. Who is right? Is it a good picture or is it a lousy picture? If Jimmy is influenced to begin thinking it's a good picture, then think what his father has done to Jimmy's standards. Could that have an effect on Jimmy's later life, especially if he becomes a budding artist? One certainly could make a case for Jimmy's standards remaining rather high.

Now, let's say Jimmy is also aware of his father's strong need to have a son who draws well. If that's the case, the effect of Dad's praise might well be that Jimmy doubts his father's honesty. He detects an intent to make Jimmy keep at his drawing ("Practice makes perfect"). Now Jimmy's reply is likely to be some variation of:

> "Oh, Dad, you're just saying that to make me feel good! You really don't think the picture is good."

Loosely translated, that message reads, "Dad, you're not honest and I see through your praise." What might this transaction do to the father-son relationship?

Still another problem can be precipitated by praise. Jan, who aspires to be a tennis champ, enters her first tournament and loses in the semi-finals. Her mother, a loyal spectator at the match, with the understandable intent to console, says, "Jan, you played a fine game." Jan, almost in tears and convinced she played poorly, angrily replies, "I did not, I feel horrible! I should have won." And from Mother, "You did your best, honey."

A likely effect of this praise is that Jan will feel her mother does not understand the depth of her disappointment in defeat. Mother denies Jan's obvious hurt, as well as Jan's evaluation that she didn't play well. So, although her intentions were to console and reassure with praise, Jan's mother missed an opportunity to show empathic understanding. She might have done that with a response such as:

"You don't feel you played well and you're very disappointed you didn't win."

Parents erroneously assume that a kid (and everybody else) always likes to be praised. Not so! Praise often makes the recipient feel uncomfortable or embarrassed, especially if friends are around to hear it. Have you ever watched a youngster react to praise by hanging her head, scraping her feet, or burying her face in her hands? Such emotional discomfort is often accompanied by responses that deny the validity of the praise:

1. PARENT: You have such lovely red hair.

   CHILD: I hate it!

2. PARENT: You're getting to be such a good little swimmer.

   CHILD: I'm not half as good as Laurie.

3. PARENT: That was such a wonderful breakfast you cooked for us.

   CHILD: Was not—I cooked the eggs too long.

Something about praise produces another troublesome side effect—it communicates to the recipient that he or she is inferior to the sender. It works that way because praising is judging, and the act of judging usually implies that the evaluator knows more than the one being evaluated. So when a person is praised he may feel patronized—by definition, "treated with a superior air."

If I evaluate another's accomplishment, by implication I communicate I'm expert enough to know the standards by which such activity is judged—that is, I know what is good and poor performance for that activity—art, music, writing, or some athletic endeavor. The act of judging establishes my superiority. Seldom do people like being patronized. And remember? Kids are people, too.

In recent years, some of our P.E.T. instructors have been insinuating into the course an alternative which can be employed by parents with much less risk of producing the negative effects of praise.

It was only natural to ask, "If the I-message is a more constructive way of motivating a child to modify behavior that's *unacceptable* to parents, could it also be a more constructive way of communicating positive feelings—appreciation, pleasure, gratitude, relief, thankfulness, happiness?"

When parents praise their children it comes out as a You-message, almost without exception:

"You're a good boy!"

"You did a fine job!"

"You behaved very well at the restaurant!"

"You're doing so much better at school!"

In our diagram of the communication process, we can represent a parent who is experiencing a positive feeling as follows:

Accurate coding of such a feeling would obviously be an I-message, certainly not a You-message:

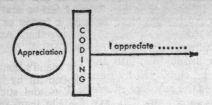

A complete three-part I-message would include (1) the child's behavior, (2) the parent's feeling, and (3) the tangible effect on the parent. Suppose the child surprised his parent by cleaning up the kitchen after making snacks in the afternoon when he came home from school. The parent's message might be:

> "When the kitchen was all cleaned up when I started to fix dinner tonight, I appreciated it, because I didn't have to spend time cleaning it up myself."

Here are some more examples of positive I-messages:

Your eight-year-old daughter phones to tell you she stopped at her friend's house after school.	"When you let me know where you are, I feel relieved, because then I don't worry about you."
Your twelve-year-old son has begun to wash his hair every day.	"When your hair is clean all the time, I get pleasure looking at you."
Your six-year-old son pitched in and helped you set the table when you were in a hurry.	"I was sure happy to have your help tonight, because without it dinner would have been late and I would have missed my TV program."

A mother describes two occasions when she sent appreciative I-messages:

"In the morning now when Caroline gets dressed by herself, I'll mention to her, 'Wow, I feel so neat when you get dressed like this, because it leaves us more time to talk and have a good time together.' And she beams and smiles."

"Today we had an Easter party at a friend's house and before we left, Caroline went around all by herself and picked up all the Easter baskets and stuff and put them in a paper sack and brought them over to me. And, you know, I was floored! And I said, 'You know, you saved me so much time, because I thought I was going to have to pick them all up myself. I'm so pleased—you've been such a terrific help to me!' She just floated on cloud nine!"

Note that this mother's messages were *I-oriented*. She sent no judgments or evaluations of Caroline. But will they still be interpreted by Caroline as manipulative and controlling—that is, as attempts to "reinforce" her "good" behavior? I think not, provided two conditions prevail:

1. The parent is not consciously trying to use the messages to influence the child to repeat the desired behavior (to modify the child's future behavior).

2. The message is simply a vehicle for communicating a spontaneously experienced temporary feeling—that is, the feeling is genuine and real, as well as here and now.

Adding this new concept to the P.E.T. model provides justification for parents to share their positive feelings when they spontaneously feel appreciative, without the risks inherent in praise. Previously, I'm afraid that when I cautioned parents against praising their kids, I left them puzzled, frustrated, and with no constructive way of communicating the positive feelings most parents feel from time to time. Now they have an effective way to tell their kids how they feel.

THE PREVENTIVE I-MESSAGE

Recently, I have come to see another significant omission in the P.E.T. model. Being an assertive parent need not be limited to sending confronting I-messages only after the child *already has caused you a problem.* When you're experiencing no problems at all in your relationship with a youngster (the relationship is in the No-Problem area of the rectangle), you may want to send a message to prevent an unacceptable behavior in the future.

For example, your family is planning a trip and you know all of you will be together a lot, often in the close confines of the car or a motel room. You'll be wanting some private time, by yourself and with your spouse. Prior to your departure you want to communicate this need to your kids, hoping it will influence them to be sensitive to your need for "alone time." Your assertive message might take this form:

> "I like to be alone sometimes, and I also need to spend time with just Mommy and me. When we go on our trip next week, I'd really appreciate having this time every once in a while."

Such an I-message might be called an I-want or an I-need message. Its purpose is to inform your kids ahead of time exactly what you want, need, or like.

> "I need quiet in the house from one o'clock until two o'clock so I can have a nap."

> "I like to know where you are when school is out."

> "The national basketball finals will be on TV all next weekend. I know some of the games will be on during the kid shows on Saturday morning. But I sure don't want to miss any of the games."

> "I wish we could use our dinner time for talking about things that are important to each of us."

"When Grandma comes next week, I'd really like the living room kept clean all the time without any messes."

These assertive messages naturally won't always get parents exactly what they want, but it's far better to let your kids know ahead of time what you have in mind than wait until they behave unacceptably out of ignorance of your needs. An I-want message in time might save nine confrontations.

A less obvious effect of the preventive I-message is that kids learn that their parents are human: they have needs, wants, preferences, and wishes like everyone else. And, of course, I-want messages give kids a chance, without being told exactly what to do, to behave so their parents will be pleased.

A mother, raising her three teen-age sons by herself, described how she sent an I-want message to her son, Don, about a PTA meeting:

"I feel Don has been closer to me—I can tell him what I feel. The other night I went to this PTA thing where he was going to play the guitar and sing. He wanted me to go, but I'd never been before, and I was feeling like I didn't want to be dumped in there and left alone, not knowing anyone. So I said, 'Don, I've never been to your school meeting before and I'm feeling just a little scared, you know. I'd like you to take care of me in there and not just leave me.' And he did! He took me in and introduced me to a bunch of people I didn't know, and he brought me a cup of tea. He just really looked after me!"

HOW I-MESSAGES LEAD TO PROBLEM-SOLVING

When an I-message fails to produce an immediate change in a child's behavior, some parents give up, feeling disappointed or resentful. They forget that I-messages sometimes are only a prelude to problem-solving or conflict-resolution. The I-message tells the youngster why his behavior is unacceptable to *you*, yet he may have strong needs to continue, for reasons unknown to you at the time. So when he does not modify his behavior, the two of you have a conflict—you don't like his behavior, but *he* does! Even if you send a stronger I-message the second time, he might not change.

This certainly doesn't call for giving up (or giving in). Your needs are still unmet, and you still have a problem. Your job is to start problem-solving, which you'll recall means: defining the conflict (what are your needs, what are the child's); generating possible solutions; evaluating each solution; and finally getting agreement (making a mutual decision) on a solution acceptable to you *and* the child.

How this works is reported by an Arizona P.E.T. mother and instructor:

"We had a really neat play yard, so all the kids in the neighborhood would come to our house and play. My problem was that I didn't want them to come on Sunday morning because that was the time I wanted to be free from watching the kids—to have quiet time and sit and drink my coffee and read my paper. So I said, 'I would really appreciate it if you wouldn't come to the door until noon because I want time to be alone and drink my coffee and read the paper!' But that didn't work, because they came and rang the doorbell every fifteen minutes asking me if it was noon yet. So my I-message didn't work. So I decided we'd problem-solve it and see what we could come up with, because I really liked the kids and wanted them to feel comfortable about being there, but I needed the time to myself. So we came up with the solution that when it was noon I'd put a flag out in front, because we had a flag holder on our porch. So when they saw the flag, that was their signal that they then could come to the yard. But until they saw the flag they weren't even to come to the door. The first Sunday we did this I went outside to put the flag in the flag holder, and here lined up on the sidewalk in front of the house were all these little kids just waiting with their eyes glued to the house to see when the flag was coming out. It really did solve the problem. . . . I don't even remember who came up with the decision—it just evolved, and it worked, and solved the problem."

In subsequent chapters, the problem-solving method will be examined more fully. My point here is: when I-messages don't work, parents may have to move into problem-solving to find a solution that will meet their needs, as well as the child's.

IX

PARENT-CHILD CONFLICTS:
Who Wins, Who Loses

Confronting a child with an I-message—even a good one—will not of course, always produce a behavior change. The youngster may have such a strong need to continue what he is doing that he will not modify his behavior, despite his knowledge that it is causing his parent a problem. Our terminology for this situation is "conflict"—parent and child have conflict, and *the relationship owns the problem* because the needs of parent and child are at stake.

We locate behavior that brings on the conflict in the very bottom of our rectangle. Observe, however, that some of the child's unacceptable behaviors already will have been eliminated by I-messages. Others that persist, because I-messages do not always work, cause conflicts in the relationship.

Faced with a conflict in your relationship with a child, how should you approach this conflict to get it resolved? We now must employ *methods of conflict-resolution*. In P.E.T. we teach parents what we call the No-lose method. This critical technique is fully discussed in the P.E.T. text book. Here I'll review its elements, contrast it with the two other methods of

173

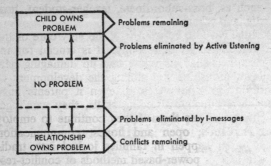

conflict-resolution that are used almost universally by parents before their P.E.T. course, and discuss some of the reasons why parents do not easily accept the new method. Then I'll offer new insights and perspectives to help parents understand and accept the No-lose method more readily.

BARRIERS TO ACCEPTING NO-LOSE CONFLICT-RESOLUTION

Most parents quickly understand that by learning how to become better listeners they have everything to gain and nothing to lose. Parents also tend to welcome the I-message skill and its promise to increase their effectiveness in getting kids to listen and modify whatever behavior is giving parents a problem. But the concept of No-lose conflict-resolution is not invariably welcomed by parents. In fact, many initially suspect that this new method of resolving parent-child conflicts requires them to give up something—their influence, authority, power, "parent prerogatives."

So the No-lose method threatens some very fundamental and traditional beliefs of parents. Even more significant, the method is not familiar to parents. Rarely do we meet parents whose own parents used the No-lose method. For that matter, we find few parents who have had *any* firsthand experience with the No-lose method in the important relationships in their lives—such as, boss-subordinate, teacher-student, husband-wife, and others.

Yet the No-lose concept is at the very core of the P.E.T. model and its philosophy. It is crucial for resolving conflicts that otherwise end up damaging parent-child relationships and stifling the development of responsibility in children. And, even if parents have learned more effective listening skills, they won't get many chances to use them if they continue to employ win-lose methods; open and honest communication does not often happen in families locked into traditional win-lose or power-based methods of conflict-resolution. *Children do not easily share feelings with parents they fear.*

Consequently, in P.E.T. we are faced with a dilemma: of all the methods we teach, the method we think parents need the most is often the one they least want to hear, because almost all parents are strongly committed either to an *authoritarian* approach for resolving parent-child conflicts or a *permissive* approach.

THE THREE METHODS FOR RESOLVING CONFLICTS

Almost without exception, the many thousands of parents who enroll in P.E.T. have been handling their inevitable conflicts with children and youth in one of two ways: strict or lenient. We call these approaches Method I and Method II. Both are win-lose approaches —somebody wins, somebody loses. Conflicts are approached as power struggles, a contest of wills, a fight to win. A review of both methods will help the reader understand why.

Here is how Method I operates:

When a conflict between parent and child occurs, the parent decides what the solution must be, hoping the child will accept it. If the child resists, the parent threatens to use (or actually uses) power and authority to coerce the child into compliance. (PARENT WINS, CHILD LOSES)

Here is how Method II operates:

When a conflict between parent and child occurs, the parent usually makes an initial effort to persuade the child to accept the parent's solution. When the child resists, the parent gives up or gives in, permitting the child to get his way. (CHILD WINS, PARENT LOSES)

In both methods the attitude of parent and child is, "I want to get my way and I'm going to use my power to get it" or "I'm going to get my needs met, even if the other person doesn't get his met." In both, one goes away feeling defeated and usually resentful or angry at the other for winning.

In Method III, unfamiliar to all but a handful of parents, parent and child together search for a solution that would meet the needs of both—no one loses, both win. Hence, the name "No-lose method."

Here is how Method III operates:

When a conflict between parent and child occurs, the parent asks the child to participate in a joint search for some solution acceptable to both. Either may suggest possible solutions, which are then evaluated. A decision is eventually made on the best solution. They then decide how it is to be carried out. No coercion is required, hence no power is used. (NO ONE LOSES)

To show how each method works, here is a conflict between a mother and her four-and-a-half-year-old son, Eric. Mother is upset and worried about Eric's refusal to eat vegetables.

Method I

M: I really worry when you don't eat your vegetables because I'm afraid you're not getting all your vitamins, and you need them to grow up and be strong and healthy.

E: I don't like vegetables—I *hate* them.

M: Well, I don't care. You're going to eat at least some of the vegetables I serve you. If you don't, then you won't get any of the other foods you like.

Method II

M: I really worry when you don't eat your vegetables because I'm afraid you're not getting all your vitamins, and you need them to grow up and be strong and healthy.

E: I don't like vegetables—I *hate* them.

M: I just don't know what to do with you! You know you need vegetables. So if you don't eat them, you're the one to suffer. I give up. Go ahead and ruin your health. You'll be sorry.

Method III
(Submitted by a P.E.T. graduate)

"One morning after breakfast I called Eric, who is four and a half years old, to sit with me at the dining room table. This was just the right time to discuss and attempt Method III to solve a problem because Eric's favorite TV program ('Sesame Street') wasn't on for another hour. I briefly described to Eric what we were about to do and what the problem was.

M: I really worry when you don't eat your vegetables because I'm afraid you aren't getting all your vitamins. [I have talked to him before about the importance of vitamins to growth.]

E: Uh, huh.

M: Your daddy and I are tired of telling you to eat them and punishing you when you throw them up on your plate.

E: I know, but I *don't* like vegetables—I *hate* them.

M: You really hate to eat vegetables!

E: Yeah!

M: Well, this is the problem and we want to do something so that we don't have to get angry with you
anymore. Can you think of something we can do
about it?

E: I could go to my room and not play with the kids
for a couple of days.

M: Well, that's really punishing you, and we don't
want to do that.

E: Well then I don't know.

M: I have a few ideas, I'll write them down so we
can see what they are and maybe we, *you* and *me*,
can decide what might be OK for *both* of us.

E: OK.

M: How about my making a list of the vegetables you
do like and a list of the vegetables you don't like?

E: Yes, do that!

M: You think that's a good idea.

E: Yes!

M: OK, you tell me what you like and I'll write them
down.

E: Well (*then he runs to the cupboard and takes out
certain cans of vegetables*), these, Mommy!

M: OK, let's see what they are—green beans, corn,
creamed corn, is that it?

E: Well, I also like corn on a stick.

M: Do you mean corn on the cob?

E: Yes, corn on the cob. I like salad and mixed
vegetables. I like cucumbers and onions too in my
salad. (*As he mentioned these, I repeated them
back to him.*)

M: OK, anything else?

E: Yes, not cooked I like carrots and cabbage.

M: OK, how about another list of uncooked or raw vegetables?

E: Yeah!

M: OK, you agree.

E: Another list—what I *don't* like (*then he points with his finger to the page*), Mommy (*here he begins to dictate to me*), write down, "Eric, does not like peas, peas and carrots."

M: OK. (*Then I repeated the entire list to him and he agreed that the list was correct.*)

E: Mommy, put down (*here he dictates again*) "Mommy don't forget what Eric likes and what he don't like." (*I wrote everything word for word and repeated it back to him.*)

M: OK and also, "Eric will eat what he likes on this like list" without Mommy or Daddy telling him to eat them. Do you agree to that?

E: What's agree?

M: That means that you understood what I'm saying and it's OK with you.

E: OK, I agree!

M: Where should we put it?

E: Up there (*points to cupboard*) where you can see it *every day.*

M: OK (*and I let Eric tape it up*).

E: Good idea, Mom!

"We both smiled at each other and he walked away happily to see his program."

Unlike Method I and Method II, the No-lose method is a "problem-solving" process, usually requiring six separate steps, as explained previously:

Step I: Defining the problem.

Step II: Generating possible solutions.

Step III: Evaluating the possible solutions.

Step IV: Deciding on the best solution.

Step V: Implementing the decision.

Step VI: Follow-up evaluation.

The key to using the No-lose method effectively is to make certain this six-step process occurs. It needn't always proceed sequentially. But it's important that parent and child complete the steps, particularly the first five.

The No-lose method can also resolve conflicts between siblings and between husband and wife. In fact, it is a universal method for resolving conflicts in all human relationships—between individuals, groups, even nations.

In P.E.T., parents not only read cases in which Method III is used successfully, but they get opportunities to practice the method in class with simulated conflict situations. Often they bring back to the classroom tape-recordings or written dialogues of problem-solving sessions they tried at home. These are analyzed and critiqued by the instructor and class.

More than a dozen years of teaching Method III have greatly increased our understanding of the difficulties parents encounter with the method—both accepting the concept and making it work in the home.

NEW PERSPECTIVES ON CONFLICT-RESOLUTION IN FAMILIES

We have learned why parents resist the nonpower, No-lose concept. We have also acquired new insights about how parents become confused about "parental authority" and its place in the home. Parents also have revealed how they got locked in to either Method I or II. We think, too, that we have a better understanding now of the typical fears parents experience when they start thinking about giving up Method I. And we have made some recent advances in our own thinking about the No-lose method, leading to some improvements and refinements in the P.E.T. model.

The Discipline Dilemma

Ask one hundred parents, "Should children be disciplined?" and ninety-nine unhesitatingly will answer, "Of course." That parents should discipline their offspring has been so commonly believed (and strongly defended) that to question the validity of the idea may seem like heresy or foolishness. Yet I know of no other belief that causes parents more trouble. In fact, I've become convinced that it is actually a very dangerous belief; it alienates parents and children and contributes heavily toward the deterioration of parent-child relationships.

Most parents who discipline their children are motivated by the best of intentions. They want their kids to be responsible, dependable, thoughtful, courteous, competent, and much more. Parents simply know of no other way to carry out their good intentions. So they use discipline. Then, when they find that discipline isn't working well, they usually decide they must discipline even more strongly. And so it goes, until the youngsters rebel, retaliate, or leave home.

What is this *discipline* parents feel they need to use? What does it mean? Webster defines discipline as "punishment by one in authority, especially with a view to correction or training." The key to the term discipline is the concept of power or authority—power to obtain obedience, to enforce orders—using *punishment,* or giving *rewards.*

Officers discipline their subordinates; animal trainers discipline dogs in obedience school; teachers discipline their students, parents discipline their children. But where do all these people get their power?

Power is acquired when one person possesses what another needs badly: *rewards.* The teacher has grades to hand out, the dog trainer has food to offer the hungry dog. Power also looms when one person possesses the means for inflicting pain or discomfort: *punishments.* The teacher can keep students after school

or send them to the principal's office; the dog trainer
can jerk the choke-chain and hurt the dog's neck.

Rewards and punishments give people power,
and power is the basis for people's position of authority
over others. So when parents say they use their authority in disciplining kids, they mean that they make use
of rewards and punishments. They offer (or promise)
rewards to get the behavior they want from their children, and they inflict (or threaten to inflict) punishment to get rid of behavior they don't want. Sounds
easy, doesn't it?

In practice, disciplining children through rewards
and punishments is not nearly as easy as it sounds.
There are pitfalls for the parents, and some are quite
dangerous and destructive for the parent-child relationship.

In the first place, parents are inevitably going to
run out of power. When children are very young, parents have a great deal of power over them. Parents
initially possess many rewards that work quite well, as
well as punishments that make youngsters toe the
mark. As children get older, however, parents begin
to run out of effective rewards, as well as potent
punishments. Rewards that once worked are now met
with disinterest. Faced with punishment, children begin
to resist or rebel. When youngsters reach the teen
years, parents come up emptyhanded. One father in a
P.E.T. class expressed it this way:

> "My son is fifteen and a half now, and the only source
> of power I have left is the car keys. And in six months
> that won't work because he'll have his own car."

The mother of a fourteen-year-old girl admitted:

> "Shirley simply ignores most of my attempts to con-
> trol her with promises of gifts and favors. 'Who needs
> it?' she says, and then she keeps on doing what she
> pleases."

Parents who have relied heavily on disciplining
their children when very young discover to their dis-

may that they have run out of power when the kids reach adolescence. And then they find they have no other way to *influence* their kids. This is why the adolescent years for most families turn out to be frustrating, stressful, and stormy.

Parents, of course, would like to see their children become responsible, considerate of others, co-operative, happy, and healthy. Most mothers and fathers know of no way to foster these characteristics other than to administer discipline. Yet disciplining children, based as it must be on the use of parental power, never *influences;* it only *forces* them to behave in prescribed ways. Discipline *compels* or *prevents* behavior, usually leaving the child unpersuaded, unconvinced, and unmotivated. As a matter of fact, children generally return to their former ways as soon as the parental power is removed (or absent), because their *needs* and *desires* remain unchanged when they're coerced.

Most parents are reluctant to give up their power to discipline because the only alternative they see is to be permissive. And few parents want inconsiderate, unmanageable, or irresponsible kids—the type produced by permissiveness.

The No-lose method can be an alternative to power-based discipline (Method I) or permissiveness (Method II). The No-lose method does not *coerce.* It does *influence.* It influences kids to modify unacceptable behavior. It influences them to be considerate of another's needs. It influences them to make commitments and stick to them, as I shall show in subsequent chapters. Likewise, I-messages do not coerce, but they do influence kids to change behavior that is interfering with the rights of parents.

When parents understand that *they will have more influence if they do not use power,* their resistance to giving up power greatly decreases.

The Myth of Benign Authority

So many times I've heard parents in P.E.T. defend their use of power on such grounds as these:

"I always use my power wisely."

"We're firm but fair."

"Dare to discipline, but sprinkle it generously with love."

"Parents can be benevolent disciplinarians."

Probably all dictators and despots throughout history have genuinely felt they were using their power wisely—for the good of the people, no less. While their intentions may be benevolent, it's not how the *dictator* feels that's critical, but how the power he wields makes the *recipient* feel. And my experience convinces me that no one feels good when coerced—children or adults.

Can a parent use power and soften the impact with love? I have come to believe that this too is a myth—one of parents' rationalizations for justifying the use of power. Is anyone capable of "loving" the person he coerces? I doubt it. Besides, I have never met a child who feels loved when his or her parent is using power to win at the expense of the child losing.

I see little possibility of love in Method I or II. In Method I, the child is not going to love the parent; in Method II the parent is not going to love the child.

Authority: One Word for Two Concepts

We have learned that many parents resist giving up their authority in part because the word itself has two meanings, and parents invariably confuse the two.

AUTHORITY$_1$:   Expertise, experience, competence. (He is an authority in his field; they consulted an authority; he speaks with authority.)

AUTHORITY$_2$:   The power to control, command, and to punish for violations. (The boss has authority over his subordinates; he exercised his authority; she rebelled against her parents' authority.)

The first kind of authority involves exercising influence; the second means exercising power by manipulating rewards and punishments. Now, if a parent decides to give up exercising power (Authority$_2$), it certainly does not mean having to give up exercising influence. It's understandable that all parents want to *influence* their children by their knowledge, wisdom, and judgment derived from long experience. And well they should. Kids often need this kind of help. In fact, children are much more willing to listen to parents' knowledge and judgment if the relationship has not been damaged by the parent using power (Authority$_2$).

Another paradox of human relationships: *If you use power in a relationship, you'll come to have less influence.*

In P.E.T. we teach parents nonpower methods of resolving conflicts, which in the long run will create such relationships that children will be more open to the parents' influence.

The Special Language of Power

We have learned that parents who rely heavily on Method I invariably talk about their role and their approach in what I have come to call "the language of power." Typical terms and phrases in this power language are:

Parental authority	Firm but fair
Parental duty	Father knows best
Setting limits	Running a tight ship
Being strict	Discipline
Parental control	Obedience
Punishment	Restricting
Establishing rules	Enforcing rules
Demands	Respect for authority
Deprivations	Spanking
For the child's own good	Compliance

Do parents who take the Method II or permissive approach talk a different language? Not exactly. What we have learned about permissive parents has almost completely altered many of my earlier beliefs and opinions. Contrary to what I was taught in my professional training—as well as contrary to what most authorities still accept as truth—we have not found many parents who are permissive. And the few who are permissive are not that way *by choice*. Most parents who at first appear to be permissive seem to fall into these categories:

1. Parents who used Method I when their children were young (when the parents possessed effective power over the kids), but reluctantly had to give it up when their kids got older and the parents ran out of power. ("They used to respect our authority when they were young, but now we have no control over them at all.")

2. Parents who approach each conflict with Method I but are forced into a Method II posture by the strong resistance of their kids. ("All right, I've tried. I give up, you win. And I hope you suffer.")

3. Parents who are quite permissive (generally use Method II) as long as the conflicts are not too serious or critical, but switch to Method I whenever the conflict is about behavior that the parents find *very* unacceptable or *very* threatening to their values. ("On this issue, I will never give in. You simply have to accede to my wishes, or else!")

The implications of these findings, while startling at first, now seem logical and valid:

> *Most parents (probably a very high percentage of all parents) believe in the Method I approach to conflict-resolution; they prefer it as their method of choice; and they use it when the chips are down and the stakes are high.*

> *Few parents ever want their conflicts with their children to be resolved so that the parent loses and the child wins. If it happens to turn out that way, it is not because the parents have chosen Method II or accepted the outcomes it produces.*

The many authorities and public figures who have been putting the blame for the troubles of youth on an overwhelming predominance of permissive parents have based their diagnosis on incorrect and inadequate data.

Previously, I referred to the "language of power" used by parents who operate under Method I. I also asserted that permissive parents do not have their own separate language. Now we can pursue this further.

I'm convinced that most permissive parents think in win-lose or power-struggle terms, too. The difference is that theirs is a posture of defeat or frustration, so they use the "language of loss of power":

No control	Our needs don't get met
Loss of discipline	We suffer
Give in	Defeated
Give up	We lose
Kids rule the roost	Kids have the power
Disobedience	Rebellious kids
Anarchy	Loss of leadership
Unmanageable kids	No respect for authority

So authoritarian parents and permissive parents are cut from the same cloth—they are not really different in their attitudes, beliefs, or values. And they both use the language of power! They differ in one respect: Authoritarian parents persist in their hope that parental authority will still work; permissive parents have already discovered it won't.

Confusing the No-Lose Method with Permissiveness

Parents are so accustomed to thinking in win-lose terms that it's hard for them to shake off the idea that the No-lose method is a form of permissiveness. Nothing could be farther from the truth. The No-lose method requires that *the parent must also truly accept the solution,* not just the child. Parents in P.E.T. need frequent reminders, when they begin using Method III, that they must make sure during problem-solving that the ultimate solution meets their needs, too. They must not stop problem-solving until a decision is reached that is acceptable—otherwise they *will* feel they've lost.

Resistance to Method III dissolves when parents finally comprehend this fundamental principle: *While Method III will enable your child to get his or her needs met, it must do the same for you.* This principle helps parents who have been locked into Method I because the only alternative they were able to see was Method II, which no one wants in relationships.

"Don't Kids Need Limits?"

Of course they do. The mistake parents make is to use this obvious fact to justify their use of power. Their argument goes like this: Kids need limits; therefore, parents have to use their authority to set those limits. The weakness in that argument is that kids resent having their parents unilaterally tell them what they cannot do, and they usually resist or rebel against the power of the parent—passively or actively. I have never known a child who wants a parent to set limits on his or her behavior—as in these examples:

"You cannot go to the basketball game because it's a weekday."

"I won't permit you to take the car to the party."

"You can't ever play outside after the sun goes down."

"One piece of candy—that's my limit."

A better principle, derived from our P.E.T. model, is the following:

Children need information from parents that will tell them whether their behavior is acceptable or unacceptable. If unacceptable, children may want to make whatever changes are necessary to make their behavior acceptable—they prefer to limit their behavior themselves. In case of conflict, children want to participate in problem-solving so that any decision that limits their behavior is acceptable to them.

Kids need limits, yes, but not limits imposed on them; rather, limits they choose to set on their own behavior or limits that are mutually set. Giving up Method I does not mean a household without limits. It usually means *more* limits and rules—and they're more apt to be followed! Once parents understand this, they're much less tenacious about holding on to parental power.

THE TRUTH ABOUT PARENTAL POWER

With all their strong resistance against giving up their parental power and authority in favor of the No-lose method, parents subsequently make some surprising admissions:

"Method I never worked anyway."

"I hated myself when I used power."

"I always felt guilty punishing the kids."

"I was afraid to relinquish my authority even though it wasn't working."

Strange, indeed, to hear parents make such statements about power and authority not too long after they defended them so very vigorously. One father and mother, Fran and Karl, told us:

FRAN: Karl was very much against the class when he first went. He made it very clear that the only way to go with kids was spanking and hollering.

KARL: Well, with Ben, you know, I could hurt his feelings just by barking at him. I could really hurt him and it was worse than spanking. But Mark was the other way around—he'd rather take the spanking. He would say, "All right Dad, go ahead and spank me, I'm still going to do what I want to do anyway. Spank me, if that's going to satisfy you."

FRAN: The night he wouldn't learn ten spelling words, remember? He said, "You can say anything

you want but I'm not doing the spelling words."
Did you spank him, I can't remember?

KARL: Yeah, I did.

FRAN: So he sat there for one hour writing those words, went to school, and got only one out of ten right.

KARL: Yeah. Only one word! That incident was a big laugh when we reported it at class the next week.

Then there was the mother whose husband pushed her hard to use Method I:

"My husband kept telling me, 'Well, it's up to you to see he gets his homework done. He should study two hours a day in his room. If you're a good mother, you should do this.' Well, I'd try everything—no television for six months, for example, which he never stuck to. And I found they were not working. I would keep him in his room, but he would only sit and stare at the floor. He was very unhappy, we were very unhappy."

Another mother admitted the impotency of her power:

"I won't allow Betty to hitchhike. *She will not do it.* Well, the only problem with that is that it doesn't work, because 'You will not do it' to her means she will sneak and do it, which I know she does."

This parent talks about how much she hated using power with her preschooler:

"I still resort to power. I cannot solve this shoe-tying problem. With day-to-day things it's so easy to give orders to the kid, but it's not easy to give those orders every five minutes, because the kid is not listening. You know, I just nag him and nag him and nag him and nag him and nag him! I just hate that! I hate doing it that way. I take the easy way out and give the kid an order hoping it'll solve the problem. And it doesn't. I think, well, I'll yell louder. And that doesn't work."

Other parents tell us how terribly guilty they feel when they use power, especially if they resort to physical violence of some kind, like spanking, slapping, hitting, pinching. Most parents, it seems to me, get no satisfaction from hurting someone smaller and weaker. In fact, it pains them to inflict pain on their loved ones. Nor do parents of older children feel good about denying the youngsters something they want to do very badly. It gives few people pleasure to play the role of a dominating dictator or a punishing parent—no matter how they try to justify their use of force intellectually and logically.

As a psychologist, I had learned in my graduate training about the "authoritarian personality," largely through a compilation of a number of research studies assembled into a massive book aptly titled *The Authoritarian Personality*. I inferred that the world was full of people whose personalities predisposed them to use power and authority. So when I started the P.E.T. program I expected that a large number of parents would fit this stereotype. True, most parents we enrolled in P.E.T. used Method I to discipline their children. Yet with few exceptions, most have welcomed an alternative. Most have expressed relief from the guilt-producing role of the punishing parent. And many later admitted their power and authority did not work well anyway.

Now I offer the hypothesis that a very large percent of parents who might be classified as "authoritarian" do not have "authoritarian personalities." They only act that way because their only visible alternative to power is permissiveness. And nobody likes that role—in *any* relationship. Show these so-called authoritarians a third method—a no-power, no-lose approach that gets their needs met, too—and they'll be relieved and grateful (at least after some initial disbelief and skepticism).

If I am right, we can all be more optimistic about the possibility of eliminating from our society much of the violence, vandalism, retaliation, and brutality so prevalent today. Behavior we have labeled "man's in-

humanity to man" (and of course, to woman) might
be greatly reduced if we can teach greater numbers of
these humane methods of resolving human conflicts.

In the next chapters, you will enter the homes of
parents who are trying to apply these nonpower methods. You will see their struggles as well as their successes. Judge for yourself whether my optimism is justified.

X

USING THE NO-LOSE METHOD:
Problems and Solutions

Not only is the concept of No-lose conflict-resolution hard for some parents to accept in principle, we learned that the method was not easy to put into practice successfully in a number of the homes we studied. Apparently P.E.T. graduates have more trouble making the No-lose method work than they do applying the listening and confrontation skills. This is not to say that all parents encountered problems with the No-lose method—we also talked with parents who were able to use the method effectively and successfully, often with dramatic results.

In this chapter I will analyze failures and partial failures and offer suggestions to help avoid similar problems in other families. In the next chapter I'll show how other parents were able to make the No-lose method work successfully and be rewarded by an enriched family life.

We discovered a wide variety of problems that parents encountered as they tried to use the No-lose method, yet certain common themes and patterns emerged from our interviews and questionnaires. In some families pressures of time interfered with No-lose

problem-solving. A number of parents found it too
easy to slip back into their old habits of controlling
their children with power and authority—in some
cases, even reverting to spanking and other forms of
physical coercion. Other parents failed to follow
through, to find ways to influence their youngsters to
stick to the commitments to which they had agreed.
With still other parents, the temptation to issue orders
and set limits could not be resisted, especially with
very young children. Finally, a handful of parents
became so discouraged with their initial attempts at
Method III problem-solving that they gave up in despair.

As one of these parents expressed it, "It was a
mess—a real fiasco!"

TIME PRESSURES AND INTERRUPTIONS

Problem-solving takes time, obviously, and some
parents could not find enough of it to use the No-lose
method effectively, as this father admitted:

> "We don't have enough of those little meetings—
> those problem-solving things. 'Cause everybody is so
> busy. I'm guilty of it. I'm gone all the time, working
> desperately trying to keep the ship afloat. And my son
> has activities he's into all the time, and my little girl,
> she does, too. So to get everybody together when
> they're not in a hurry and are relaxed is difficult."

A mother talked about her lack of success getting her
kids into a problem-solving session:

> "They didn't want to agree on any specific date—
> they just didn't want to talk about it. One of them
> was reading—that was a bad time to bring it up, now
> that I think of it. The other child said, 'Why do you
> bring it up now?' So it was probably a bad time. But
> it's kind of hard to find any time when they're just
> doing nothing."

A father commented about the time pressures:

"Gary, my son, has complained about the length of problem-solving, too. The youngsters have a pressing need of some kind—like having to leave at a certain time; and maybe the problem comes up when we're practically going out the door. There's a kind of time pressure there. And the problem loses its punch if you wait and make an appointment to do it at some later time."

It's not at all surprising that so many parents have trouble finding time to get their kids into a problem-solving or conflict-resolution session. In the first place, kids (and adults, too) seldom relish the idea of facing up to a conflict and going through the often painful process of being confronted; working through to a solution; and making a commitment to modify their behavior. Most people prefer to avoid conflict-resolution. It's easier and more comfortable to read, watch TV, or otherwise postpone or avoid the problem, hoping it will go away.

Parents must send pretty strong I-messages if they're going to get their children into a conflict-resolution session:

"I need to get this problem solved right now, because I'm not willing to have my needs ignored much longer."

"This problem has to be resolved, because I'm darned unhappy!"

"I know you're busy right now, but I want us to get to work on this problem as soon as you're through. When will that be?"

"I know you don't want to talk about this, but I do! I'm not willing to go on with things the way they are."

Some parents whom we interviewed shared their techniques for preventing interruptions: taking the phone off the hook, making sure no friends would drop in, setting a specific time the following day, picking a time when no one had a favorite TV show, and so on.

One parent gave us a strong clue why her children usually resisted getting into problem-solving sessions. See if you, too, can detect the reason:

> "I said, 'Well, when I tell you to lock the doors and it's my understanding that you're to do that and if I have to remind you every night, then it's a problem to me. I still have the responsibility, but I want you to have the responsibility. . . . Then also there's the problem of discipline in the home—you're not minding me when I ask you to do something.' So he said, 'Well, I don't know what to do about it. . . . You want me to mind, and I'm not minding.' And I said, 'That's right. I want to be able to tell you something that needs to be done and know it will be done.' "

This report clearly reveals why the youngsters in this family drag their feet when it comes to problem-solving. This mother still talks in "the language of authority"—she wants obedience from her son, wants him to "mind," and when she tells him what needs to be done she wants to know "it will be done." These attitudes are incongruent with the No-lose method.

Principle: The No-lose method will not work when a parent's intention is I-win, You-lose.

The fact that No-lose problem-solving takes time is certainly recognized by those who use it effectively—executives and administrators as well as parents. But they also know from their experience that it will actually *save* time in the long run. Why? Because when a problem or conflict between persons is resolved so that both get their needs met and both accept the solution, there is much less chance for the problem to come up again. Having solved their problem to the satisfaction of both, each person is motivated to carry out the solution.

"IT REALLY WON'T WORK WITH KIDS"

Unlike Active Listening and I-messages, the No-lose method is criticized by some parents as a tactic that just won't work. Whether it's their lack of trust in their kids or that the method seems so foreign to them in family life, some parents initially could not bring themselves to try it:

> "As to starting the problem-solving, I thought, 'Oh, no, this is really going to be ridiculous—I'm not going to be able to sit down and really do this thing.' I couldn't see myself dealing with the kids in this way. They're not going to listen or they're not going to care. They're going to want their way, and that's going to be the only way. . . . I'd feel totally defeated. I'd think, 'Oh, it'll just never work.' "

Another parent felt totally unprepared to try the new method:

> "She's not to ride her bicycle out in the dark, but sometimes she does, and she has a tendency to go visiting from house to house without letting us know . . . that's a problem. I know we should sit down and discuss it, but . . . I know I went through the method in class and everything seemed so neat and straightforward. But it just doesn't work that way in real life. Of course, I have to admit I haven't tried it. . . . That's why I have to read the book again. It's because I'm really lost. I've forgotten half of what I learned."

A father contrasted his feelings about problem-solving at work with using the method at home:

> "It takes a lot of work, a lot of time. At work I can go and sit in a meeting and Active Listen and tell people how I feel, but that's just not the way it is at home. . . . I don't have any patience or the fortitude to follow through."

Undoubtedly, using the No-lose method of home seems foreign or impossible to some parents because they never had the chance to experience the method as children in their own homes. Their evaluation that "children aren't going to care" or "they'll want their own way" must derive from the memories of how they felt as children in the win-lose climate of their own families. How can such people, now parents themselves, be helped to take the plunge and break the pattern?

I have no sure answers to this question—only some suggestions that might work.

First, try the No-lose method initially when there is no "here-and-now" immediate conflict—no strong emotions such as anger or frustration or resentment. Examples: "How shall we as a family spend our time together on the long Fourth-of-July weekend?" "When your friend Amy comes to visit next week, what sort of rules do we need to make your life pleasant, and ours, too?" "How can we solve the problem of my having to wake you up three or four times in the morning to get you off to school on time?"

By starting with such "preventive problem-solving" situations, not only will the method seem less complex but parents will get a chance to see how willing youngsters are to accept solutions that will help their parents (provided, of course, *their* needs get met, too).

Second, choose a problem that's making a child unhappy because his or her needs have not been met in the past. With such problems, the child really has something to gain from problem-solving. Examples: "You hate to have Mommy or Daddy tell you when you should go to bed each night. Let's see if we can find some solution that will be acceptable to you and also acceptable to us." "You don't like eggs very much and I hate to nag you every morning. I'd like for you and me to find some solution so we would both be happy."

Once kids have a few experiences when *they* gain a great deal from problem-solving, they'll be much more willing to enter into problem-solving when their *parents* are not getting their needs met.

WHEN KIDS WALK OUT DURING PROBLEM-SOLVING

A few parents reported that their kids got restless or bored with No-lose problem-solving or actually walked out:

> "The first time we negotiated the chores problem, I remember the kids got tired in the middle and said, 'We're tired of this now.' . . . The job was not finished and they were ready to go out and play. We talked about it later and finished it."

A mother had a similar experience when she tried to problem-solve her need to get help from her children:

> "I said that I wished there were some way I could get additional help around the house because it seemed I couldn't do it all. 'I'm working at the church and I really need help—I don't know what to do, so could we come up with some solutions?' And they were not receptive—they didn't want to talk about it right then. 'Let's talk about it later,' they said. So I replied, 'That's fine, when would you like to talk about it?' One of them said, 'Never.' They didn't want to get into it, and the other said, 'I hate it when we have these little talks.'"

In such situations, parents can try several courses of action. I recommend first "shifting gears" to Active Listening, primarily to understand better why they want to escape. You might learn something about *why* they find the problem-solving boring or unpleasant, so you can take corrective action.

Secondly, get a commitment for later, provided you genuinely feel comfortable with a postponement. If you don't, then a strong I-message is called for—such as, "When I have a problem and you kids ignore me or want to walk away, I really feel hurt and feel you don't care about me." Don't be afraid to be honest.

Most kids much prefer a comfortable status quo over having to make a commitment to change their behavior. Who doesn't? It takes effort to problem-solve (and it's seldom pleasant for kids to hear how their behavior is making their parents unhappy). Consequently, you'll need to let them know how serious the problem is to *you*.

A warning: If you permissively let your kids walk away from a request to problem-solve, they will quickly learn to handle your subsequent attempts to problem-solve in the same evasive way.

One mother, a schoolteacher, summed up her feelings about the importance of problem-solving with kids:

> "It's kind of like being married, because if you're to have a good relationship, you're always working on it. *And you never let there be times when you can't be open and get things cleared up, if you want it to be a good thing.* It's always successful, the problem-solving, unless there's something that comes up and somebody is not willing to share their feelings so you can work it out."

WHEN KIDS DON'T STICK TO THEIR AGREEMENTS

While the No-lose method greatly increases the *probability* of children carrying out their commitments, it certainly does not guarantee it. Parents quickly learn this, particularly with younger kids. Our interviews provided many such real-life examples, as well as unique and creative solutions generated by parents.

One mother described how one of her two daughters failed completely to keep her part of the bargain, and provided us with an example of how parents should not handle such a problem:

> "Barbie had agreed to keep her bathroom clean—it's often used for guests. It was often a mess! Sue said she'd pick up the newspapers around the house. But the very next week, while Sue did her job every time,

Barbie never did get around to hers. Her intentions were good, but she had a busy week—lot of things going on at school. By the end of the week it was apparent that it was not going to work. After a while, Susie stopped doing her job, too. I'd say something like, 'The papers are still out' or 'Would you put the papers away?' Or maybe I'd just start doing it myself. That's more likely what I did. So it was a failure, I have to admit."

What this mother inadvertently taught Barbie and Sue was that if you agree to a decision or make a commitment (promise, agreement), you really don't have to stick to it because eventually Mom will carry it out for us. A completely different lesson would have been learned by the two girls had their mother sent a strong I-message representing accurately how she felt about the girls reneging on their agreement—such as, "When we make an agreement and you don't keep it, I end up not getting the help I need, and I feel resentful."

Some parents fall into the trap of resorting to Method I, using their power to solve the problem of broken Method III agreements, as in this incident:

"In the morning the kids would raid the refrigerator. Now we're on welfare food stamps and the food is rationed out for the week. So we problem-solved it, deciding on a mutual decision; put a 'wake-up box' in the refrigerator—a shoe box with fruit and snack food, peanut butter sandwiches, and some surprise. They could eat from the box—nothing more. I thought it was great and they thought it was great. The next morning there was a pack of hot dogs missing—just like nothing had been solved at all. . . . I don't even want to tell you what we did: we put locks on the kids' doors, so they couldn't get out of their rooms until we get up."

Resorting to power when kids break commitments defeats the very purpose of No-lose problem-solving: to get kids to be more responsible and self-disciplined. Besides, when these parents put locks on the kids'

doors, in effect they used punishment, risking all the
effects of punishment: resentment, hostility, retaliation,
cheating, and so on.

In such a situation, I again recommend that parents try strong I-messages instead of reverting to power.

Perhaps it would help parents to recall their own lives as children—how hard it was to remember to keep a commitment and how tempting it was to hope that parents would overlook failures to stick to agreements. Being responsible and trustworthy does not just happen with one lesson—it takes practice, not unlike learning to play the piano or tennis.

Parents have several options to speed up this learning process:

Send an I-message.

Shift gears to Active Listening.

Send a stronger I-message.

Problem-solve again to see if a better solution can be found.

Problem-solve why the child is not keeping the commitment.

Even with all these options, parents may still ask "But what if nothing works?" In all our interviews only one incident was reported of a youngster continuing to renege on an agreement after repeated attempts to influence her with nonpower methods. This was an eighteen-year-old girl who agreed that if her parents bought her a horse, she would keep the stable clean. She didn't. She was confronted. She said she was willing to clean out the manure. Days go by, the stall is not cleaned. More confrontation. Again, promises to do better. Here is how the girl's father, an articulate physician, described the situation:

"Finally, my acceptance area is no longer there, so the horse was removed from the stall. Three months later, she wanted the horse back in the stall. Well, the same thing happened. She didn't follow through with the contract. What do you do? How do you renegotiate something like that? When I have to deal with people like that repeatedly, then I start turning off. I feel they really don't care about me or about our relationship or they wouldn't do that to me. . . . You know, trust in relationships and that's the whole essence of living—that's part of learning for young people, I think. And sometimes it's a hard lesson. If our children can learn this now, they're going to function so much more effectively as adults and be so much happier. . . . Finally, I told her, 'Dottie, my acceptance level is completely exhausted. I've told you repeatedly about your horse and if you didn't do a minimum of care in the barn your horse had to go. You refused to do it. I'm sorry, your horse goes. By Friday I want the horse off the premises.' By Friday the horse was off the place. . . . I mean, this girl is eighteen years old, and if you can't be responsible at that age, it's too bad. It's really too bad for her. Will she ever learn? Sure, she's learning slowly. It's a question of her value system versus somebody else's, and she's got to put that in perspective."

Probably few parents would disagree with this father. I don't think I do either, based on his perception. Experience cautions me, however, to suspend judgment in the absence of knowing what is going on in Dottie's head. Perhaps there is a deeper problem—a hidden agenda. We don't know from the transcript of the interview. Nevertheless, I do know that negotiation is impossible (say, between two nations or between labor and management) when one party repeatedly refuses to keep agreements. The No-lose method is a two-way street. It does require mutual satisfaction of the needs of both parties.

UNREALISTIC SOLUTIONS FROM KIDS

More amusing than serious are problem-solving situations when kids agree to solutions that are too unrealistic or too difficult for them to carry out. In the warm glow of a problem-solving session they offer, and agree to, impossible solutions which the parents know from experience will never be carried out. A five-year-old proudly and with the best of intentions agrees to clean off the table and wash the dishes each night, a task few adults would find easy. Or your twelve-year-old agrees to wash both of your cars every Saturday.

Here is the story of a five-year-old who made a commitment to go to bed at 7:30 P.M. when she was accustomed to staying up until 9:00 or 9:30 each night.

"I told Jan that in the morning when I wake her up she says she doesn't want to go to school because she's too tired. I said, 'It's frustrating for me to keep coming in all the time and to help you get dressed. That cuts into my time to get dressed and your time to eat breakfast.' At any rate, she understood and we sat down and talked about it. She said she really is tired in the morning. It was so cute, because she doesn't know how to write but she said, 'OK, let me write my suggestion down.' Right off she said, 'I'll go to sleep right after my TV program or after you read me a story—I'll go to sleep then.' Well, that would make it 7:30, and she's been going to sleep at 9:00 or 9:30. To adjust would be impossible—a very unrealistic solution. . . . So that night she got into bed at 7:30, but after five minutes she said she wanted to put on a record. She did, but five minutes later she came out and said, 'I don't think that was such a good solution.' "

Compassionately, the mother agreed to problem-solve again the next day. "It was unrealistic to begin with, but the solution seemed so simple and direct to her she just agreed to it. She felt different at night."

While I admire this mother for biting her tongue and not intervening when Jan came up with her radical solution, another option was open to her. She could have said, "Honey, are you sure that's what you want to do? It sounds awfully early to me for a girl who's used to a nine-thirty bedtime." And Jan then might have taken another look at her first solution. One advantage to this type of message is that the child most certainly would be convinced that her mother was vitally interested in Jan's needs.

Just remember: young children lack the experience to visualize how easy or hard a task might be, so don't rigidly hold them to their first commitments.

Another kind of solution to be alert to comes from a child who you know has difficulty asserting himself, a child typically too willing to deny his own needs to please others—like Tim:

> "Tim and Gina were pushing this cart around the living room, making a lot of noise and interfering with my conversation with a friend. I called them over for a little problem-solving. After my I-message, I said, 'We'll need to think of a good idea so we'll both be happy.' And Tim said, 'We won't play with the toy anymore,' a typical Tim comment: try and satisfy whoever the adult is. And I said, 'Do you think you'd be happy not playing with the toy? Is that a good solution for you?' And Gina jumped in and said, 'No, no, no, Tim, you be quiet; I'll do this.' She pushed him aside and said, 'We can't play in the kitchen because the trash is in the way.' And I replied, 'OK, if I took the trash out, then would you be able to play in the kitchen?' She agreed. And Tim said, 'Yeah.' I took the trash out and they did not come in that living room once."

The lesson here is that some kids may be too willing to give in and adopt a solution that does not meet their needs. Tim's sister, Gina, rescued him in this incident, but parents may have to be sensitive to this type of solution and double-check to determine whether it represents too much submission and unassertiveness.

ARE POWER AND PUNISHMENT EVER JUSTIFIED?

Some parents in our study reported how, for a variety of reasons, they chose (or were driven) to use power or punishment. Their interviews or questionnaires provided a great deal of information about when they used power and why they thought it was necessary. Sometimes their power brought the desired results, as one would predict, but sometimes it backfired, which we also would expect. Some of the parents regretted using power and felt guilty; some defended using power and felt justified.

One father, a physician, clearly understood the pitfalls and damaging effects of power, yet rationalized its use when the health of his children was an issue:

> "If you bring them up in an atmosphere of authority and command and control, you're going to lose them . . . and that's changed my way of thinking—trying not to run their lives for them. . . . P.E.T. made me feel better about letting go of that control. . . . I figure bedtime is my problem, basically. They can have feelings about it, and I'll listen to their feelings, but there comes a point when I have to direct them, for the sake of their own rest and health and growth. . . . As a physician I know the time for your body to rest and that's the time your body does most of its growing—when you're asleep. . . . Sometimes it's absolutely necessary to use a command or specific advice."

While this father's logic is clear and his motivation benign, I cannot help but wonder whether his objectives could be accomplished just as effectively by involving his children in a problem-solving session about going to bed and getting enough sleep; certainly his special medical knowledge could then be communicated to his children as essential data for them to consider.

So power or punishment is used by some parents not because of the failure of the No-lose problem-solving but in lieu of it. Another example from an interview:

> "Sometimes I pull a power trip on them—we're gonna do this and too bad whatever you feel! I use it because I feel my needs are much stronger than theirs. . . . I tell them, 'When you're finished with something,

put it away.' . . . And sometimes, like on Saturday, when I'm having a rough day, I'll say, 'OK, you're not doing what I asked you to do.' And sometimes Chris will agree to it and not follow through, so I'll say, 'OK, I'm going to punish you.' Then I'll take whatever it is and put it away for two or three days."

Here again, no problem-solving was even attempted. Instead, the mother *chose* power and the threat of punishment (and, finally, actual punishment) as her *initial* method. This may seem a small point, but it is critical and deserves thinking about: some parents use power or threaten the use of power *even before any conflict is apparent.*

In another kind of relationship, say between husband and wife, this would be ludicrous. Suppose I say to my spouse, "Honey, I'd like for you to take the clothes to the cleaner today—I just won't have the time to do it because of my meeting." So far so good, but then I add, "You're going to do this and too bad whatever you feel!"

I'm convinced she would not feel motivated to take the clothes to the cleaner. She'd be furious at my using a "power trip" on her. Our relationship would be bruised. There is no reason to think children will react differently.

Several parents told us of occasions when they felt justified using their power to protect the child from some dangerous situation:

"I still think that a circumstance like carrying a .22 rifle out of the house and transporting it to the rifle range requires specific rules and regulations that must be dogmatically and militarily applied. Or else someone's going to get shot. An accident can happen and that's my problem. I'm responsible for my ten-year-old using a .22 rifle. . . . If I couldn't quickly direct him with an I-message, then I'd immediately revert to a command."

Is this father using his power? Some P.E.T. graduates think so, because they often bring up similar situations to refute the validity of what is taught in P.E.T.—or, more accurately, their interpretation of what we teach. Apparently, in the minds of some parents, confusion is created between the P.E.T. model and what seems to be appropriate parent behavior in such real-life situations.

Here's how I analyze the situation with the .22 rifle. Say the ten-year-old son was seen by his father getting into the car with the rifle loaded and not in the safety position—obviously a very dangerous act, and certainly unacceptable to the father. The father's rectangle would look like this:

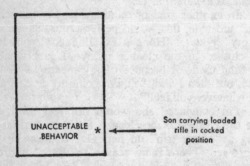

We recommend using an I-message to modify unacceptable behavior rather than any of the Twelve Roadblocks. Instead of a command, which the father felt necessary and justified, P.E.T. theory would call for an I-message, such as

> "I really get scared when you carry the rifle loaded and not in the safety position—it could go off and *kill* someone!"

I'm convinced some such message would be as effective as a command such as

> "You put that rifle in the safety position right now!"

Yet even if the father had sent this command, I wouldn't classify it as using power. I'd say the father only sent a strong You-message, but from experience I'm convinced this has a higher probability of provoking resistance and hurting the relationship with his son. Hence we favor the I-message.

Now, suppose the I-message failed to produce the desired corrective behavior. The son might say, "I'm not going to shoot someone, I know how to handle a rifle safely!" At this point, a conflict has emerged, and the father has a choice of three methods:

METHOD I: "Put it on safety or we don't go to the rifle range." Or, "Hand me that rifle, right now!"

METHOD II: "Well, OK, but just be careful."

METHOD III: "I'm not satisfied with your feeling safe. I don't, unless the safety is on. We have to settle this before we go one step further."

While I'm certain that Method III would work here—and risk less damage of the relationship—I certainly wouldn't fault a parent who chooses to use the drill sergeant approach, especially because I am deathly afraid of guns myself. The Method II approach is the one I'd find hard to condone.

Should the father use a command in this situation, I'd strongly recommend that, after the son puts the rifle in safety position, the father say to his boy, "I'm sorry I yelled that command at you, but I was really scared, and I didn't want to take the time to talk about it." Most kids would understand this easily.

Other parents described similar incidents, but the principles are the same. One parent thought she was using power when she said, "OK, kids, as soon as you fasten your seat belts, I'll start the car and we can go." As you'd expect, no conflict arose; all the kids fastened their seat belts quickly. There was no necessity for the driver to use *any* of the three methods for resolving conflicts.

What about using physical force? Is this the use of power? Take this incident:

> A nine-month-old baby developed otitis media (inflammation of the middle ear). Liquid Ampicillin was offered, but the infant would have none of it. The mother mixed it with strawberry ice cream, but still the baby refused to eat it. The pharmacist gave them a plastic gadget that went into the baby's mouth and allowed the medicine to be poured down her throat. It worked but only when the mother put the baby on her back, held her arms and legs. The baby took it all, but acted darned angry and upset.

Is this parental power? Was there a conflict? Yes, to both questions. Was the parental power (Method I) justified? I say yes, especially because the parents first tried everything they could think of that would be Method III. In view of the seriousness of the infection, I'm sure most parents would have used their power to get that medicine into the baby's system.

IS SPANKING JUSTIFIED?

A handful of parents in our study told us about spanking their children. Frankly, I was surprised that any parent who had completed P.E.T. would still resort to spanking. It also made me very curious to find out why, especially since P.E.T. provides parents with so many alternatives to physical violence against children. I'm aware how prevalent spanking is in every part of the country, with parents from every socioeconomic level. Seldom do I speak to parent groups without getting some variation of this question:

> "Dr. Gordon, certainly you're not advocating that parents shouldn't spank children, are you?"

That anyone would even *question* the almost universal practice of spanking children—at home and in school—makes most parents incredulous. Most parents have a fear that if someone took away their freedom to spank, their children would turn out to be unmanageable, wild animals, impossible to live with and destined for delinquency. One P.E.T. graduate we interviewed gave this view on spanking:

> "The P.E.T. course either implied or the students in the course implied that you should not spank. If that is true, I think it's vastly wrong. In fact, we got into serious problems with our children by being too lenient. We came close to losing control."

As an aside, we can only speculate why in our classes it's the fathers in greater numbers than mothers who defend spanking. The father in the excerpt above reveals his fear of loss of control, implying that the only alternative to losing control of children is physical punishment. However, the value of P.E.T. is that it teaches parents so many influential alternatives to prevent losing control: skills for developing a warm and loving relationship: I-messages for teaching kids their parents have rights, needs, and feelings; problem-solving to find solutions so that parents' needs are respected as well as the child's; methods for setting rules in the family to prevent disorder, chaos, and unbridled license. These are the very same methods and skills that prevent "loss of control" in all human relationships.

From our interviews, some critical insights emerged. First, I learned that some parents had a misconception that we offer Active Listening as an alternative to spanking or other forms of punishment. This confusion is apparent in what this father is saying:

> "Maybe a child has to be older before he appreciates the respect his parent is giving him by Active Listening. Because to our two-year-old the Active Listening was just meaningless. Here he is writing with crayons on the wall, and I say, 'Jimmy, you want to write on the wall.' It didn't work with him because he's too young."

This father had not grasped a basic principle—*a parent should not use Active Listening when a child is engaging in unacceptable behavior*. The appropriate skill would be an I-message.

It's no wonder, then, that he complains that Active Listening didn't work! Of course it won't! Jimmy's response to his father's Active Listening ("You want to write on the wall") would be a resounding, "Yes, I do!" It's more understandable now why the father feels some other method is needed to stop Jimmy from writing on the walls. He advocates spanking for this; P.E.T. advocates an I-message.

I think Jimmy might have stopped writing on the wall if his father had sent an I-message such as, "Hey, when you write on the wall I'm afraid we can't get it off and I'd hate to have a dirty wall!" Perhaps I need to add that Jimmy's father also might have given him some big sheets of paper to draw on (Modifying the Environment).

One mother told how she spanked her six-year-old daughter, Melanie, for the first time, while she was taking the P.E.T. class. Her reason is interesting:

"One day I spanked Melanie for the first time in her life. She was six years old. This shocked everyone in the class. But I realized that I raised my first two children with Method I and my second two with Method II, including Melanie. My resentment toward her had built up and built up until I learned in P.E.T. about kids' power and it made me so furious at that kid I spanked her. . . . In spanking her I was saying to her in effect, 'I'm no longer willing to let you do whatever you want to do.' I didn't want to be walked over."

It seems unlikely that this special spanking, so meaningful to this mother, would be repeated. She probably needed just once to give vent to her anger at being permissive for six years.

Another parent reported spanking a four-year-old who resisted efforts to get him potty-trained:

"I just couldn't see a four-year-old not potty-trained, almost ready to go to kindergarten. Before P.E.T.

we'd shame him, take things away from him, spank him, punish him and promise him a Cheeta if he'd start going poo-poo in the toilet. Nothing worked. . . . But the P.E.T. didn't help on the potty-training either. One day my husband Clark got so upset at Tod—he had changed his pants six or seven times in about three or four hours. Tod was holding it purposely, you know, and then he would let a little out in his pants, and Clark would change him. And then he'd let a little more out. I mean it was *terrible*. And Clark just went berserk and spanked him, really hard —I mean super hard. Since then he's never done it again. The listening and understanding had never helped."

While it is not clear just what Tod has "never done again," one can certainly be sympathetic with this father's plight in that situation. The question is still unanswered whether Tod's continued resistance to potty-training might have been overcome with No-lose problem-solving. The mother admitted that shame, deprivation, punishment, and promise of reward had not worked. Why didn't they give problem-solving a try? Again, it seems clear that parents tried "listening and understanding," but what was called for instead was *problem-solving,* because it was the *parents* who owned the problem, not Tod. We can only surmise what the outcome might have been if the parents had used Method III, starting out with:

> "Tod, we have a problem. You haven't learned yet to go potty in the toilet, for some reason, but Mommy and I are getting tired of changing you all the time. We hate to do it but we can't stand the smell. This is a real problem for all of us. Let's see if we can find a solution to this problem so you'd be happy, and we would too."

In many families parents have had outstanding success problem-solving with four-year-olds—even with children as young as two. I see no reason why the method would not have worked with Tod, *had it been tried*.

Why do parents spank children? To my knowledge, this has never been investigated by research studies. My hypothesis, based on working with parents in P.E.T., is that three factors operate when a parent spanks, hits, pinches, shoves, thumps, slaps:

1. Their own parents used these physical punishments on them.

2. They don't know that there are nonpower alternatives to physical punishment.

3. They employ these methods out of feelings of severe desperation, panic, frustration—they are at their wit's end.

One mother analyzed her use of spanking in some detail:

"I was getting very spanking-oriented. It was the kind of raising up I'd come up out of. . . . Both my husband and I had been raised in families that had very, very rigid discipline, where spanking was *the* method of discipline. . . . I knew I didn't want to use physical punishment, but I hadn't found some other way yet. . . . So I took the P.E.T. class, but it wasn't instant change. It took me a long time to get beyond wanting to spank her. But that's been accomplished—now that she is twelve years old. I tended to jump in, and if I spanked, I spanked, following whatever sort of instant rage I had gone into, but wishing I hadn't. . . . This particular child and I had a very difficult relationship from the very beginning. I'm sure of myself now, but I was panicked when at two and a half we were having constant run-ins, where she would either be sent to her room or be spanked. . . . The thing I learned the quickest in P.E.T. was the I-messages. They worked very well for me. I could stand in the hall and scream at her, 'I really feel like hitting you right now—you're really bugging me'—and be able to control that urge to spank. I was verbalizing it rather than doing it. . . . It took about five years to really incorporate this and make it a part of me."

Another mother touches on some of the same points:

"With Ann, who is four years old, we really get along pretty well, except she whines, which gets on our nerves. A whiny child is enough to drive you up the wall! I'd say, 'You just have to go to your room and when you come out and not whine, then fine. But we can't take it!' It happens a lot around dinner time —I'm tired, she's tired. . . . The biggest change from P.E.T. is that I've found a way to let out my anger, to express my anger verbally rather than express it in a more damaging way to her."

Note the utter desperation experienced by this mother, many years prior to taking P.E.T.:

"When I was pregnant with Paul, Gene was a year and a half. He began waking up during the night with mournful wailing in a penetrating voice. And I'd go to him and try anything I could think of to meet his needs. He wouldn't talk about anything and nothing would stop the loud wailing. First, twice a night, then four times a night. The rest of the family was going down the drain. And I was getting desperate— getting closer to having my baby and on top of this getting up in the middle of the night. I ended up spanking him, but I felt that was not the right way."

Despite the few instances of spanking reported by P.E.T. graduates, I am encouraged by how many parents did find in P.E.T. viable alternatives to physical punishment. Many broke the pattern established by their own parents, many welcomed the I-messages and No-lose method of problem-solving as alternatives to the physical punishment they already hated, and even those who did not stop spanking altogether reserved it only for situations where the child's health was endangered.

XI

HOW PARENTS MAKE THE NO-LOSE METHOD WORK

Our follow-up study of P.E.T. graduates provided overwhelming evidence that parents can make the No-lose method work. Parents reported a large number of conflict situations that were successfully resolved by No-lose problem-solving. Some were simple and brief; others, much more complex, took longer. Some involved conflict between one parent and one child; others required the entire family in a problem-solving meeting. And even though most parents first think that Method III will work only with older, more verbal children, many parents told us how they used the method with toddlers, sometimes even infants.

We also collected cases of the No-lose method being used to resolve conflicts between siblings, where parents play a role not unlike a neutral arbitrator. In some families we learned how they used Method III problem-solving in a preventive way—to make decisions or set rules to prevent conflict arising in the future.

These real-life applications of the No-lose method will provide the vehicles in this chapter for discussing some of the fine points required to make the No-lose

method work. After all, resolving conflicts so that no
one loses is a *process*—a step-by-step sequence of
specific procedures that parents must follow. I'll point
out, for example, how important it is to set the
stage so kids are willing to get involved in problem-
solving. I'll also discuss why parents need to send nonblaming I-messages rather than judgmental You-messages, which make kids resist the problem-solving
method. I'll show the importance of generating a lot of
alternative solutions. And I'll offer parents some new
insights and suggestions that will help them avoid some
common pitfalls.

SETTING THE STAGE FOR NO-LOSE
PROBLEM-SOLVING

One important lesson we learned over the years is
that parents who have the most success introducing the
No-lose method in their families (particularly where
kids are older and therefore accustomed to Method I
or II) are those who made an effort to explain the
new method before they start using it.

Some went into considerable detail, explaining
the difference between Method I and II and how neither had been successful. Some even drew the diagram
of each method to help their children understand. A
mother described how they introduced Method III
when they were tackling the problem of the kids not
eating their dinner:

> "We had dinner and, after the table was cleared, we
> all sat down. . . . We said we'd like to try problem-
> solving the eating problems we had. So first we listed
> the problems together. We took the blackboard in
> there and stood it up. I said, 'Daddy and I feel that
> things have been unhappy and all of us were getting
> upset and we'd like to know if there isn't something
> we could do to change that.' So then I said, 'We're
> going to try a new method that Daddy and I learned
> in our class. It starts with everybody having a chance
> to say what's a problem they would like to work on.'

And I added, 'I'll list all the problems on the board. Then we'll decide how we want to solve the problem. . . . We want to do this so no one loses in this situation—so nobody feels bad about it. . . . If it's a solution that not everybody is happy with, then I don't think that'll be good for us.' "

To children lacking previous experience with the No-lose method, "Let's problem-solve" is not enough to make them willing to get into it. To them, problem-solving in the past meant: parent wins, child loses. So it's extremely important to explain the new ground rules. No one is to lose. Everyone must be happy with the solution. We want to get our needs met but also find a solution that will meet yours, too.

A father told how his teen-age son responded to the first attempt at problem-solving when the parents had not explained the method adequately:

"When we suggested problem-solving, my son said, 'What kind of a new psychological technique have you learned now to let you get your own way?' "

In addition to making sure children really understand what Method III is all about, parents must be certain to start out with I-messages rather than You-messages. The reason is logical: You-messages point the finger of blame at the child, so it is only natural for him to expect that problem-solving will result in his having to be the one to change; after all, his parents already feel the problem is "his fault."

How a problem can be effectively stated in I-messages was reported in our interviews:

"I feel upset when you wiggle around in church, because I can't concentrate."

"Now that we have a nice big family room, I'm working very hard to keep the living area upstairs looking neat. It upsets me when I look down the hall and see in plain view the desk and bureau top in your room all cluttered and stacked high with toys, day after day."

"I'm worried that when we play catch in the living room, one of the lamps will be knocked on the floor and break."

"I'm troubled because you kids watch TV during dinner and I enjoy talking with you at dinner time about your day and about my day. I'm hurt a little because I can't do that."

When you start out problem-solving sessions with messages like these, you greatly increase the chances that the kids will be willing to enter into the process and feel they have a chance to win, too.

WHEN NEEDS ARE CLEAR, SOLUTIONS COME

Parents frequently find it hard to believe that the No-lose method will work when a situation suggests that the only way for this conflict to be resolved is to have one person get his way and the other not.

Dad needs the car tonight, but Mark was counting on it for an important first date with a girl.

Mom has to go to work in the morning but Bonnie refuses to go to school.

Judy won't wear her raincoat to school because she hates the color, but Mother insists she wear a raincoat on rainy days.

Both parents want the kids to be at the supper table with them, but the kids want to watch their favorite TV shows.

Thinking about such conflicts, parents often say, "Either I get my way or the child gets hers," or "There can be no solution acceptable to both parent and child; someone *has* to lose," or "Either Dad gets the car or Mark gets it"; "Judy wears her raincoat or she doesn't." So it seems. But minds are set that way because most people are so accustomed to thinking in terms of *competing solutions* rather than *competing needs*.

When you think of the raincoat problem as a conflict of competing solutions, naturally it appears that only two solutions exist—she is made to wear it or she is allowed not to. Win-lose. However, when you think of competing needs—such as your finding out that Judy doesn't want to wear a raincoat whose color she dislikes, yet you have a need to prevent Judy getting sick—many different solutions open up: Judy could take an umbrella, she could buy a raincoat of the color she likes, maybe the raincoat could be dyed, maybe she could trade raincoats with a friend, and so on.

We learned from families who successfully used Method III that it works when needs are clearly identified and shared, but it often fails when parent and child think narrowly in "either-or" terms. Nowhere is this illustrated more clearly than in the following incident submitted by a father with two children, seven and nine:

"TV was interfering with dinner hour. The children wanted to run to the TV with their plates, or wouldn't come to the table. There had been a lot of hassling about this. At a family problem-solving session, I brought up the problem. My wife and I shared I-messages. The TV watching troubled us because:

"1. I enjoyed talking with my kids at dinner time—hearing about their day, sharing mine. I was hurt when I couldn't do this.

"2. For my wife, preparing dinner was a problem—keeping it hot, knowing when to serve.

"3. If we tried to enforce their eating at the table, there was a hassle, hurt feelings, and then no one enjoyed the meal; if they ate in front of the TV, dishes were left there, my wife and I were both uneasy because we couldn't share with them.

"In response, the kids expressed their needs:

"1. The very best programs for their ages came on from 6:00 to 7:00 P.M.

"2. They would get started on a program and get interested, and then we called them for dinner. They felt this was unfair. If dinner could be at the same time every day, they wouldn't get involved.

"We began to search for solutions:

"1. Dinner could be at a more regularly scheduled time. This was OK with my wife. The kids would avoid programs at that time.

"2. There were usually two nights per week when I was working. My wife said it was OK with her if they watched during dinner hour when I wasn't home. This was OK with me.

"3. The children *volunteered* to avoid all TV during weekdays. I nearly fell through the floor. My wife and I responded that this was not acceptable to us because we thought it went too far. It was a proposal they probably couldn't keep.

"4. They responded that they would limit themselves to one TV program each evening from Sunday through Thursday. This was agreed to—with exception for 'Specials.'

"Outcome: The TV hassle at our home really stopped. The children selected their programs carefully and stuck to their limit of one. This was an agreement we never even anticipated—however, it was beautiful. We had evening time for family games. The kids had time for homework and they got to bed earlier. This plan went on for probably one and a half to two years. By this time habits were formed, the kids were older, and there was not a need for any *rules* on this. The problem just ceased to exist. The TV at our home continues to be used sparingly."

Another problem-solving, by four-year-old Stan and his father, illustrated how important it is to understand a child's need and avoid a stalemate over competing solutions. Stan and his father were home alone; the mother and the two-year-old had gone out of town for the weekend. The first day Stan and Daddy spent a lot of time doing things together. But now Daddy was beginning to feel tense and frustrated over not getting his own work done:

STAN: Daddy, will you build a house with me now?

DADDY: I really feel like I need to do my own work now.

STAN: Please, just one more house, OK?

DADDY: You just aren't ready yet to play alone, are you?

STAN: (*Pouting*) No.

DADDY: You'd still like me to be with you.

STAN: Yeah.

DADDY: But I just don't feel very good about playing anymore right now.

STAN: Well, maybe you could do your work in my room.

DADDY: Well, I want to work here in the living room where all my books and papers are, and my comfortable chair.

STAN: (*Pause*) Would you help me move my blocks out here?

DADDY: You'd like to be in the same room with Daddy while I do my work?

STAN: Yeah.

DADDY: OK. Let's go get your blocks.

Stan played with his blocks for an hour or so. Daddy was able to get a good chunk of his work done, and this put both in the mood to play together later in the day.

In this next exchange, notice how, one by one, Ann's needs get identified and how this frees solutions to emerge:

MOM: I feel upset when you wiggle around in church because I can't concentrate.

ANN: I don't like church.

MOM: You don't feel happy about it.

ANN: No, I can't sit still that long.

MOM: You get tired of sitting.

ANN: Yes. It's not that I don't like listening. It's just that it hurts to kneel and get up and down.

MOM: It's hard for you to move in a small space.

ANN: It's not too bad. Mostly I'm too hot.

MOM: Is there anything you can think of doing about that?

ANN: We could leave our coats outside.

MOM: Good. Let's try it. Anything else?

ANN: Well, I don't always know what's going on.

MOM: Could we get there a little early and read everything first?

ANN: OK. And perhaps you could help me mark my prayer book like you do yours.

MOM: OK. Let's take your own book to church, that's less bothersome than using two books.

ANN: Good. No problems, huh Mom?

PROBLEMS USUALLY HAVE MORE THAN ONE SOLUTION

Nothing contributes more to the failure of Method III problem-solving (or the reluctance to even try it) than the attitude that there is only one solution to a problem in human relationships. The biggest danger of this "one-answer" freeze is that it tempts parents to manipulate a child into accepting a preconceived "right" solution—and give up on the method if the child does not buy the parents' solution. We try to teach parents to keep an open mind to the likelihood that every problem has many possible solutions. Their task is to see to it that, after a conflict has been defined, a variety of solutions are generated. Here are guidelines to accomplish this:

1. Allow the child to generate one or more solutions before you offer any.

2. Don't expect the child to come up with all the solutions. You have a stake in the problem-solving, too, so feel free to toss in your ideas. With younger children, parents usually have to offer more solutions.

3. Don't evaluate any suggested solutions until after a number have been generated. Evaluation stifles creativity and discourages kids from offering their ideas.

4. Encourage your kids to come up with any solution that comes to mind, no matter how silly or impractical. Quantity is what's needed. This is called "brainstorming," a technique used extensively to solve problems in business and industry.

In the following situation, note how many solutions were generated until finally one was acceptable to the child:

"One warm afternoon Danny was in a neighbor's yard with two other children. The mother offered them all popsicles. Danny said something silly to her which implied that he didn't want one, so she didn't give him one. He ran home crying that he wanted a popsicle and demanded that I go get one from the neighbor. My reaction was to want to say, 'That'll teach you not to give such a smart answer again!' Instead, I decided to problem-solve. In the beginning this was not my problem, but it became my problem when Danny demanded that I go ask the neighbor for a popsicle. I listed the possible solutions: his solution that I go get the popsicle; he could go ask her for a popsicle; we could make homemade popsicles with juice; the next time we went to the grocery store he could get a popsicle; he could have a cookie at home. Danny immediately chose to make homemade popsicles after I told him that the first solution was unacceptable to me."

A husband and wife in their twenties, with only one child (two years old) found that P.E.T. skills apply in different relationships, and expressed their

feelings about how the problem-solving process fosters
creative thinking:

F: It was the strangest feeling I ever had, because
I went in to the meeting expecting him to
change, and it turned out that the best solution
was the other way—for *me* to change.

M: I think P.E.T. opens up a whole new world of
solutions to you. It's a process, and after you
decide what the problem is, now you need the
solution. And there are just a million different
solutions. It's not black and white. All of a
sudden it is way different. Things that you just
wouldn't have thought about . . . More creative.
Just way more creative solutions.

In interview after interview, parents reported being surprised by their kids' creative capacity to come
up with good solutions. We underestimate children in
this respect because we have given them little chance to
demonstrate their creative-thinking capabilities. It
stands to reason: Method I gives children no opportunity to participate in generating solutions—the solution is dictated by the parent. You can sense the mother's surprise in this incident:

"One of the problems we had was the kids coming
to the back door with muddy feet. At first we made
them go all the way around the outside of the house
and come through the garage. Yeah, that was my
solution. But they countered with the fact that they
were cold and wet and it's a long way around, and
would it be OK if they took their shoes off on the
back porch and carried them into the muddy shoe
box. . . . It was not a solution I would have thought
of. Once I had told them my solution it was chiseled
in stone as law. . . . It was kind of an eye-opener. I
got what I wanted even though it was not the solution I felt *had* to be. . . . They're much smaller and
younger than me and therefore I'm supposed to be
all-wise and know the answer. And here they had a
pretty darned good idea. It got them what they

wanted and I got what I wanted. . . . It was not a hassle anymore."

Another parent talked about how problem-solving had made her daughter seem more like a person—with good ideas:

> "It taught both of us and my four-year-old daughter, Mary Ann, that she could come up with some good ideas. Before, with us it was just a flat, 'No you can't do that.' Now she contributes new ideas. I think it has made us realize that children are people, and they have the same rights we have. . . . And lots of times she'll come up with ideas. One time I remember she wanted to water every plant in the pots in our back yard. I explained that with some plants all that water killed them. So she then came up with an idea that I would tell her which ones she could water. We worked it out—some she could water as often as she wanted, some she couldn't. And before it would have been, 'No you can't,' and there would have been a lot of crying and everyone would have been unhappy."

And then there was the mother who used Method III to resolve the ubiquitous problem of her five-year-old never eating vegetables. The creativity in their solutions is obvious in the following dialogue:

> "When we learned about problem-solving, I decided that this approach was the one to use on our five-year problem of getting Jay to eat vegetables. In contrast to Barbara who cheerfully ate anything, Jay hadn't eaten vegetables willingly from the day they had first been offered to him as an infant. Most other foods he ate well and with little fuss—but vegetables, they were a lost cause! We'd tried everything from cajoling, to ignoring, to threatening. Nothing worked. If I tried to force him to eat vegetables by threatening to withhold other foods, he simply refused to eat altogether. He'd endure anything rather than eat vegetables.

"Obviously this was a case for P.E.T. problem-solving. We were eating dinner one evening and Jay, as usual, refused to eat peas. I suggested that I wanted to talk with him about it. So after dinner we went into the playroom, and as nearly as I can recall, this dialogue occurred:

M: You remember I said at dinner that there's a problem about you and vegetables.

J: Yeah, I don't like to eat them.

M: I guess I know that by now. Now Jay, this is a problem we need to work out together. You don't like to eat vegetables. But I'd like for you to eat them because they contain certain vitamins that your body needs. Do you have any ideas about what we should do about this problem? Do you have any suggestions for a solution?

J: No.

M: Well, try to think of something. Isn't there something you can think of?

J: (Sort of whining) No, I can't think of anything.

M: OK, Jay. I'm going to suggest a solution, and then you tell me what you think of it. We won't settle on anything until we both agree to it. OK?

J: (Somewhat skeptical) OK.

M: What would you think of this? Would you be willing to take at least one taste of the vegetable at each meal? If you didn't like it, then you wouldn't have to eat anymore.

J: No.

M: No?

J: I don't like that idea. I'm not going to do that.

M: You don't think that's a good idea? OK. Then you think of an idea.

J: I can't.

M: Well, then . . . uh, Jay, are there any vegetables you *do* like?

J: Yes, I like raw carrots.

M: Anything else?

J: Celery sticks.

M: And?

J: And beans. Not beans from the garden, but beans from a can.

M: Any more?

J: Nope. That's all.

M: I see. Now I wonder what we could do.

J: Could you fix one of those vegetables for me every time?

M: (*Slowly*) Yes, I suppose I could. It really doesn't matter to me which vegetables you eat. I'm just concerned that you eat some vegetables. Yes, I think I could agree to that.

J: (*Lightly*) OK.

M: Now there's one other thing. Sometimes you don't like to eat the main dish either.

J: Yeah, if it has onions in it.

M: Well, what could we do about that?

J: I don't know.

M: Well, would you be willing to taste the main dish?

J: But what if I don't like it?

M: What could you do if you didn't like it?

J: I could fix myself a sandwich.

M: A sandwich? Yes, I guess you could. At least you'd get something to eat that way. So you would try at least one bite, and then if you de-

cided you didn't like it, you would make a
sandwich. OK. That sounds good to me. Do
you suppose we should write down our agreement?

J: Yes, let's make a sign and hang it by the table
so you'll remember it.

"Our sign said: The Problem: Jay doesn't like to eat
vegetables and sometimes the main dish. The Solution: Jay will eat raw carrots or celery or green beans.
Mother will fix one of these for him each night for
dinner. Jay will taste the main dish; and if he doesn't
like it, he will fix himself a sandwich to eat.

"We both signed the document with a flourish. I
felt very good about our problem-solving experiment.
Even though it had not been perfectly executed, I
felt as though, in the end, we had both won. Our
solution may not have been acceptable to another
family, but for us it was right. My concerns for an
adequate diet would be fulfilled, and Jay evidently
felt that his freedom of choice would be respected.
Now we simply had to wait and see whether or not
the whole thing would work.

"The next evening when I passed around a plate
of carrot sticks, Jay took one without comment. The
following night he said, 'No thank you,' and passed
them on. Forgetting the role I should have taken, I
lapsed into my former directiveness and reminded
him of our agreement. He took a carrot grudgingly.

"Later I realized my mistake and resolved to meet
such situations in the future with an appropriate
I-message. The next time it happened, I said, 'I'm
disappointed, Jay. I thought we had made an agreement about eating raw carrots.' Jay responded positively.

"Several nights later I fixed a main dish which
Jay eyed very suspiciously. He gamely took one bite
and pronounced it horrible. Then, as though he had
suddenly remembered our agreement, he jumped up
from the table, gleefully ran for the bread, jam, and
peanut butter and began making himself a sandwich.

"I was much amused by his obvious pleasure. It
meant so much to him to be able to have this au-
tonomy. I was beginning to get an insight into his

repressed feelings of the past and realized that, despite our very good intentions otherwise, we had succeeded in making him feel quite oppressed."

This mother added an interesting postscript:

"The vegetable-eating episode has a happy ending. We no longer hold to the original agreement—it served its purpose for helping us get through a difficult time. Now, most of the time, Jay will eat a small amount of vegetables without any urging."

MODIFYING THE ORIGINAL DECISION

Not all decisions made by the No-lose method turn out as well as expected. Method III can hardly guarantee a perfect solution each time. Not only in families, but also in business and industrial organizations, problems often have to be re-solved, after you discover that the first solution was inadequate. Parents should not make the mistake of rigidly adhering to a family decision in the face of evidence that it's not working out, for whatever reason. Here is an anecdote illustrating how parents need to call another problem-solving session to find a better decision:

"My two girls, Gina and Laurie, had problem-solved with me the problem of clearing the table and setting it up for dinner each evening. We agreed, using Method III, that they would take turns a week at a time, one clearing the table and wiping it off, the other setting the table. For the first week it worked fine. Then Gina, the four-year-old, began balking and fussing, but only when it was her turn to clear and wipe. She loved to set the table. So we called another family conference on the floor of our family room with a big piece of newsprint taped to the paneling. . . . I learned that Gina, naturally quite short, found it hard to reach up to the table to get the dishes off, and so she was afraid she'd drop them in lifting them down and carrying them to the sink. She didn't mind wiping the table but she didn't like being left alone in the kitchen doing it. So the whole family decided to help her with her problem. Below is exactly what we wrote on the newsprint, ending up with a new decision that the girls would take turns as before, but when it was Gina's turn to clear and wipe, Daddy would do the clearing for her and she would wipe as usual. That was over four months ago, and there's been no problem since."

PROBLEM: How to get the table set, cleared, and wiped off every day.

Needs:

Laurie	Mommy	Gina	Daddy
Not to be bugged by Gina about whose turn it is and wanting to trade jobs Needs job to have allowance to buy things	Needs help Doesn't need to have to take time to talk people into doing their jobs Needs to have table cleared faster, so she's not just standing around	Laurie not to yell at me I like to set table best Don't like to clear table (The last two are not needs but we accepted them anyway.)	Needs girls to take part in housework Needs not to have to argue, yell, listen to crying and get mad when someone doesn't clear table

Solutions:
(taken from girls first)

1. Laurie let Gina set table tonight.

2. Gina always sets, Laurie always clears and wipes.

3. Take turns by the day, not by the week.

4. Person who sets always wipes.

5. Daddy helps by clearing when it's Gina's turn to clear and wipe and by wiping when it is Laurie's turn to clear and wipe.

NOTE: Needless to say, No. 5 was acceptable to all when we evaluated; and as I said before, that has been months ago and there have been no further problems.

GETTING DOWN TO THE REAL PROBLEM

So often what appears to be a problem (or conflict) turns out to be merely an initial "presenting problem," not the real one. During Step I of the problem-solving process, parents need to do a lot of Active Listening so kids will open up and communicate more. That way parents get more data to help them find out what's really going on in the kids' minds. A mother described a conflict situation which on the surface appeared to be caused by her seven-year-old hating school:

"My son could not get off to school happily in the morning. He angrily announced he hated school, asked why he had to go, left late and in tears every morning. This scene upset everyone in the family, especially me. After *decoding* his 'I hate school' message to 'I hate getting ready to go to school,' I examined the morning routine. I lingered in bed until the last possible minute, then went to waken him. By that time he had to get up 'this very minute' and decide immediately which clothes to wear. He wouldn't get up and refused to pick out his clothes— anything I selected was rejected. From then on it was more pressure to hurry and eat, brush teeth, tie shoes, comb hair, until the tearful departure. Here is the solution we worked out: we select his clothes as he goes to bed in the evening. This is a happy time of the day and he agrees to anything I pull out of the closet. An alarm clock is set early enough that he can linger in bed for a while. The results? He awakens *before* the alarm rings and has his clothes on before I'm out of bed. He's very proud of himself and helps me in the kitchen; brings in the milk and feeds the dog. The change in his disposition is very dramatic and makes our mornings a pleasant, happy time together."

As this solved problem shows, once the real issue has been defined, the other steps usually go quite rapidly. The importance of *using a lot of Active Listening dur-*

ing the first step—defining the problem—cannot be emphasized enough.

Another incident revealed how Active Listening to the presenting problem helped a toddler discover the real problem:

> "It was a bad scene, Mal waking up and getting into bed with his parents around 3:30 A.M. That had to stop. So he told us, 'I don't like to sleep in my bed.' But, he used to love his bed—thrilled with that bed when he got it. 'Well, I don't like my bed, and I want to sleep with Mommy and Daddy.' So we Active Listened and learned that the problem was that his baby brother Greg was waking him up—it wasn't that he didn't like his bed. So we said, 'It's too crowded when you get in our bed and we can't sleep.' So we asked what we might do to solve it. He said, 'Well, we could leave Greg downstairs in his portocrib, then there won't be a problem.' We answered, 'But what if Greg woke up and he was all wet and cold and he cried and we couldn't hear him?' Mal said, 'That wouldn't bother me.' But of course John and I saw that as a problem. . . . He suggested sleeping on the floor in our room and we didn't like that because he might catch a cold. We thought about other beds, eventually agreeing he could sleep in the double bed in the guest room."

KIDS CAN BE SO REASONABLE

We collected incident after incident that demonstrated how reasonable children can be in accepting solutions far less advantageous to them than their originally desired solution. Often parents could hardly believe their children's willingness to agree to solutions that the parents thought would be totally unacceptable.

Method III does something quite remarkable to kids—it seems to move them out of a "I must have my way or nothing" posture. As they see their parents' willingness to unfreeze, to negotiate—to consider seriously the needs of the child—the children are put in a negotiating mood. "Either-or" thinking decreases.

"Me-against-you" attitudes are dropped. The "win-lose" motivation is replaced by genuine feelings of consideration for the needs of parents.

In the following conflict-resolution session, you can sense the youngster's strong need to ride his bike on the street as well as his subsequent willingness to accept a less preferred solution:

"My son wanted to ride his bike on our residential street. After watching him and his reactions to traffic and changing situations, my husband and I realized it simply was not safe for him to ride in the street. We told our son how we felt and he was crushed. Bike riding on a hard surface was exhilarating—so much fun! We listened to him and he realized we wanted him to ride, and then we restated how we felt about the situation. The three of us started to problem-solve and our son decided he would enjoy riding on the black-top in his schoolyard. It was his suggestion and it was fine with us. The agreement was that he'd wheel his bike to the schoolyard and then ride on the black-top, where there was no traffic. He was pleased and we were satisfied. This continued for several weeks until he gained the skill and confidence he needed to ride responsibly and safely in the street."

Here is a session that actually took place a few minutes before our interview with a mother in her home:

"Just a few minutes before you came, Randy felt like playing Halloween. He closed all the curtains in the whole house. I didn't want it to be totally dark while you were sitting here with me. But he felt very strongly that he wanted it to be all dark. I told him, 'We have a visitor coming in a few minutes and I don't think it would be good for us to sit all in the dark; we couldn't see each other and plug in the tape recorder.' He said, 'I really wanted to play Halloween.' Then we talked about it for a while. He agreed that he'd play in the kitchen, because the kitchen isn't visible from this room. As soon as the interview was over he could come in and darken everything. *But he was very understanding about this.*"

PROBLEM-SOLVING WITH INFANTS

Parents of infants and toddlers often comment that the skills they learned in P.E.T. were not as applicable to them as to parents of older children. They view No-lose problem-solving, particularly, as requiring a relatively high level of verbal skills on the part of the child. So parents and P.E.T. instructors have usually assumed that Method III could not be used much before a child was three or four years old. However, we know now that parents *can* use the method with infants and preverbal toddlers. Problem-solving with infants moves through the same six steps except that they're essentially *nonverbal* rather than verbal. All six steps are clearly identifiable in the following incident submitted by a parent:

"My baby was crying and screaming in the playpen, rattling the slats and putting up a fuss as if to try to get out. I didn't want him underfoot because I had to clean up the house before friends arrived [Step I: DEFINING THE CONFLICT]. I thought I'd try Method III, so I began thinking of different solutions. First, I gave him his bottle, half-full of milk [Step II: GENERATING SOLUTIONS]. But he threw the bottle down and kept crying even more loudly [Step III: EVALUATING SOLUTIONS]. I then tried putting a rattle in the playpen [Step II], but he ignored it and kept crying and rattling the side of the playpen [Step III]. Finally, I remembered a little colored trinket I'd bought and wrapped up some time ago. I went to the closet, took it out, and handed him the ribboned box [Step II]. Immediately he stopped crying and started to play with the box, trying to get the ribbon off [Step IV: DECISION-MAKING]. He occupied himself happily for half an hour while I did my housework [Step V: IMPLEMENTING THE DECISION]. Every time I'd come back in the room to check on him, he was still involved with the trinket [Step VI: FOLLOW-UP]."

Mother did not lose, child did not lose—both won! All accomplished nonverbally.

Another incident was described in some detail by the mother of a baby boy:

"Bobby, at fourteen months old, was loving his bottle. When he sucked on it, it looked as though he were in a trance, recharging his batteries so to speak. He'd suck for a few moments and then move on to another activity, leaving the bottle on the floor wherever it happened to be. Well, the problem was that the full bottle, lying on its side, dripped milk from the nipple and left dots which eventually turned black on our new, expensive carpeting. First I tried modifying myself. I promised I'd get the rug professionally cleaned after Bobby outgrew his need for the bottle. But a couple of months passed and the rug looked worse and worse. I couldn't stand how ugly our new rug looked and I started to become uncomfortable every time I looked at it. My next step was to buy all new nipples, figuring that the holes in the old ones were worn and that was the reason they were leaking. That didn't work, though, because the new nipples leaked as much as the old ones. My third effort was to try a new type of bottle Bobby wasn't used to, but which didn't leak. Bobby didn't like that idea because he couldn't drink in his favorite position: the bottle upright on the floor, and Bobby sitting over it, his chin leaning on the nipple and sucking as he examined the floor, his fingers, a book, etc. Bobby cried when I gave him this new bottle. He handed it back to me and walked over to the refrigerator where he knew I kept the old type of bottles. My next idea was the winner. I reviewed my needs. 1. I had just spent many hours scrubbing the black milk stains out of the rug and I didn't want them back. 2. I spend a lot of time on the family room floor and I really enjoy looking at a pretty, clean rug. You might say it was almost esthetically pleasing to me. Bobby's need was obvious—to suck on his bottle any time, any place, any way he needed to. So I decided to fill his bottle with water when we were downstairs and to give him milk upstairs, where I didn't care whether or not the rugs got stained. I tried that and he never complained.

It was the bottle and not the drink that mattered to him. I didn't mind water dripping on the rug because those dots dried up and left no stains. I think we're both happy with those results. I value the P.E.T. ideas that Bobby was respected for his needs, as I was for mine. The long-range effect is that, hopefully, Bobby will grow up feeling he's a person who is important, who has a right to have his needs met, and I have those same rights, too."

The attitude of this mother stands out clearly: "I have my own legitimate needs and the right to get them met, but I respect Bobby's needs. He too is a person who is important, who has a right to have his needs met."

The discovery that parents can use the No-lose method even when their children are infants has far-reaching implications for the prevention of child abuse and child-battering. Only in the last few years has the public been made aware how many children in our society are victims of parental violence. A very high percentage of these victims are infants. Could the explanation be that, because infants obviously cannot be influenced by *verbal* communication (threats of punishment, fear-producing commands, and warnings), messages which most parents employ with older children, parents of infants then resort to nonverbal acts of power (slapping, hitting, spanking, beating, pounding, burning)? If this is true, child abuse might be drastically reduced if parents are taught how to use nonverbal Method III. It certainly would be worth a try.

USING THE NO-LOSE METHOD TO RESOLVE SIBLING CONFLICTS

The No-lose problem-solving method works just as effectively to resolve conflicts between children as it does with parent-child conflicts. The same six steps are involved. The only difference is that the parent, not a party to the conflict, plays a somewhat different role. In sibling conflicts the parent attempts to get the *kids* to go through the six steps of problem-solving. They own the problem, the parent does not.

The No-lose method was successfully employed by the father of Gary, age seven, and Steven, age eleven, when they got into a conflict over baseball cards:

> Steven owned some baseball cards which Gary wanted to take to school to "show and tell" in his second-grade class. Steven was certain Gary would lose them or damage them.

GARY: *(Crying)* Steven took my cards.

STEVEN: They're mine; he took them from my room.

GARY: Make Steven give them back to me.

STEVEN: They're mine. Make him leave them alone.

DAD: *(Arms around both)* You boys are really upset. *(More accusations and crying)* Gary, you're crying so hard you must be upset, but I can't hear what you are saying.

GARY: *(Plainly now, explains how he wanted to take the cards for sharing)*

STEVEN: *(Interruptions and accusations that Gary would lose his cards)*

DAD: Steven, you're really worried that your favorite cards will be lost. And, Gary, you feel badly that you can't take the cards to your class. You feel badly that you won't have anything to share with your class. Gary, do you have any suggestions about how you can get some cards? And, Steven, do you have any ideas how Gary can get cards?

GARY: I have fifteen cents. I could buy them from Steven.

STEVEN: That's fine. I sure can use the fifteen cents to buy new cards and gum.

DAD: Gary, Steven feels he can buy new cards
            and keep the gum and give you the cards.

GARY: I should get the gum, too.

STEVEN: Gary, because I'm going to ride my bike
            downtown to buy the gum and cards, I'll
            keep two pieces of gum for making the
            trip, but you can have one piece of gum
            and the cards.

GARY: Can I take the cards today?

STEVEN: Yeah, if you give me the fifteen cents now.

DAD: Steven, why don't you buy each pack of
            cards and gum separately, so you won't have
            to pay any sales tax.

Did you notice the father's extensive use of Active
Listening (except when he made a suggestion after
the conflict had been resolved)? Also, did you become
aware of how the communication gradually changed
until the boys were talking directly to each other?
While the father's Active Listening facilitated the
problem-solving process, he did not get into the argument or take sides. As a result the boys took over the
process themselves.

Two quite serious problems involving three young
children were resolved by Method III in the next episode:

"It's April now, eight months since I took P.E.T. The
process of problem-solving was the most difficult for
me and my family to employ. My children are now
four and a half, six, and eight, and an incident occurred just the other day that made me realize how
much, despite numerous setbacks in trying to solve
problems, we have all developed—and this despite the
fact that for the past six months we have been in the
process of a divorce.

"There were two glaring problems that had been
building up—one was the difficulty in getting to bed
without a lot of fighting and hassling. Another was the

more and more frequent physical and verbal abuse between the three children. So the first thing one morning (when everyone was fresh and relaxed and there was reasonably good interaction) I brought up my concern on the two issues. My daughter (eight) suggested we use the blackboard and try to find some solutions. Over the months they had become familiar with the concepts of 'solutions,' taking turns offering suggestions, and the need for a solution 'agreeable to us all.'

"We listed 'Bedtime' first, and under it, wrote down everyone's suggestions. Even my four-year-old had several ideas and originally he had been easily intimidated by his verbal older sister and dominating older brother. They all readily accepted that we weren't to judge the solutions as they were offered. Next we discussed each briefly and finally settled on a compromise between two—that each would move back to separate bedrooms and share the playroom if they could each have a corner in the playroom for their special things.

"Next we tackled the problem (and they labeled it) of Name-Calling, Teasing, Hitting, Kicking, Complaining. Incidentally, the boys were not satisfied to leave it at just the physical, more overt interaction. My daughter does very little of this. But she contributes her fair share more subtly and, hence, the labels of 'name-calling' and 'complaining.' I was delighted as the problem really did involve *all* of us and if one felt they didn't contribute to the problem, then a vested interest in the solution wouldn't be there.

"Anyway, using the blackboard and the same process, we arrived at some conclusions. They felt that they needed to do some 'rough-housing' as long as it was in fun, and that was to be done outside. When they were fighting and using any of the above labels, they were to separate and go to their rooms to 'cool off.' And instead of calling names or complaining, they were to practice stating 'I-messages'—what *really* upset them—instead of using names or inappropriate griping.

"I transferred our conclusions to a chart, which is now in the playroom and we refer to it frequently. I'm not pretending that there are never any more hassles, but there has been a lot of improvement and I'm convinced because we shared in the process rather than Mom handing down an ultimatum.

"My hope is for all of us to continue using the process until it becomes 'second nature' to all of us and can ultimately be transferred to problems with friends, spouses, businesses, etc.

"Incidentally, using the blackboard seemed very effective, particularly for my younger ones. They could actually *see* each step rather than trying to absorb it all auditorily even though they couldn't read all the words."

In one family it was the mother who had to step in to apply Method III in a serious conflict involving her two "kids": six-year-old Jack and thirty-four-year-old John (her husband):

"They had real conflict over the TV, especially every Monday when the 'Monday Night Football' was on. Fighting, crying, screaming, and John ending up being the bad guy because he ended up, of course, getting his way, because he'd say, 'I earn the money that buys the TV.' Jack sits by and clenches his fist and grinds his teeth and kicks Robbie a few times. And Robbie slams a few doors and goes off to his room. And so I went in and said, 'All right now, this is really bugging me.' I suggested that the problem was, 'Jack wants to see Zoom and Electric Company, while you want to watch football. We have only one TV and we can't afford to buy another one. What are we going to do?' And we began to think of solutions. It ended up that John agreed to limit himself to the one football game on Monday night, but not watch football or basketball on Tuesday, Wednesday, Thursday, or Friday, unless there was something special and he got agreement from Jack. This way Jack could watch Zoom and Electric Company without fear of John coming in and switching to whatever he wants to see. It worked out fine. The problem had been going on for maybe a month and a half."

REGULARLY SCHEDULED PROBLEM-SOLVING MEETINGS

Some families institute regularly scheduled problem-solving family meetings, much like staff meetings in organizations. One mother described theirs:

"After I first took P.E.T., for the first two years we had an agenda sheet posted on the cupboard door where everyone could see what we were going to problem-solve. We'd meet once a week, and I'd put down things on the list so everyone could start thinking about them. Also I let the kids add to the list, so they felt that they had a part in it too. We'd always write down our solution and keep track of each problem in a folder and review it to see if it was still working for us. And that helped refresh the kids' memories—it was a reinforcement."

While the advantages of regularly scheduled problem-solving meetings are obvious, here are some guidelines for making them more effective:

1. Don't make them last too long. Remember how quickly kids get tired and restless.

2. Some conflicts need resolving right on the spot, so the regular meetings should not replace sessions about conflicts that are urgently in need of resolution.

3. Use family meetings only for issues and conflicts involving *all* the kids. The other children get bored in a meeting when time is spent on conflicts between a parent and one child.

4. When the agenda is long, decide as a family which problems have highest priority and should be tackled first. Low-priority items can be carried over to the next meeting.

PREVENTIVE PROBLEM-SOLVING

The families who successfully used Method III to *prevent* conflicts held meetings that produce rules and agreements for pleasant daily family living and special events planned for the future.

Here is how such a planning meeting worked out in one family:

"My aunt and uncle are flying in Wednesday night to visit my mother. They're coming to dinner here Thursday night. I decided to confront my two sons with my problem of wanting to have the house in tip-top condition by then. Tim is twelve years old. He is cautious and looks a situation over carefully before leaping. He is also observant and says he knows when I am 'Active Listening' because my voice changes. Marvin is eight years old, enthusiastic and apt to leap into things feet first and then look back. I explained to them that Mr. Miller, my teacher, suggested that I discuss *my* problem with them and get their suggestions about what to do about it. They were delighted with the idea that I wouldn't just tell them what I wanted done, but that we would discuss it.

TIM: *You* can work hard.

ME: Yes, I can work hard.

MARVIN: After you clean the house, don't let any of us in!

TIM: We can come in!

MARVIN: I can help you clean the house. How about you clean three rooms and we can do the rest.

MOTHER: OK. I could clean the living room.

TIM: Oh no! The living room is the easy one—we can do that.

MOTHER: How about I do the dining room, den, and kitchen?

MARVIN: Oh no! The kitchen is the easy room. (*I suppose my eyebrows raised*) OK, Dad, you do the kitchen.

TIM: I suppose you mean we should clean our own rooms.

MARVIN: I can get Jeff to help me clean my room. He's not much interested in the things in my room, so we won't play.

TIM: Well, I'll clean off my bureau, but I'll only clean off half of my window seat. (*The window seat is about eight feet long and covered with treasures like partly done and done models, ink bottles filled with colored water, a cranberry juice gallon jug, pencils, marbles, etc.*)

MOTHER: Don't you think all of it could use it?

MARVIN: Where can he put all that stuff?

TIM: Oh, Marvin!

MOTHER: He has all those shelves around his train table.

TIM: I'll still just clean off half the window seat. It's a long time until Thursday.

MARVIN: Let's do it all on Monday.

TIM: OK. I'll do it on Monday if I have time. (*Pause*) You always clean the house top to bottom on Tuesday so we'll just keep it clean until Thursday.

MOTHER: Should we say no children can play in the house after Tuesday then?

MARVIN: Ohhhhh. (*Horror*) Nobody?

MOTHER: You could play at Jeff's house for one and a half days.

MARVIN: Well. OK.

MOTHER: Mr. Miller says that we should all carefully read the agreement and sign it like a con-

> tract and that I should not remind you be-
> cause that would be nagging.

MARVIN: Ohhhhh no—can't you even remind me a *little?*

"There was more conversation, but I cannot remember it exactly. We left the room with a warm friendly feeling. Tim's parting words were, 'Now, how about your "Active Listening" me on my going with your Cub Scouts on their ice skating trip?' When I went to class last Monday, Marvin had not finished his room, but he had by the time I got home. Tim worked on his room after school and did straighten up all of the window seat. Marvin was so pleased with his room that he cut out paper footsteps and taped them from the front door to his bedroom to show Aunt Helen and Uncle Bill the splendid cleanliness. It was a fun and interesting experience."

Another family generated rules and agreements in preparation for a vacation outing.

"Last summer we decided that we and our four children (nine, eight, four, and two) would go to the Canadian National Exhibition, a huge annual event in Toronto. We live nearby, but the decision was made somewhat reluctantly because my husband Dave and I didn't know whether we really wanted to face up to thousands of people, four tired children, attractions to spend lots of money, whining, etc. But we decided to sit down the day before with the oldest three, to lay out our concerns and to problem-solve.

"Through Method III we got out everyone's needs as far as what each one wanted to see and do at the exhibition and how we would handle temptations to overspend. We all decided on five dollars per person for the day for food, rides, and souvenirs. Each person could decide for himself how he wanted to spend his own five dollars. (For example, if a child chose to spend it all on rides and forget meals for that day, it was OK.) Lisa (nine) and Jennifer (eight) carried their own money and looked after it themselves; Dave and I helped the younger two manage their five dollars. Much to our amazement and delight, we spent *eleven* hours there (plus an hour of travel each way) and did not have one fight or one hassle! Everyone saw and did what he had expressed an interest in during problem-solving, we stayed longer than we would have predicted, and we all enjoyed being there together. Great!"

XII

HELPING PARENTS HANDLE VALUE COLLISIONS

"I remain a frustrated parent," a father writes. "Do I just sit back and let him solve his own problems? He doesn't feel he has a problem! One good example is that he likes to play tennis for his school but will not practice to improve his game. He then comes home all depressed because he lost a match. . . . I love him very much, but I can't find the right combination to use."

Another parent, a mother who took P.E.T. six years before we interviewed her, expressed sheer hopelessness: "I think everybody who takes P.E.T. knows that where you and your kids have a different set of values, P.E.T. is not going to work, and I think we've found it doesn't work. Nothing works when you have a different set of values."

Both these parents apparently received little from their P.E.T. experience to help them handle the inevitable value collisions in parent-child relationships. Both feel they were left with nothing to help them cope with children whose beliefs and values conflict with those of their parents.

While many other parents *did* acquire skills to handle value collisions far more effectively than before, as I will document later in this chapter, the P.E.T. stance on what to do when values clash does leave some parents perplexed and disappointed. What do we teach parents about value collisions? Let me review this briefly before I analyze where parents go wrong. Then I'll illustrate effective methods for dealing with conflicts over values.

WHY A VALUE COLLISION IS DIFFERENT

Very early in the development of the P.E.T. course (and in the first P.E.T. book, as well) I recognized that the No-lose conflict-resolution method seldom worked when parents and children fell into conflicts over certain kinds of issues—values, life styles, tastes in dress, choice of friends, esthetic preferences, morals, political beliefs, life goals, personal habits. Many kids saw no reason why they should change their behavior—even enter into a negotiation with their parents (agree to Method III)—because they felt that these particular conflicts (we later called them value collisions) are conflicts over *behaviors which do not concretely or tangibly affect the lives of their parents.*

They said to their parents, "Why should we change what we believe or value—it doesn't concretely interfere with you or do you any harm."

When their hair was long and they liked it that way, they couldn't be convinced to cut it just because their parents preferred short hair; how they wore their hair was none of their parents' business. The same was true for their choice of friends, the way they dressed, the kind of music they listened to, how much makeup they wore, how short they wore their skirts—or how tight their pants. No wonder parents encountered the strongest of resistances to their I-messages as well as their attempts to get kids to enter into No-lose conflict-resolution. For the kids, there would be no compromising whatever they valued or believed—after all, their behavior was not interfering with the needs of their parents. So kids fought to preserve their *rights.*

The principle at work here is an important one,

yet difficult for parents to accept: kids are usually willing to enter into the No-lose method only if it is clear to them that their behavior in some *tangible and concrete way* (the key concept) interferes with parents getting their needs met.

Remember how strongly I stressed the third part of the I-message, "the tangible and concrete effect." For people to be motivated to change, they must be convinced that its effect is some *real* (believable) deprivation for the other person. Our experience in P.E.T. classes has shown that in the case of most value collisions, parents have difficulty sending a three-part I-message; they cannot come up with a real (concrete or tangible) "effect," or at least an effect that is believable enough for the kids to motivate them to change. Try it for yourself in the following examples. Fill in the blanks:

1. If you get your ears pierced, I'd really be upset because _____
   —Unacceptable Behavior
   —Feeling
   —Tangible Effect

2. When you wear those old jeans, I get so irritated because _____
   —Unacceptable Behavior
   —Feeling
   —Tangible Effect

Like most parents, you probably could not come up with any plausible effects—at least none that would be convincing enough for a youngster to modify his or her behavior.

Our Behavior Rectangle represents that certain un-

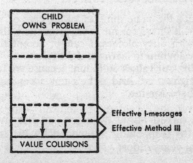

acceptable behaviors of kids *will* persist, even after you have tried I-messages and Method III. For value collisions, parents need other skills.

PARENTS WHO WON'T GIVE UP

As convincing as we try to be to dissuade parents from using methods that have a high probability of failing, some won't give up on such methods. A mother and her husband argue about the mother hassling her son to get him to stop using a bean bag chair as a plaything:

M: Kim has a bean bag chair—paid almost thirty dollars for it—a lot of money to me. The kids roll on it and romp on it. Even though I know that it's his "chair" and it's made of heavy vinyl, and they can have fun with it and romp around on it, I cannot accept that. I mean I have gone through this bit, many times, going into his room and explaining that it's to sit on.

F: To you it's a chair, because you and the decorator wanted a chair, but he doesn't look at it that way. To him it's a fun play toy.

M: It's very hard for me to accept that I have the problem and he doesn't.

F: I learned in P.E.T. that she has the problem and our son doesn't have the problem. The values he places on the bean bag are different from the values she places on it. . . .

M: It's the same thing as taking care of your clothes —it's hard for me to see someone walking around with dirty clothes. I cannot accept that value. I want him to learn the right values. . . . We're passing our values on to him because we feel they are right. . . . And if he's not accepting it, that is hard for me.

A mother talked about trying to get her five-year-old son, Tod, to stop being influenced by his friend, who was several years older:

"I can tell Tod that Dan is doing the wrong thing and that his mother is going to be upset with him, too. I'll say things like, 'It doesn't make me happy when you do things like Dan does. Dan is a very mean little boy and people don't like mean little boys. They like nice little boys.' Tod's answer is, 'But Dan is my friend.' And I'll say, 'He's not really your friend.' And Tod says, '*Yes*, he is!' There's really not much I can say to him to convince him Dan isn't his friend."

Parents probably find it hardest to stop hassling their children when it comes to value collisions about schoolwork and studying. An incident that illustrates this was described by a parent who placed high value on school performance:

"We would say, 'All right, you should try hard in school, because you have a fine mind. It's been tested and you have a high IQ. You have a fine mind and this is your opportunity to use it. This is your formal education.' He'd say, 'All right, but I'm not so sure formal education is the way you really need to be educated.' And I reply, 'You may not think so but apparently the world does.' And from him, 'Well, I'm not sure that I really want to get out in the world that much.' 'Then what would you do?' And he said, 'I don't know, live in the forest with the trees.' "

This same mother's evaluation of her children goes to the heart of the whole problem of trying to push kids to change their values:

"I found in dealing with my children, especially the older one, that he could outdo Mahatma Gandhi with his passive resistance. He'd say, 'All right, fine, but I'm not sure what you mean by that.' Or he'd find ways of dissolving an argument or a conflict. It's like handling wet spaghetti."

Yes, with most kids it *is* like handling wet spaghetti when parents try to change behavior that does not tangibly and concretely affect the parents. I-messages seldom work. Then, when parents switch to moralizing and preaching, lecturing, shaming, and other forms of hassling, they're met with similar resistance.

The most bitter battles and the most tragic outcomes occur when parents in their frustration and desperation roll out their big guns—power and authority. They threaten, deprive, punish. In retaliation, the youngsters walk away from discussions, go into isolation, lie, and sometimes leave home.

Our experience confirms that battles over values produce the most damaging effects in families. Relationships deteriorate, communication ceases, families disintegrate. In their stubbornness to win battles over values, parents lose the war. Their kids divorce them, so to speak. Predictably, kids then refuse to enter into Method III problem-solving for anything—even for conflicts that ordinarily would be amenable to No-lose conflict-resolution.

EFFECTIVE METHODS FOR DEALING WITH VALUE COLLISIONS

Contrary to the conclusion reached by the mother quoted earlier ("Where you and your kids have a different set of values, P.E.T. is not going to work"), many parents successfully applied P.E.T. to become more effective in handling value collisions. A significant attitude change is necessary, as described by a father:

> "I'm kind of realizing with the long hair thing and their clothes that we have been telling them what to do so they will conform to *our* peer group. I wanted them to look right when I introduce them to the people in business that I know. But that's not *their* peer group. They're people, and they're just as entitled to operate in their peer group as they are in mine. That's kind of a tough realization for me. I don't think some people accept that. I'm not sure I accept that all the time, but at least I'm willing to modify some of my values to allow them to be accepted in *their* peer group."

A mother describes her changing attitudes about long hair:

"My feeling was that I liked his hair shorter, but I said, 'It's your hair and I want to accept that you need to let it grow longer.' . . . Maybe I had a fear of losing that last bit of control of my children—that was scary."

This father is beginning to be more accepting of the fact that kids may have to learn their own lessons:

"The age-old problem of parents—they want kids to take the parents' advice. But the kids have to learn themselves. So you are frustrated when you can't pass on your great experience. . . . Again, I think he's old enough that that's the way he'll learn from now on, period."

With such changes in basic attitudes, parents are more able to stop hassling their kids and rely on methods we teach in P.E.T. for dealing with value collisions effectively.

Modeling Effectively

It is clear to me now that in the P.E.T. course we made insufficient efforts to teach parents how powerful modeling is in shaping and influencing children's values and beliefs. True, we tell parents that kids are bound to learn some of their parents' values by observing what their mothers and fathers do and by hearing what they say. We say that parents will in fact teach their values by actually living them, and we caution them about the inadequacy of "Do as I say, not as I do."

Unfortunately, parents somehow do not trust this process. They fear that their offspring might not buy the values they see their parents living by. What we did not stress is that *kids are much more likely to learn from the parental model if their relationship with the parent is a good one*. Kids seldom model after adults they dislike or fear. They adopt the values of people they admire, respect, love—those people are the ones kids feel they want to be like. It figures!

So to insure the maximum benefit of parental

modeling, parents would do well to learn all the skills
we teach in P.E.T. because they are relationship skills:
what it takes to foster and maintain a relationship in
which the child can develop as a person—and the parent, too. To quote the P.E.T. Credo:

> "Thus, ours can be a healthy relationship in which
> both of us can strive to become what we are capable
> of being. And we can continue to relate to each other
> with mutual respect, love, and peace."

By learning the P.E.T. skills parents will be doing
everything they can (to my knowledge, at least) to
foster a relationship of mutual respect and love, and
thereby increase the probability that their children will
adopt the parents' values.

See how the power of the parent model operates
in this incident reported by the mother of a five-year-
old:

> "I was lying on the couch because I didn't feel very
> good. The kids just forgot I was there. This particular
> child who worries us about her bad influence on our
> kids, said, 'Let's pretend this man is stealing that man's
> wife.' And I was taken aback when I heard that, be-
> cause Sharlene is only five. It seemed like a strange
> game for a five-year-old to be playing. I lay there
> stunned. But then I heard Sharlene say, 'No, let's just
> pretend they're going to a meeting.' She switched the
> whole thing. . . . I always worry about other children
> influencing ours, but maybe our kids might have an
> influence on someone else's children."

A mother felt gratified observing how her child treats
other children:

> "When you see your child treat other children with
> respect, you know that you've been treating them right.
> Just in their dealing with other children I have seen
> this. Listening quietly at the door when they're talk-
> ing, I can hear my child using Active Listening. A kid

says, 'I don't like this toy.' And I'll hear my son say, 'It sounds like you really don't like it, huh?' They just begin to use it themselves."

Another parent made a similar observation:

"Some of the cutest things that have happened have been when I heard Sharon and Joey use I-messages on each other. . . . They've modeled that a great deal, they send a lot of very clear I-messages. It seems such a natural thing for them to do now."

Although the effects of modeling sink in only with time, your children will adopt far more of your values than you think, provided your relationship is a good one. But don't expect your kids to buy *all* your values, even in the best of relationships. Some they may find unacceptable, inappropriate, or not compatible with how they see life.

Being an Effective Consultant

What people value and believe, and how they behave as a result of their values and beliefs, unquestionably can be changed. People do not remain the same —values, beliefs, and patterns of behavior are not cast in concrete. And, as everybody knows, marked changes can be brought about when people are influenced by someone who has knowledge and facts or has a vast amount of experience, wisdom, demonstrated competence.

For such a person to be an *effective* change agent he must follow certain proven principles and practices. In P.E.T. we say that an effective change agent is one who has learned to be a good "consultant," because, more than any other group of people, successful consultants follow these principles and practices. That is why they're successful in changing people.

So if parents want to influence their children's values, beliefs, and behavior, they should take a leaf out of the book used by successful consultants.

Be Prepared with Facts and Information

Successful consultants approach their job adequately prepared with convincing data relevant to their expertise. They do not try to tell "the client" what he should believe or how he should act without marshaling evidence and knowledge that will convince the client he will be better off changing.

Parents often try to influence kids without adequate facts—on such matters as smoking grass, choice of friends, style of dress, or tastes in music. Our advice: stay out of the consultant role unless you have a lot of experience and are armed with convincing facts. If you want to influence your children not to smoke cigarettes, for example, get the Surgeon General's Report, collect authoritative articles, talk to your family doctor—anything to be prepared. People have to be convinced before they change, and remember again, kids are people!

First Get Hired as a Consultant

Successful consultants make certain their clients are ready and willing to hire them as consultants—that they're in the right mood to listen and have time available. Again, parents can learn from successful consultants:

1. Ask your kids whether they would be interested in hearing your facts and opinions.

2. Ask them to set a time convenient to *them* as well as to you.

3. Tell them you think you have some valuable data which they might find useful.

Leave Responsibility with Your Client

Successful consultants only *offer* their experience and expertise, leaving it up to the client to decide whether to buy or to reject. *This is crucial.* Successful consultants share, they do not preach; they offer (rather than impose) their ideas; they suggest rather than demand. Equally important, they usually offer their expertise no more than once; they do not cajole or hassle clients, shame them if they do not buy their ideas, relentlessly push their point of view. If they did, they'd get fired by the client—and fast.

Too often, youth fire their parents by informing them that their consulting services are no longer wanted. Why? Because most parents push, hassle, cajole, persuade, implore, preach, and blame. They assume responsibility for their kids changing. Their attitude is, "My kids *must* buy what I am selling." And if they don't, the parent feels like a failure.

Parents are guilty of the "hard sell," which, as consultants know full well, fosters resistance and resentment. No wonder kids respond by saying, "Get off my back," "Stop hassling me," "I know what you think I should do, so stop lecturing me every day."

If parents would only let themselves be guided by the rules of effective consultants, their children would be more open to parental experience and wisdom, more inclined to ask for their parents' consulting services again.

A mother told us how she tried to be a consultant to her daughter on the issue of wearing a coat when it was cool so the youngster wouldn't catch a cold. It was amusing because the mother, instead of talking face-to-face to the youngster, offered her opinions to a group of women visiting in the home, making sure she talked loudly enough for her daughter to hear:

"Friday a couple of friends were over with their kids. Well, the kids all decided they were going out without their coats. Though it had been warm the previous day, that day it was cool. One of my friends saw her son on his way out without a coat and said, 'Bobby, you put your coat on!' He looked at me and said, 'Lisa doesn't have her coat on—is she going out without her coat?' Very loudly, so Lisa would hear every word, I said to my visitors, 'I've got to stop worrying about Lisa as much as I do. I've got to stop trying to force her to do things, and instead let her learn that she's responsible for her own actions. She has to start learn-

ing from the natural consequences of her behavior.
Now, if she goes out without her coat, chances are
she'll be more susceptible to catching a cold. She
has dress rehearsals coming up this week and a ballet
recital on Friday, which I wouldn't like to see her
miss. That'd have to be the natural consequences of
going out without her coat today. . . . But I just
have to leave that up to her.' *And, man, she ran and
got that coat!*"

On a much more serious matter, a father demonstrated that he had also learned to be a consultant:

"My son had decided to grow a plot of marijuana with
two neighbor kids. One of the kids had been growing
the stuff a lot—he has pretty severe emotional problems. So I shared with my son one time, and one time
only, how I felt about that: 'I think growing grass is
your decision as long as it's not on our property,
where we could get in trouble. And you must think
about the fact that if this kid gets caught, it could
involve you. More than likely, he's going to be dealing in it to make money and that could make you a
dealer too, which is a felony.' And that's all I said;
one time, right out loud how I felt about it. Haven't
said a word since. I don't know what happened, but
I feel I've done my consulting job—it's about all I
could do. . . . Before P.E.T. I would have hassled
him to death about it."

Another parent was confronted with this chilling
question, "Mom, how would you feel if I went into
crime as a full-time activity?"

"That took some thinking. . . . I had to do some real
soul-searching to give him an answer that was the
most valid I could find. I said, 'I think maybe I would
tend to lose respect for you because there is so much
injustice in crime—someone else is always wronged.
This is the thing I would regret the most. I'd also feel
extremely anxious about you, because of the risks in
terms of the law. But the thing I'd regret the most
would be that I couldn't hold my respect for you.' He
reported later that he felt pretty good about that—

didn't go into details about either his question or my answer, except to say he felt good about the way I had answered it."

Here is how a parent handled a different value collision: a conflict about her son's responsibility to his school's track team:

"He decided he'd rather go skiing than go to track practice. He was determined to go skiing instead. He called a friend and the friend couldn't give him a ride. He asked his father and his father said no. Finally, he said, 'I can't go skiing because I'd have to leave at three or four o'clock in the morning.' But he said to us, 'Well, I'm not going skiing, but I'm certainly not going to that track practice.' So I said to him, 'When you use this way of dealing with this problem, I feel you are retaliating against me because you know how I feel about your responsibility to your track team. When you have the skill and they are counting on you, then I feel you're letting them down, and it's a cop-out for you not to go. I know, when I tell you that, I'm not helping you get what you want [to go skiing], and so I feel like you are retaliating against me and using power on me.' He said, 'Well, don't bother to wake me up—I'm not going.' Well, on his own he got up and went to track practice. On his own! I never said another thing about it. Someone else has to explain why they make the decision like that—I don't know."

This mother is right—parents often do not know, after they consult, why their children buy their values and make an appropriate decision. All we know is that sometimes they do.

Re-examining Your Own Values

Value collisions between parents and their children often disappear or get resolved happily when the parents modify *their* values. Until now we have shown only how parents can be more effective in modifying a child's values, yet we know that change can be a two-way street. Parents *can* change their position on issues, and they do—more frequently than we think.

A mother changed her posture toward how neat and clean her son's room should be:

> "We sat down and talked a couple of months ago. I said, 'Tim, when you leave your room like that, it bugs me. I hate to walk in that room and see it looking like that.' 'Well, why don't you shut the door?' he answered. And I asked, 'Do you mind it that way?' And he said, 'It doesn't bother me a bit.' And so I said, 'OK, that's what we'll do then.' . . . So I'm just shutting the door and waiting. The kids know how we feel about the rooms being messy, but what's the point? Why should I let it bother me? I'm more able to accept it now. . . . And do you know, since then he's kept it nicer. I couldn't believe it, but it did work."

Of course, not all such changes in parental attitudes produce such a change in behavior. Sometimes the child continues to hold on to his or her value, but the value collision disappears only because the parent changes. This is what happened when a child decided he wanted to sleep with the light on:

> "It's a very simple solution to leave his light on, but I reacted negatively at first. You know, nobody is supposed to sleep with a light on. But then I thought, 'Sleeping with the light on doesn't interfere with my needs. It's a problem that I own. . . . Just because everyone sleeps in the dark. But why should he, just because everyone does?' I've found with a lot of things that if I can just live with something like that for a while and overcome my own hang-ups about that, then pretty soon the problem just ceases to be."

Parents sometimes change as a result of questioning the usefulness of their values or re-examining just how important they are. Understanding where your values came from may help you clarify whether you want to change. One mother did just that in a value collision about peanut butter sandwiches, of all things:

> "Everything has to be peanut butter and jelly sandwiches. And it has to be on brown bread, and it can't

be cut in half, you know! Why does it bother me that he won't let me cut his sandwich in half? Because I worked in a restaurant, and in restaurants you give somebody a sandwich nicely cut in half with an olive and a pickle. . . . If I can just remember that he has every right to have his food served the way he wants it, what difference does it make to me?"

Accepting What You Can't Change

"You have to bite your tongue and shut up."

"I'm going to have to live with it."

"Don't rob them of the chance to make their own decisions."

"If we haven't taught them right from wrong by the time they're teen-agers, nothing more I can do is going to change."

"What law says my kids have to conform to what I I think?"

These are statements from parents who somehow found the serenity to accept what they cannot change. P.E.T. does help parents see their children as persons, separate from them and with the right even to choose to be different from them. Many behaviors and values of children parents simply may never be able to change. The only logical alternative is to accept this fact. No amount of power will change what people believe or what they value, as long as others are not injured in any tangible way. Kids cherish their rights and their freedoms, which I predict will someday be guaranteed them.

Does P.E.T. help all parents accept what they can't change? I doubt it. And I am at a loss to know how we could do better. Hopefully, in the future we may better understand how to foster in *all* parents the basic attitude of acceptance of others that is clearly illustrated in this interview of one P.E.T. graduate:

"Our son is living with a gal who has several children but has never been married. And these children do not even have a common father. She is also several years older. But I'm able to see her now, realizing that this is my son's choice and if he sees something in her, then, because I love him, I'll have to accept her. And it's very freeing! One day he said, 'Mom, what if I marry her?' And I said, 'Well, honey, then you marry her and she'll be your wife.' I was able to say it without really lying to myself. . . . I really thought, yes, he can bring her here and she will be his wife and that will be a fact."

Where does it come from—this capacity to continue to love someone who has chosen to be different from you? How can we better foster this deep attitude of acceptance? Others may disagree, but I firmly believe this is the principal attitude people must learn if we are to build a society that is truly democratic. Not only will it provide freedom for others, but it will bring freedom to self, as this parent experienced:

"It frees you from judgment, and when you're freed from judgment you're quite a bit freer than you can imagine. P.E.T. helps parents get a new perspective on how to look at the world."

XIII

WHY SOME PARENTS SEEK TRAINING AND SOME REJECT IT

Who needs parent training? Only certain few parents, many parents, or all parents? For sure, training for parenthood is a relatively new idea. It has not been around very long, nor is it widely accepted as something that would benefit parents, much less improve our society. Is it an idea whose time has come? Or is it another of those fads that suddenly come into prominence and quickly become history?

All parents need answers to these questions to help them decide whether parent effectiveness training is something that would benefit them and improve their family life.

From the many reports submitted by the P.E.T. graduates we contacted we learned why they made the decision to take P.E.T. They told us where their families were before P.E.T., and they talked about their reasons for seeking help through training. Some were skeptical and delayed their decision; others were eager for help and jumped right in when they saw the opportunity to become more effective. Some mothers enrolled while the fathers refused.

We also have acquired a lot of information about why parents reject the idea of parent training or why it threatens them.

In this chapter, I will report what we have learned, with the hope it might help parents think more deeply and with more clarity about training for parent effectiveness—whether it would be beneficial to them and our society.

Certainly, the notion of achieving greater parent effectiveness through special training flies directly in the face of many traditional views about parenthood that are almost universally accepted as truth. For as long as I can remember, when parents encounter minor difficulties in rearing their children, they blame their troubles on the child—Jimmy is a "problem child," Sue is "maladjusted," Dave is "incorrigible," Kevin is "hyperactive," Linda simply will not "accept authority," Ray is "emotionally disturbed," Peter is "bad."

Rarely have parents of such children asked whether their problems might have something to do with their own lack of skill or their ineffective patterns of parental behavior. So when serious breakdowns in the parent-child relationship occur, parents usually take the child someplace to be fixed up—"counseled," "adjusted," "disciplined," or "retrained." In recent years, parents have even accepted doctors' prescriptions for drugging hyperactive children.

Another persistent belief embraced by most parents is that changes in our society are at fault for their family problems: the ubiquitous TV, the breakdown of authority, the availability of drugs, the disappearance of the extended family, the increase in the divorce rate, the questioning of basic moral values, increasing affluence, and so on. While not discounting any of these factors as having some influence on family life, I feel they represent a rather traditional and limited way of thinking about what causes the deterioration of parent-child relationships so frequently experienced in today's families. Such thinking has tended to divert parents from considering the idea that their own lack of skill in parenting could be the significant factor in damaging their relationships with their children.

We have discovered many other reasons why parents do not seek out training for parenthood. When P.E.T. instructors give talks to parent groups to explain the P.E.T. program and how it will improve family life, they hear why parents tend to resist parent training:

"Loving your children is enough." This belief assumes that love is like some medicinal substance that you have in nearly unlimited supply and dispense daily no matter how you feel or how the children behave. (As I will show later in this chapter, many parents experience their love for their children running thin as problems get serious.)

"We don't have any serious problems now." This belief is not unlike the resistance to most preventive efforts. If you have no serious symptoms of illness, why eat properly, exercise regularly, or quit smoking? If your car runs pretty well, you don't feel much like taking it for maintenance check-ups.

"Other parents need training much worse." Usually those "other parents" are thought to be the poor people, the uneducated or "culturally deprived." Many parents persist in the belief that only in such families do children become delinquents, dropouts, or drug abusers. The evidence refutes this—such trouble can occur in all families.

"We've got plenty of time—our kids are still young." This attitude fails to recognize that it's in the first few years that children begin to develop their patterns of behavior, such as thoughtfulness of others, self-esteem, a sense of responsibility, self-confidence— or the opposites of these traits. Parents need skills when their children are very young—this is when they pay off the most.

"Troubled kids come mostly from broken homes." This is another mistaken belief. Broken homes (divorce) can also be *caused* by trouble with kids. And people who lack the skills to be effective in the marriage relationship are likely to be ineffective in the parent-

child relationship too. This means troubled kids and broken homes may occur together, but it does not mean that broken homes *cause* troubled kids.

"We're not emotionally sick people." Unfortunately the idea of training for parent effectiveness carries the stigma of "getting therapy," especially if parents see anything "psychological" in the training program. Going to a parent training class doesn't mean a person is "sick" any more than going to Sunday School means a person is sinful. Parent Effectiveness Training is an educational experience—it's not therapeutic treatment.

"Nobody is expert enough to tell me how to raise my kids." This attitude reflects a misunderstanding of what the P.E.T. program is all about. *It does not tell parents how they should raise their children.* Rather, it teaches parents proven skills and methods for fostering effective two-way communication, for getting kids to solve their problems themselves, for resolving conflicts between parent and child so nobody loses. These are the same skills you need to have good relationships with anyone—your spouse, your friends, your co-workers, your in-laws.

Why do other parents *accept* the idea of training and make the decision to enroll in P.E.T.? Who are the parents who feel they need parent training? We wanted to find out. The interviews with P.E.T. graduates gave us some answers.

First of all, we learned that these parents were not at all a homogeneous gorup—there were far more differences than similarities in our sample. Some took P.E.T. when their children were very young, some had only teen-agers; some felt they already were pretty good parents, some saw themselves as utter failures. We found some families in which no serious problems had emerged; some in which there were only signs of beginning problems; and still others where the parents were already experiencing rather serious difficulties. A few parents enrolled in P.E.T. primarily because they saw the course as another opportunity for self-development and personal growth. A larger number of parents felt desperate or were facing some serious crisis. Some came on their own; others were referred by pediatricians or ministers and a few by juvenile court authorities. A number of the parents had experienced considerable success with their first child (or children), but their methods were not working with their lastborn. Some parents accepted parenthood as a challenge and had high aspirations to be competent; others approached parenthood with fear and trepidation, certain they were in for real trouble.

"YOU CAN BE BETTER THAN YOU ARE"

The optimism implicit in the lyrics of this hit song from *The Sound of Music* came through clearly in interviews with a few parents. One mother, a retired nurse in her late twenties, whose home is filled with paintings done in her spare time and Indian artifacts collected from her years as a nurse on an Indian reservation, spoke of wanting to be a better parent of her two boys:

> "I think that everybody probably has a feeling that they can do whatever it is they're doing a little bit better. I felt comfortable with my kids, but I always had the feeling that it could be better, or that maybe I could hear more of what my kids had to say so I might better help them and help myself and our relationship."

A father of four—three girls and a boy, seven to thirteen—owning his own carpet and drapery business and living in a woodsy suburban home, said:

> "We've always had people tell us what nice children we have—how well behaved they are and how conscientious—and this always made us feel good. But Mary's reading the P.E.T. book was an eye-opener to me. The course was a chance to further our understanding of our children—a chance to gain a little more knowledge."

A petite, well-educated mother of two preschool girls, working part-time in a local bookstore because of her love of books and an interest in doing something outside the home, had this to say:

> "You know, I have a Master's degree—five years of schooling—but I didn't take anything to teach me how to be a mother. And Joe felt the same way. We thought it would be a good idea to have some guidelines. I read every book that comes out, but I was finding I had so many different philosophies—one would say do this, another you shouldn't do it. I began to feel I needed one philosophy. And because I don't have much patience, too many philosophies just wasn't helping."

Another book-reading parent was a mother/homemaker/student working on her B.A., with three children—girls of six months and three years and a boy of six years. She expressed similar feelings of being confused by the books she had read:

> "I needed more communication with my children. It helped me not only with my children, but with people in general. I was confused. I'd read one method of bringing up children and that would be my way. Then I'd read another and I'd kinda sway over that way. And my children would get a little bit confused, so I needed something that would work for me and that I could practice and stick with."

A mother of a teen-age son, whom they had sent to a psychiatrist, said she had luckily stumbled onto P.E.T. at that time:

> ". . . and it made the book *I'm OK, You're OK* clear, and it made Dr. Ginott understandable. It just explained everything."

Parenthood was felt to be a challenge by a mother of three girls (ten, eight, four) in a well-to-do family. She took P.E.T. as a program brought into their church by her husband, a psychologist:

"I find it a huge challenge to be a good parent. I guess most parents do. I read a lot of books on parenting, and at the time I'm reading a particular book it sounds great and I can do it that day and maybe even the next day. But then little by little I return to my old ways—I hope I'm not alone in that. I think the difference with P.E.T. is that the techniques are so simple and definite and clear, with good reasons behind them, it makes sense to me. And so it's easier for me to stick with it. I can't say I've stuck with it perfectly. In fact, in going back and reading the book I find I've forgotten some things. However, there are certain things I've held on to that have really pulled me out of some tight spots with the kids."

Early in their marriage Bob and his wife began to realize their family life could be better. Now that their children are seventeen, eleven, and five, Bob, a minister, talks about how his recent experience with P.E.T. filled a void:

"So, way back there when we were married only two years we could sense there was a need, there was something better, a better way of living—something to this idea of better communication. You know, two people just didn't stand before a minister and get married and then go out and live happily ever after. It just isn't that easy, and we found that out. Then June and I got into the P.E.T. class and all of a sudden the things that were stirring way back there were suddenly crystallized. But when I say crystallized I don't mean it's once and for all but I mean it's something that is ongoing and something which must be continually re-evaluated in your own life."

These parents represent an apparently growing number of people who welcome the P.E.T. course as yet another opportunity to grow as persons, to enrich all their interpersonal relationships, to develop intellectually. One father put it eloquently when he said, "P.E.T. has been one of the many catalysts that is helping me in my pilgrimage towards being a more real and actualized person."

"I'M NOT GOING TO MAKE THE MISTAKES MY PARENTS MADE WITH ME"

"I felt very inadequate as a mother, for I was eighteen and a half when I was married, and I was pregnant. I hadn't particularly liked either of my parents' parenting, and I didn't want to use either of their methods, but I didn't have any alternatives," reported one mother.

A thirty-one-year-old divorced mother of two (ages twelve and ten) had taken P.E.T. about nine years ago when she was feeling very much unprepared to be a parent and in need of help and guidance in her parenting patterns. Now, working on her Master's in psychology, she looked back and recalled, "I can remember having a real fear when my kids were very young that they would grow to hate me, you know, the way I hated my own mother."

Today's parents, yesterday's children, vividly and often angrily remember the methods their parents used and the pain and resentment they experienced as children. Many are determined not to inflict the ineffective methods on their own kids, as did this parent:

MOTHER: I had a very authoritarian father and a mother who tried to control me by using emotional blackmail and you know, various kinds of guilt-producing phrases. And I hated it. I hated them for doing that. And I didn't want to be that kind of parent.

INTERVIEWER: Were you already falling back on those methods?

MOTHER: Oh yeah, yeah. I was the typical, you know, prototype of the authoritarian or the permissive parent—more the permissive until I couldn't stand my kids. Then, authoritarian until I definitely couldn't stand myself.

The same theme was expressed by another parent, a thirty-two-year-old mother of two (ages three and one), who also spoke of her unhappiness with the way her parents treated her:

I: You took P.E.T. because your parents were such a bad model, is that it?

M: Bad model, yeah. I decided to take P.E.T. because I didn't have a good relationship with them. . . . I felt I was manipulated quite often, and I learned to do pretty much what they wanted, because I felt that was the only way I could be loved, I guess. And I really didn't want to pass that on to my children.

I: You remembered what it felt like to you, as a child?

M: Yeah. Never feeling you had a voice in what went on, and always expected to be something that you weren't. . . . Not able to make a lot of choices because I had this, you know, fear, this panic which was so great I just always went back and followed their path. It wasn't a happy path for me because it wasn't using a lot of my talents my gifts. So I didn't want to pass this on to them.

I: Uh-huh.

M: Oh, and another thing. Because I felt they were authoritarian, I found myself being a liberal (permissive) parent. I was going to be the other extreme. And yet I didn't like this liberal bit I was into. . . . I didn't want my kids to do all the things I was letting them do, but I was afraid to go the other way—being too strict. . . .

These parents want to break the vicious cycle: parenting the way they were parented. Something much better for their kids, they hope. Yet a danger lurks within such a motivation—going too far in the other direction! Sharon, the mother in the dialogue above, discovered the pitfall of overcompensating by being permissive. The result? I have seen it many times. The parent begins to feel resentment toward the children— even grows to dislike them.

"PARENTHOOD IS A SCARY, DIFFICULT JOB"

The P.E.T. course for some parents held out a promise of making them better prepared for the difficult and scary job of parenthood. "I felt I needed all the help I could find," one parent revealed, "I was kind of scared with what I had to cope with."

Penny and John, a couple in their late twenties, became parents deliberately after being childless for the first five and a half years of their married life. Still, they felt they wanted guidance in this new life and didn't want to give up their individual needs for valued time alone with each other. They didn't want to give up their marriage relationship for one with their child. Penny expressed her need for advice:

> "The reason I took P.E.T. was that parenting was a new thing. I didn't remember what my folks did, it was so long ago. I figured I could use all the advice I could get. This sounded like a good plan, but if I was going to institute it, I'd better do it right from the start." (When her child was only two years old.)

Starting as early as possible to learn the skills of being an effective parent was a principal reason given by another parent for enrolling in P.E.T. Sally is an elementary school teacher working on her Master's. She shares the rearing of her two boys (ages three and a half years and seven months) with her teacher husband. Coming into parenthood deliberately after establishing their career and personal goals, they sought parenting help through P.E.T.:

> "I knew in the case of my own family [her parents] that boys a lot of times break away in rebellion, and don't come back. And both my husband and I were really concerned about keeping an open relationship

with our two boys—forever, you know, even when
they become adults. And I figured now would probably be the best time to start."

Alice, the mother of two teen-age girls, looks back
at her reasons for enrolling in P.E.T. about four years
ago. She had a special reason for being scared of the
responsibilities of parenthood—in her case doing the
job alone, without her husband, who had recently died.

I: I generally start out by asking why you took the
     course—if there was anything specific that you
     wanted to change.

M: Well, my husband had just died. And I had teen-
     agers who were twelve and fourteen years old. I
     was not used to making all the decisions myself—
     having the whole responsibility. Because we had
     really worked things out together so much. You
     know, when you have another sounding board,
     that makes a difference. When my husband
     drowned, my children were with him in the
     ocean when it happened. I didn't know what the
     effect would be on them. So I felt I needed all the
     tools I could get to cope with whatever might
     come up.

Getting prepared for the "terrible teens," the
storm and stress of the "dangerous" adolescent years,
motivated some parents to seek parent training early.
Karen, a "domestic engineer" and mother of three
(thirteen, ten and a half, two and a half), who's been
involved in numerous training programs and courses
—values, Montessori, child development—but never
attained a college degree, said:

"I had a pretty good relationship with the kids. I really
took the course because I knew I could use it. I had a
lot of friends who had teen-agers and I could see the
problems that came up, where communications get
shut off with teen-agers. And I got to thinking it would
be kinda neat if that never had to happen with my
kids."

Surprisingly, only a handful from our sample of interviewees told us they were thinking in such preventive terms—that is, getting "training before trouble" or preparing for expected problems in the distant future. Apparently, as in other areas of peoples' lives, it is not easy to make a heavy commitment of time and energy to prevent problems long before they are expected to occur.

"WE READ THE WRITING ON THE WALL"

It's different when parents are observing danger signals. Unacceptable and worrisome behaviors are cropping up; the youngsters are beginning to get wills of their own; a child is becoming increasingly unhappy with himself; parents are feeling a growing sense of helplessness in coping with nitty-gritty daily conflicts with a child; parents are beginning to get worn out and irritable. Many parents told us that they sought help because they were reading the writing on the wall. Nothing terribly serious, no big crises, no tragedies. Rather, early signs of impending trouble.

The taped interviews illustrate these gnawing fears and doubts:

"I think our approach had sort of worn out. . . ."

"My husband told me I was picking on them all the time. We both had sort of thought we're not quite getting the job done; there's too much friction; we're always coming to sword's point."

"Freddy, the second oldest child, was more of a rebel. The oldest son went according to the rules. But Freddy wouldn't do any of these things. That's when things started getting really bad."

"I remember having a feeling about David when he would have something bothering him—I didn't know how to help him to get it out."

"Another thing that I remember was that it often bothered me when Ralph was unhappy. I wanted to help him and talk about it. It was hard for him to let me know what was bothering him. It made me feel very helpless. And it was hard for me to accept that I couldn't help him get it out—what was bothering him and making him feel down and depressed."

In one family, a mother who took P.E.T. about six years ago, when her four boys ranged from five to fourteen, said she was embarrassed and took it as "a personal affront" when a friend suggested she take P.E.T. Then two particular poignant events caused the mother to sense something was wrong:

"I'll tell you one comment my son made to me which was a little startling. One day I asked him to do something. To me it was my normal voice, but he said, 'All right, but don't whine.' I was not aware of it, but apparently when I asked for something it sounded like a whine to him. I thought, Gee, if that's how I sound to him, there's something that's not really good there."

". . . And, oh yes, we were having a big to-do about the oldest boy not doing his homework. It was just slipshod. My husband kept telling me to do something—make him study in his room for two hours a day or no television for six months. And then, you know, I would try all those things and they just didn't work. I could keep him in his room but he'd sit and stare at the floor. His schoolwork was going downhill; he was very unhappy; and we were all unhappy. After that I got into a group and then right after that into P.E.T."

Some parents reported how they began to get disillusioned about parenthood—it wasn't what it was cracked up to be and things were getting out of hand. Steve and Ann described their growing disenchantment and frustration with being parents of a ten- and seven-year-old:

M: I was nagging them and heard myself doing it, and didn't stop. I felt that motherhood couldn't possibly be just one constant hassle after another —no one can live through all that.

I: What kinds of things were you nagging about?

M: Oh, goodness, everything.

I: Everyday simple things, like toothbrushing, like haircuts?

M: Mm-hmm.

F: Like picking up their room. Like making their beds, requests we made for dinner table manners or taking care of their plates after dinner or jobs around the house. All these things seem silly but they're practical, they're everyday little things. . . .

I: How were you feeling about it?

M: Very angry. I'm sure, anger within myself and anger directed toward them. I really felt I was capable of handling this whole thing at a much higher level . . . it just takes a lot of time to be a good parent. P.E.T. can cut that time down because what you do, you do more effectively.

Fortunately, these parents listened to their feelings of helplessness and anger and responded constructively to the "writing on the wall." They acted on their perceptions that things were getting out of hand and their conviction that families need not have such constant hassles. Many other parents fail to take corrective action when early warnings occur. They bury their heads in the sand, hoping these signs and symptoms will go away. Helplessness turns into hopelessness; disappointment is replaced by disillusionment; parenthood becomes a burden instead of a joy.

WHEN THINGS GET DESPERATE

For some parents in our sample things were getting critical, minor problems had become serious ones, conflicts escalated into battles, tempers flared, the parents felt run over, the children felt dominated, power struggles became frequent, communication had broken down, kids were rebelling or withdrawing. Parents often take their children to psychologists, psychiatrists, or

family counselors at such times, hoping they might be
fixed up or straightened around. Unfortunately, too
many of these therapists concentrate their efforts on
working with the youngster, all but ignoring helping
the parents to change. In some cases a therapist does
recognize the importance of the parent and tries to be
influential in getting one or both parents to modify
their behavior toward the child. This was the case with
Ruth, deeply involved with her middle child and only
son, then fourteen, who had been withdrawing more
and more.

> "Our psychiatrist used methods of having us read a
> tremendous amount of things and seeing what this did
> for us, and, as I said, I just stumbled onto P.E.T. . . . .
> It just explained everything."

Many parents wait far too long before seeking any
kind of help. Some resist the idea of seeing a therapist;
many feel they can't afford the high fees charged for
individual consultation. The usual pattern is for parents
to try to handle their problems alone, often using trial
and error based on very little knowledge of the dynamics of their troubled relationship with their child.
Too often the problem is not alleviated, and parents
feel helpless.

Laura and Daniel related their experience with
their fifteen-year-old daughter, Janice. Dan is an engineer, Laura is a housewife and part-time Avon Lady.
They have two younger children and live in a large,
stately home. They come from England, where they
were conditioned to be very proper with strong values
about right and wrong. Daniel said, "I had some fixed
ideas about how I was brought up. I was trying to live
by a set of rules that I'm sure my father got from his
father and his father before him. And those rules were
that a child is to be seen and not heard."

I: Let me ask you why it was that you took P.E.T.

M: Well, mostly it was for our older daughter, who
     is fifteen, and we were losing contact with her

fast. She had a terrible summer—you know, just crying and bad temper, miserable. All sorts of things. . . . She wasn't communicating to us and we weren't with her. And it was very frustrating, you know.

F: I think that what upset you was that we acknowledged that she and I couldn't communicate—very rarely even talked to one another. But you thought you could always talk with her. But then came the time when my wife couldn't talk to her. . . . We could see her going away from us.

I: How do you mean, going away? Withdrawing?

F: Yes, withdrawing.

M: Yeah, she would come home and shut herself in the bedroom all night long, and never speak unless she was spoken to. And she never spoke to her father at all, except in a grunt or something like that. And it was really getting on my nerves, and it was getting to both of us. And then when I heard about the P.E.T. course, it sounded so marvelous that I thought, oh golly, any straw, we really need help. I really felt we needed the help in the summer but we didn't start until October.

F: I have to admit I didn't think I needed any help.

M: I had to talk him into it.

Note Daniel's strong resistance against attending a course for parents, despite his almost total lack of communication with his daughter, Janice, for months on end. This is not atypical. Yet it continues to perplex me that parents delay so long before biting the bullet, and accepting that they need training.

Another family found themselves in a power struggle over values with their seventeen-year-old daughter, Clara. Clara's mother describes her fear of what was happening to her teen-age daughter and her anxiety in not knowing how to handle it.

"That authoritarian stance is so hard for parents to let go. . . . We were trying to be authoritarian and clamp on her in our way—the way we thought things should be done, and how she should live, and how she should look. . . . We learned that Clara smoked. We were devastated. We took her car away from her, and that made her all the more rebellious. She was going to smoke, by George, no matter what, even if that's the way we were going to be. Her clothes! We would give her these dirty looks—we didn't have to say anything, our looks were the messages. All about her sloppy dressing and everything. She was our first teen-ager and this was the time when the Beatles were popular, and all this was so new to us, so foreign to the way we were raised. I always thought that if you took your children to church and were good people and followed a certain straight road that everything would be all right. It was such a shock to me that Clara wasn't living the way I felt she ought to live."

This mother's anguish because "Clara wasn't living the way I felt she ought to live" is the same anguish thousands of parents experience—in all kinds of families and all parts of the country—when their youngsters begin to embrace styles of dress or styles of life different from their parents. These value collisions plague most families, and without the skills to handle them constructively parents inevitably go on fighting these battles and end up losing the war. Relationships deteriorate, kids shut their parents out, they live together in sullen silence, or the kids walk away from the relationship, as in this family:

"Well, mostly there would be either silence; and rarely, unless maybe he was punished, would he change his behavior. Sometimes punishment would change it for a short time but not over a long period. . . . Like I say, he was quite hostile, sometimes he just has a terrible temper. I think it is just rebellion against having a lot of authority used over him. . . . One time when he was upset and threw the key at the car and I said, 'You pick up that key,' he just walked off. Walked away! He walked twenty-six miles to a friend's home."

THE PARENT DILEMMA

"As they were getting into the teen-age years, I was getting tighter when I should have been releasing them more. . . . With the hazards of drugs, drinking and sex, and whatever, I was feeling that if you didn't tighten up and keep tight control, you might get into some kind of problems."

"I guess I felt the father-image had to be the boss—strong and forceful. . . . they're going to do what I tell them to do."

"I was being run over as a parent, as a person. I was doing the permissive thing, particularly with our second child. And this little kid was really running over me. I was simply not standing up for my rights . . . so much that I hated her, really."

One of the most frequent themes in the interviews with our families was that they sought help because they were caught in the dilemma of whether to be strict or permissive. Frightened by the "hazards of teen-age years," some parents became dictators, some doormats. Neither way worked. Furthermore, the dictators felt guilty and hated themselves; the doormats felt impotent and hated their kids.

Some parents swung back and forth between these two postures like a pendulum, as did this mother, a soft-spoken minister's wife, with her seven-year-old daughter:

"She'd need transportation and I'd be her transportation for this and for that, here and there, whatever. It was as if I wasn't hearing my own needs, allowing her more freedom than she needed to have, and than I needed to give her. Maybe my needs to do something in the afternoon would be shot, but I would go ahead and do it. . . . Then all of a sudden—it might be just one incident—she would break the camel's back. She'd do one thing that would really be destructive, and then I'd just really come on hard and heavy on her . . . and then I would feel so bad later. And the cycle would be, 'Oh, how awful—this is such a heavy thing that I'm doing to this little kid.' All my week's hostility coming out, and then I'd feel very guilty about it. . . . And then if she would do something that would show she was feeling bad—you know, tears or withdrawal—that would trigger me to put myself down because I'd really done this heavy thing to her. . . . It was not a healthy cycle, for either one of us."

A similar kind of cyclical power struggle was described by a vivacious mother of three teen-age boys, who took P.E.T. soon after her divorce from her policeman husband:

M: I really haven't had a good background on how to deal with anyone because my own family life wasn't ideal by any means—my parents never got along very well and then obviously my husband and I didn't get along very well either. I saw I didn't have any skills to keep from repeating this. When I was rather desperate for something, I was told about the P.E.T. class. . . . There were definitely power struggles between the boys and myself, and I honestly didn't know there was a third way to handle things. I felt the only way to cope with situations was either "I win and you lose" or "I lose and you win." In the past I usually lost, but I was getting tired of losing, so I just learned to yell a little louder and then I usually won. But I found it was not really a very good victory—it's only a stalemate for a while. . . .

I: Over what kind of things would you have power struggles?

M: My youngest felt it was always my job to have all the meals ready at a certain time. He'd say, "You have to." And I was rebelling against my having to. I'd say, "No, I don't have to—I have to die and pay taxes and that's it. You'll starve before you shove me into a mold of having to fix meals." So it was meals—his trying to buck my authority, not being willing to listen to anything I had to say, his wanting to have the upper hand and my not knowing how to handle it.

I: And how were you feeling about it?

M: I don't know if I can even say how strongly I
      was feeling. Frustrated doesn't even come close
      to how I was feeling. Angry, because I didn't
      know how to handle it. And I'd gone to a coun-
      selor twice, but at twenty-five dollars a crack, I
      just couldn't put out that money. . . .

I: So what did P.E.T. do?

M: Well, they took care of it for a lot less. I felt
      then I got some tools to work with. I mean, I
      just couldn't believe the way you could go about
      it. It was like knowing I could build the building.
      Finally I had some tools, and it was just terrific.
      I was really excited about it. Now this didn't
      happen all at once . . . and I'm still working on it.

CRISES AND TRAGEDIES

Some families unfortunately experienced a serious
crisis, a traumatic event, or a terrible tragedy before
they enrolled in a P.E.T. class. Not to place blame on
all of these parents, it must be made clear that some
had not even heard about P.E.T. until too late. Others
apparently waited too long to seek help, not ever sus-
pecting anything so serious would happen in their family.

Listen to this father, a dentist, talk about his feelings of desperation when his daughter (the oldest of
three) left home, shunning every value and hope he
held for her:

"I think the main motivation for me [to enroll in
P.E.T.] was because we had a major upheaval with our
daughter. She was finishing high school and my pressure was that she go to college and get an education,
but she wasn't sure she wanted to go or not. She
started to go with a kid I disapproved of. I went along
to a certain point, but I eventually let her know that
I really did disapprove of this kid and his life style.
The conflict eventually got to the point where she left
—packed her clothes and took off, went to live with

the kid and his parents, who gave them a bedroom. They're still living together now in the mountains, living in a truck, the very classic hippy sort of way of living. . . . I was feeling a miserable failure as a parent."

Another parent was confronted with an unexpected teen-age runaway. This mother of three takes a new look at her expectations and role as a parent and how her power and influence have diminished over the years:

"There was quite a breakdown in the relationship between us, especially our sixteen-year-old son. We were not dealing with the problems effectively, mostly using our authority, but a lot of permissiveness, too. Well, he ran away from home once, and he almost went a second time. . . . The problem was stealing, and smoking marijuana and hair length had become quite a divisive thing—I suppose old-fashioned parents have a hard time accepting such things. Also clothing issues, messy room, not following up on any responsibilities, sassy talk to me. He'd feel that since he was now as big as me, he didn't have any fears."

This parent points to a phenomenon that most parents do not understand—as their children get older (and "bigger"), parental authority, which often worked fairly well when the kids were younger, suddenly becomes an ineffective method for the simple reason that parents *run out of power*. Their teen-agers no longer are willing to be bossed or bullied. To their chagrin, parents discover their big guns have run out of ammunition.

A serious auto accident shocked one family into taking constructive action:

"He was getting a lot of traffic tickets, and he and I were in constant fights with each other. . . . He'd go into his room and slam the door, shutting me out of his life. I was a very controlling mother—I had to be in control of everybody. You know, Super-Mother. . . . And then he turned the car over, and he acted as if nothing had happened. . . . This terrible power struggle he and I were in. I was trying to control him, and he was trying to get out from under his controlling mother. . . . Boy, was I desperate."

Two other kinds of crises were recalled by parents we interviewed:

"I asked her to pick up the horrendous mess in her bedroom. . . . She'd just give me a flat, 'No, I won't.' And I ended up just popping that kid on the fanny and then throwing her on the bed so hard that I could have hurt her really badly. At that point I hated that kid so badly. I just hated her, you know, thinking about putting her up for adoption."

A high-achieving, high-status executive told his P.E.T. class why he had taken the course. His oldest son had achieved almost every available honor as he grew up—Eagle Scout, graduating from an Eastern school summa cum laude, president of his Junior Chamber of Commerce, and being named the young businessman of the year. Three weeks after the last honor, he shot himself to death, leaving a note which read, "Father, I can't go on any longer because I don't know who I am. I think maybe I'm you."

WHO DOES NEED PARENT TRAINING?

Obviously the parents we interviewed felt they needed special training to become more effective, although for many differnt reasons: self-improvement, prevention, to do better than their own parents, out of fear of the "terrible teens," after getting early storm warnings, or after the occurrence of a major crisis. The vast majority of parents probably never consider taking a course for greater parent effectiveness, or, as we have discovered, reject the idea when the opportunity is offered them. Their resistance, as we found out, is rooted in certain commonly held beliefs about parenting, most of which are not based on fact.

It puzzles me that those who reject the idea of parent training readily accept the logic that if they wanted to become effective or competent in any other endeavor or activity, they would take lessons, get coaching, or enroll in a training program. Those who aspire to become good at tennis take tennis lessons from a pro; competent bridge players invariably have taken bridge lessons; few persons would go out on the ski slopes until after they have had several lessons from a ski instructor. Most people accept the idea of getting professional help when they learn how to drive, sew, paint, be a gourmet cook, do interior decorating, become an effective manager, learn to swim or fly an airplane.

With parenthood it's different. People somehow assume they're going to be good parents when they get their children. Or perhaps they cannot accept that anyone knows enough to teach them what it takes to be an effective parent. In fact, what we now know about parent effectiveness has been learned rather recently. Behavioral scientists only about twenty-five years ago began acquiring knowledge about what it takes to foster and maintain good relationships. By now much is known. We know the skills required to bring about effective two-way communication in an interpersonal relationship; we know a method for resolving interpersonal conflicts so that no one loses and both win; we know how a person can influence another to be considerate of his needs; we know a method that will help another person work through his personal problems and find his own solutions; we know how power and authority erode personal relationships.

Until very recently, very little of this knowledge ever got applied directly to the parent-child relationship. It's as if that relationship is somehow very different from other kinds of interpersonal relationships —such as friend-friend, husband-wife, teacher-student, boss-subordinate. Now we know better.

Furthermore, until the last ten years or so, most behavioral scientists talked only to each other or wrote books to be read primarily by their colleagues. Not too soon, this also has been corrected. With our new knowledge more readily available for parents and with train-ing programs going on in thousands of communities in every state, perhaps training for effectiveness will have an impact on society sooner than we think.

XIV

THE PERSONAL STORIES OF FOUR PARENTS:
How P.E.T. Changed Their Families

The following four accounts were selected from a group of thirty-four personal documents written by parents in response to our request for detailed accounts of how families changed after the parents took P.E.T. The documents are quite different, yet all are very personal and moving. They are presented here substantially as submitted to us, except that the names have been changed to preserve the anonymity of the family.

IT CAN MOVE MOUNTAINS

"I don't know what they taught you when you went to Chicago, Mom. But it works. I can hardly believe how good I feel when you just listen to me." Chicago was where I had taken my P.E.T. instructors training.

Just minutes before he had been crying in choked angry sobs, and I'd been thinking, "My God, can I

handle this?" Now I know that I can handle a lot more
than I ever gave myself credit for, and so can our sons.
Affirmation in myself as a worthy and caring person,
along with skills in honest communication and confrontation, were two gifts P.E.T. gave to me during
that week in Chicago.

I now believe that parents in situations such as
we have in our home can often be much more effective
than an outside helping person could. Since my P.E.T.
training I am closer to my sons in an intimate way that
I would never have dreamed of, and at the same time I
am happier about their independence. I can listen to
their feelings and fears and allow them to speak their
anger and frustrations.

When you're living with a terminal and chronic
disease, that's a real plus for creative living day by day.

The incident I just mentioned came on Mark's
sixteenth birthday. It was late at night. John, my husband, had gone to bed as had Mark and Stan, age
twelve. I was cleaning up the kitchen when Mark
walked in and sat down at the kitchen table.

"I can't sleep," he said. "Too much on my mind, I
guess."

It wasn't unusual for Mark to have a hard time
getting to sleep. Mark has cystic fibrosis. Often when he
lies down he coughs more. Night-times had always been
bad. When he was a baby, John or I would often sit up
into the night holding him upright so he could breathe
easier. As he had gotten older he would just get up and
read or watch TV. Sometimes he would work on an art
project. He'd become very good at that. But tonight
there was an obvious clue to do more: "too much on
my mind." I heard it loud and clear.

Cystic fibrosis is a serious lung disease. Often it is
fatal before the age of eighteen. Mark had been diag-
nosed at three, a week before his infant sister died of
the same disease. Children with C/F produce a thick
sticky mucus that clogs the ducts of the pancreas and
other body organs. In the pancreas it creates difficult
digestive problems. Most devastating is what that mucus does in the lungs and bronchial tree: blocking tiny

areas, setting up infections that can mean gradual deterioration of the lungs. It's a constant battle with antibiotics and therapy to keep those lung infections in check.

With Mark, as with many others who have C/F, it was often a losing battle. Each year he'd spent more and more time in the hospital. His daily bucket of pills ranged between forty and fifty. He is unable to go without antibiotics.

Mark knows he has trouble running. Two years ago he gave up playing Little League. He knows kids die of C/F, because some of the friends he met at the hospital have died. Obviously, he knows he can't do as much this year as he did a year or two back. We've kind of accepted that, without talking about it much. Actually, I think we spent years talking around it. I'd been wanting Mark to have his say on the subject of C/F, but I didn't think he wanted to talk about it—he'd never brought the subject up—or more likely, I'd never heard the clues. That night I did.

He said he wanted to thank me for the poem I'd written him and the card I'd made for him. [They're printed at the end of these pages.] I explained how I'd looked everywhere for just the right gift, but kept remembering how he'd always said he disliked it when people bought gifts just because it was a special day. I told him I'd been afraid to share the poem with him because it was happy/sad writing. He nodded. "But," I said, "I decided to trust you with my thoughts because it kept coming to my mind that it was the gift that would mean the most." Not just to him, but to me also.

He started talking then about the importance of people sharing what is real with each other, and how many people he sees that are phonies. His voice went from disgust to anger. He spoke in bitter words against the people in school and in our church, making accusations I felt were too harsh about "those damned Sunday Christians." It became very hard for me to listen. I had to fight my impulse to defend those people, to ask him to be more kind toward them.

When I didn't stop him he said more. Now it was

not just the people . . . it was also the teachings of the
church that were "stupid." Then it was that people
were cruel. "Where do they get all their answers on how
to live a beautiful long life?" he spit out angrily.

I was getting really uptight. I couldn't remember
having heard him swear before. He did now. "They
think they're so goddamned smart," and "How in the
hell do they know what it's like to be different?"

I was afraid I couldn't stand to hear any more.
My throat felt like it had needles in it, and when I realized how tightly my hand was clutching the kitchen
chair, I also knew how badly my feet wanted to carry
me away to another place. I kept saying to my head:
"Don't buy into the problem. Let him own his own feelings so you can listen to them."

Finally he just broke down and sobbed. He
pounded the table so hard I was afraid he'd hurt himself, and he screamed, "I'm afraid to die. I don't want
to die."

After moments that seemed like hours, as I wondered what to do now, he lifted his head from his
arms, and met my eyes.

"I had to say that, Mom," he said. We hugged
each other and cried together. Then, after we'd sat in
silence for a while, he looked up, half sheepishly, and
said, "Well, let's get those dishes done now."

Just like that.

If I'd been directing the scene, as parents are so
wont to do, I'd have probably suggested I'd come up to
his room and say good night. Mark was having none of
that. It was midnight as we washed those dishes and
talked about our feelings and fears. Many of them, we
discovered, were honestly very joyful. It felt like a
celebration. Like we were having communion together
over the kitchen sink; and why not?

"I feel so good," Mark kept saying. He told me he
was happy I'd be teaching P.E.T. "That stuff is really
important," he said. "You know, sometime maybe I
could help you out with it.

He already had. More than he'll ever maybe
know.

Talking about feelings the way Mark had that night, only once, isn't enough, as I've come to know. We need to keep the door open for new discussions. Since Mark discovered that his feelings will be allowed, he talks to me more often. He talks to others, too, and is finding out that as he honestly discovers what his feelings are, he communicates differently. And he looks at his feelings to clarify what he really believes and values. He's channeling some of his discoveries into action. At sixteen, Mark is very capable of solving his own problems. When I try and take over, he's developed some pretty neat "I-messages" of his own to let me know what I'm doing. As for C/F, well, nothing has changed; we just seem not to be so controlled by it.

A chronic disease affects the entire family. Lots of times it's harder on the healthy siblings than on the child with the disease. Especially when there are only two children in the family, being sick almost becomes more the norm than being well.

Not long after Mark's birthday, Stan began having nightmares again. This had happened off and on over the years. We'd sought professional help, but still he'd wake up screaming and be unable to go back to sleep. He'd never talk about the dreams. He said he couldn't remember them. This time he didn't want to go back to bed alone. For two nights I stayed with him until he went back to sleep. After this had happened the third time I talked to him about it the next day, wondering how the skills I had learned could serve me.

I began by saying, "Stan, I'm concerned that your dreams are causing me a problem too. We're both losing sleep. I'm worried and Dad feels I should be in our bed. I do, too, but I also don't want you to be afraid, and I feel really torn. I feel we need to talk about those dreams in the daytime." So we did—sort of. The scene went something like this for about the next five days:

At some time during the day Stan would give a deep sigh and look down or off into space. I'd say . . . "Do you feel troubled now, Stan?" He'd say nothing. I'd say, "Stan, I feel something is happening with these dreams that we should talk about. I'm very troubled. Can we talk?" He'd nod yes and we'd go alone into the den.

The first four days our conversation went like this:

STAN: I can't help it, Mom. I just get scared, and I can't go back to sleep.

MOTHER: Your dreams are awfully frightening.

S: I'm afraid to go back to sleep alone.

M: If I lie down with you, you're not so afraid.

S: Yes.

And then silence. Dead end. I had some feeling what it was about, but something told me not to push. I was thinking, "It's his problem, he'll have to state it himself." But I did try and make our conversations go on longer. I'd ask him to try and remember the dream. He'd cry and say he couldn't, or that he was afraid to try. We'd leave saying, "Well maybe tonight there won't be a dream."

But he'd wake up screaming. On the sixth day I said, "Stan, I'm afraid. I don't seem to be helping you get over your bad dreams. I feel so helpless. I'm tired and discouraged, and I just don't know what to do. I'm wondering if maybe we should go to someone else who might be able to help both of us with this problem."

This time he said, "I don't want to talk to anyone else. I only want to tell you."

"About the dream?" I asked.

"No," he said, "about being afraid."

And so we began. We talked a long time, and there were many long silences. It went about like this:

S: When I wake up and it's dark, I'm afraid I'm all alone in the world.

M: (Wanting to reassure him) You're frightened that everyone else has left you.

s: (*Angrily*) Well, you can't count on anyone to be around.

m: You feel you can't depend on us to be with you.

s: Well you or Dad are always leaving to go to work or some place.

m: You feel we're away too much.

s: (*Aggravated*) No. It's just that I can't depend on things to always be the same.

m: Things change, and you feel unsure about that.

s: Yeh, like you and Dad. You won't always be here.

m: (*Puzzled, and defending myself*) But, Stan, Dad and I don't go out in the evenings often, and when we do we always come back.

s: But things don't stay the same. (*Crying now*) I can't depend on anybody. People die, you know.

m: You're afraid that Dad and I might die and leave you and Mark alone.

s: (*Shakes his head no*) (*Silence. More crying, and then . . .*) You and Dad are healthy. Mark isn't. . . .

m: You're afraid that Mark will die, and you'll miss him, and feel all alone without him.

He nodded yes. My God, what pain, what fear he had kept down inside him! We talked more then. He told me he knew he was afraid of that for a long, long, long time. I asked him if it was six months, a year, or two years. "A lot longer than that," he said. I cried with him then.

He told me he was afraid that if he talked about Mark dying, it might make it happen. We talked about a lot of things. About how I was afraid too, and Mark, and Dad. About how it was all right if he had friends, and did things Mark could no longer do. We talked about research, how people were working so hard to find a cure, how things might not change, but also that they might.

After a while he said, "I think I'll go play now."

It was ended. I sat on the couch feeling very awed by what had just happened. A few moments later he stuck his head back around the corner and said, "Hey, Mom, betcha I sleep tonight." And he did. No more "dreams."

I don't know if I always use the P.E.T. skills correctly, but I do know they've taught me some beautiful things about other people, and they've opened up some pretty honest communication in our home that I'd have roadblocked with all good intentions only a year ago.

Stan came to me a few weeks ago one night and said he was having a hard time getting to sleep. "Wanna talk about something?" I asked. He did. He'd quarreled with Mark that day and now was feeling very badly about it. Mark had been quite sick for a week or two, and today he'd been especially short-tempered. We talked about how hard it is on all of us when someone is sick. Stan said it must really be hard for Mark when he'd see him playing basketball and he can't. (Stan had a tournament game coming up soon.)

Then Stan said, "I guess I'm just going to have to realize that it's not my fault that Mark's sick. He said some really mean things to me too, and I've got a right to let off steam just like he does." And with that, a hug and a "good night."

As the boys and I began to talk more, it became apparent that John was being left out more. That's one of the real hazards when one person parents in a new way. We've had to talk about what's happening. John was at first skeptical, but as he sees what's happening he has become less so. When I comforted Stan in the night, that seemed permissive to him. He implied that I would make Stan a "sissy" by all that attention. But when John saw that Stan did want to talk, and sees the changes taking place as Stan becomes more confident and speaks up for his own needs more often . . . well, P.E.T. makes its own credibility.

I think we need to keep talking about it, though! And I'm hoping that John soon will take a P.E.T. class himself. Meantime, there is great freedom in knowing that we don't always have to come to parenting with a mutual front. John can be John. I can be me. It's being congruent that seems to matter most. That and knowing who owns what problem.

Our experience in our home may be unique. But I find as I teach P.E.T. that we also share most of the same things other families do. And as a result of the insights I've gained, I've become much more effective outside my home also.

I've been promoted and have taken on a new job, and I find my new skills an integral part of my daily relationships with the staff and community. And because I saw how healing it was for us to talk of our real feelings about C/F, my volunteer work for our foundation has taken a new, and I feel, very exciting dimension. I organized and chaired a session at a state workshop entitled, "Parenting and C/F," using active listening to allow parents to ventilate feelings and decide some of the directions they needed to take.

In February a psychiatrist from one of our state universities joined me in addressing a conference held for Special Education workers in our state. We held a one-hour discussion with two complete families who had children with C/F. It was shown to the conference members on closed-circuit TV. These families shared deeply their pains and joys in their special way of life with a terminal disease in their midst. As a result, it looks as if a very important research project will soon be under way.

Speaking to an inservice training session for one of our local helping agencies a short while back I was sharing with their staff some of the feelings parents of C/F children had shared with me.

"Look," I said, "mostly they're just saying they're hurt and they're angry, and they're tired. They need to know that they're doing OK, and everyone keeps trying to give them a million other problems or a dozen other answers."

"Why didn't you tell us that before when you talked to us?" the director asked.

Because, I said, before P.E.T. I didn't know it either.

The last time Mark was in the hospital, I gave my business card to the visiting chaplain. He read it out loud slowly and then said, " 'Parent Effectiveness Training.' Does that stuff really work?"

"It's just like in your business," I replied. "If you believe in it, and practice it, it works. It may not always move mountains, but it sure helps build a lot of bridges."

To Mark

as we celebrate the 16th year since your birth.

Special Person
                Whom I love.
                Whom I find
                        great joy in
Be blessed this
                day by sunlight
                dancing on your cheeks
                and in your eyes.
What darkness
                we have known
                and must prepare for
                But, oh what
                        living there is
                        yet for us
                                to do.

The card read:

                You have given
                me more than
                I could ever
                return

                A light always
                glowing to warm
                the darkest day.

                I love you.
                        Mom

BEYOND SKILLS: A P.E.T. JOURNAL

I remember when Alice was born. It was just two years ago, and neither Joe nor I knew the first thing about babies. We were really afraid we might do something "wrong"—that we might not fill her needs. We wanted to give her the best possible start in life, particularly in the emotional sense, and often we would sacrifice our other interests and needs in order to do what we thought would be best for her. Yet we didn't know what was the best.

At Alice's eighteen months checkup I asked her pediatrician if there was a book I might read that would help in coping with the "battle-of-the-wills." The doctor suggested Thomas Gordon's *Parent Effectiveness Training*. I totally devoured the text! I felt so comfortable with the concepts that I was convinced P.E.T. was for me, and that it ought to be available to everyone with kids—or without them!

Convinced as I was about the effectiveness of the skills, I found it really hard to implement them on my own (we lacked the funds for taking a P.E.T. course). One day I was really shocked when I found myself screaming at Alice and threatening her with a spanking —an aspect of myself which very rarely surfaces. I was aware that whatever it was that she had done really did not deserve my anger. It was *my* problem, and it was a part of myself I didn't like. I didn't want Alice to suffer because of my inability to deal with an everyday conflict of needs.

Shortly thereafter I noticed that the University of California Extension Program was offering a P.E.T. course, and I found a benefactress in my mother. Maybe with some help and constant effort, the P.E.T. skills could work for me. Here is the journal I kept during the nine-week course—what I thought about, the difficulties I encountered, and the joy of learning:

January 11, 1975

(Note: Alice will be two years old 1/15/75. She doesn't totally talk yet—mostly nouns. She is, to date,

an only child.) Alice awakens from her nap crying and
looking scared. I go into her room to see what's wrong:

MOTHER: Did you have a bad dream?

ALICE: Yeah ... Bert ... Ernie!

M: You dreamed about Bert and Ernie? (Sesa-
            me Street "muppets")

A: Yeah. (*Cries some more.*)

M: They scared you?

A: Yeah. (*Crying subsides slowly.*)

Later, when she's more awake:

M: The dream scared you.

A: Yeah, Ernie!

M: You know ... dreams aren't real. (*I don't know
            how to go about explaining it to her.*)

A: Toy!

M: Toy?

A: Yeah!

Then I remember a couple of days earlier, when
we were at my mother's house, Alice found a fake insect where my mother had it hanging on a curtain for
maximum effect. She was a little afraid of it. I told her
it "wasn't real," that it was a "toy" insect, whereupon
she touched it and laughed. Her linking of two incidents was her way of understanding my very inept
explanation of her nightmare. Baby metaphysics!

January 14th

I remember my brother's evaluation of my "Active
Listening" with Alice. If she fell and hurt herself or
caught her fingers in the door and came crying to
Mommy, I'd say something like, "Oh! that really hurts
you!" Or if someone took something from her and she

was upset, I'd say something like "You really wanted that, didn't you!"

His reaction: "Why are you always rubbing it in?"

I can see it might look that way to someone who's never tried Active Listening. But the fact is, that Alice *does* seem to appreciate my efforts at communicating some understanding of her feelings, and it *does* seem to reduce her distress a bit.

January 17th

I found myself using a rather perverted type of Active Listening this morning as a subtle form of diversion or evasion. Even as I consciously began to Active Listen, I realized that my feedback message was deliberately distorted from the message I received, in order to divert Alice from her line of thinking and to evade the point at hand:

As we passed the bagel shop in the car, she said with some urgency, "Bagel . . . Alice!"

Knowing full well that the message was "Alice wants a bagel!" I tried to evade the issue by saying, "Oh, Alice likes bagels a lot!" I was ignoring what I didn't want to hear.

Not being a pushover, she corrected me: "Bagel, NOW!"

I said, "Now!" in a rather half-hearted parroting, realizing that *this* kind of Active Listening, if you could even call it that, was no better than the "Twelve Roadblocks" to communication—it was, in fact, one of them. Maybe an honest "I-message" would have been more to the point.

I think that I tend to do this often with her. Under the guise of Active Listening, I push my own will. I'll have to watch out for that!

January 19th

When I use Active Listening with Alice she certainly seems to respond well. But I've also grown extremely aware of every time I tell her what to do or give her suggestions. I've noticed how often she asks me if it's OK for her to do something, making me think my bossing and suggesting have somewhat suppressed the development of her own resources and the assumption of responsibility for herself. I'd really like her to develop in *her* own way, and at *her* own speed. I *do* like it when she *does* care how I feel about something! And I guess she feels the same way too!

January 20th

I find I'm becoming very aware of how people communicate with their children, and with each other. I must say it really bugs me when I'm around my friends and I hear them using all the "Roadblocks" in communicating with their kids, and with mine. And, since most people *do* use these traditional ways of talking, I find I feel unaccepting of *that* behavior a lot! Which, I might add, bothers me because I don't like to go around feeling so negative toward others' behaviors. I'd like to let them feel that they can do their own thing, and I'll do mine, and what's right for me doesn't have to be right for them. That doesn't come easy for me when it has to do with raising children, which to me is so important. Well, maybe when I get over this darned cold, my level of acceptance will increase!

January 21st

Active Listening works well with Joe (my husband). He appreciates being listened to and finding that I really want to understand how he feels about his problems. And I like it because I *can* see better how he feels about something, and don't have the feeling I have to solve the problems for him—which I can't do anyway!

There is an element of being aware that we are using a method of communicating, which is rather strange. But knowing we're doing it because we *want* to understand each other makes that part not so bad. I figure as our skills improve and we become more fluid with them, we will become less conscious of it. I hope so!

I also notice that I sometimes feel downright resentful when people won't let me solve my own problems when I mention them! I've gotten so I don't like being directed, preached to, having solutions suggested (sometimes, yes!), criticized, analyzed, and being consoled, etc., because I feel it's the other person horning in on my trip, so to speak, and what I want from them is Active Listening!!! It is seldom that I have the luxury of being Active Listened to! This awareness will hopefully reinforce my learning not to do the same "nonlistening" to others—they'd probably appreciate being listened to as much as I do.

January 22nd

Active Listening requires total attention of the listener. Both Alice and Joe respond positively to my efforts with it if, and only if, I'm giving them my undivided attention. You can't wash dishes and Active Listen—not too well! I think the other feels you're not really listening nor that you care that much if you aren't face to face, eye to eye, listening. And rightly so!

January 24th

I find that I'm becoming more aware of whether specific situations are appropriate or inappropriate for Active Listening. I think sometimes I've been feeling guilty for *not* Active Listening when somebody's had a problem and I haven't come through with the "goods." But I see now that if I don't feel like listening, I really had better not, and that it's OK! Today a neighbor was sounding off, and I thought, "Well, here's a good time to Active Listen." But I became also aware of my feeling of nonacceptance—she was just kind of irritating me today. So I decided the situation just wasn't right, that my Active Listening would be phony.

Something that bothers me when using Active Listening with adults is that I'm so extremely conscious of using it, and it makes me afraid of continuing for fear that the sender will become aware of it and think I'm using some "method" on him. I think the self-consciousness will disappear as I become more skillful

and plain old used to not using all my old methods of
responding. And as for the sender, I'm more sincerely
interested in helping him than before.

January 26th

Alice seems to respond (or change her unacceptable behavior to some degree!) to my "I-messages." It
seems to be something she can't argue against: i.e., *my
feelings.* She somehow understands that I'm not *telling*
her what to do, what *not* to do, but that the behavior
is something that I don't like, or bugs me. And that she
can choose to change it however she pleases, *if* she
pleases. She doesn't have to bother with defenses or
revenge. I think she appreciates that. An example
(Alice was playing in the bathtub):

Me: "I sure hate to see the water spill on the floor
from your beaker, because I'll have to clean up the floor
again, and I'm tired of doing it over and over." (Alice
moves her beaker to the other edge of the bathtub
where it won't spill on the floor.) Everyone's happy!

January 28th

I see Alice bossing cats a lot! Even pictures of
them! I wonder whether she's bossing them because I
boss her, or whether it's because I, and others, boss
cats. She doesn't boss other animals or people (demanding, yes; bossing, no!), nor does she boss her toy
animals, so it leads me to think perhaps she is copying
our behavior of telling the cats what to do: "Get down!"
"No!"—those are *her* favorites, and ours too, I guess.
Interesting how quickly behaviors and attitudes are
adopted, and how strong a model we are for behaviors.

January 29th

I don't feel as mean these days communicating
what is unacceptable to me, or standing up for *my*
rights. I think I was sort of afraid of dealing with
Alice's negative reactions—afraid to allow her to experience negative feelings and frustrations. I find she is
very competent in developing frustrations (as always!)
but is *also* competent in dealing with them *herself,* if I

let her know what I like or can cope with, and what I can't. Situations don't get blown way out of proportion if I let her know right away how I feel about it. She's always been quick to let us know where *she* stands, but I think I've tended to hold back 'til the blowing point! I'd like to show her the same honesty she shows me.

January 30th

I really like the idea of using NO POWER in raising children and in my relationships with others. I *don't like* using power, and it's an exciting prospect to think it *is* possible *not* to use it!

February 2nd

Evidently we've been using problem-solving techniques often without realizing it. Those are the times the conflicts have been resolved in the happiest way for all of us! For instance, here I am writing this in the bathroom while Alice bathes—she likes baths about two or three times a day! And I don't like bathing her that often. So, we've worked out something we're both happy with: She gets to play in the bathtub, often without being washed, while I just sit in the bathroom with her and read a book—or do whatever *I* want, which is something not always possible when she's awake otherwise. This is a solution very acceptable for *both* of us.

February 3rd

Another conflict-resolution situation that works!! I'm surprised, because I thought the Method III technique wouldn't work so well with a two-year-old. But, delight of delights, it does! It takes some imagination to come up with a solution both she and I are happy with, but often a process of elimination and some creative thinking bring results! Alice awakened at 4:00 A.M. today wanting to come sleep in our bed (something she hasn't requested in a while). I told her that wasn't acceptable to me (after some Active Listening), that I wouldn't be able to sleep with her in our bed, and that I really needed my sleep to be able to function

properly during the day. Her bottle of water wouldn't
satisfy her, nor my singing, but she was very happy to
stay in her bed if I would hold her hand *and* sing to her
for a few minutes! How much *nicer* than if I'd just refused and left her crying, or if I'd given in and let her
ruin my sleep!

February 4th

An interesting occurrence today—a testing of
what was mentioned in class last week: "Relationships
may not be as fragile as we think." I let my husband
and mother-in-law (*she* was the real test) know how
uncomfortable I felt with them pushing me to join
into their "fun" fantasies of a vacation trip I may—or
may not—take. Their behavior was really bugging me
(my acceptance level was at a minimum), and I finally
got the nerve up to tell them via the best "I-message" I
could muster at the moment. They saw how strongly I
felt about it, and stopped. I felt I was exposing a side
of myself I don't particularly like, and which I assume
others won't like (i.e., too serious a lot of the time—
instead of easygoing, devil-may-care). But it was accepted without much ado. Whew! I was really relieved,
and pleased that I took the risk to send the "I-message," and that it was well received.

February 5th

Another interesting thing happened today. After
dinner at my parents' house, Alice was tired and
cranky. We were waiting for "Daddy" to finish his coffee before going home to bed. Alice wanted "Grandfather" to give her some orange juice, but got pretty
upset when he started pouring it into her cup. He
couldn't figure out what was going on, so I translated
to him what Alice was indicating. She wanted to drink
out of the big pitcher of juice, *NOT* her cup (like she
sees Mommy do at home on occasion!). Grandfather
said "No." Alice said "Yes!", then threw herself on the
floor crying. He called her spoiled, and warned *me*
that I better start doing something about "training" her
before it was too late! I turned to Alice, who was still

on the floor building up a storm, and said, "You're really mad that Grandfather won't let you drink out of the big pitcher!"

"Yes . . . Alice . . . big . . . NOW!" she cried.

"You're big enough to drink out of the big pitcher, *now!*" I said.

"Yes!!" And with that she stopped crying, got up from the floor, and said, "Night-night! Home!"

I turned to my father and asked him whether there was any problem anymore because throughout my conversation with Alice he'd been carrying on about how something was going to have to be "done" about *her* carrying on! He had not really noticed what had occurred, but conceded that there no longer seemed to be any problem. I was surprised that he didn't seem to be aware of how quickly the problem dissolved (my knowing how well these incidents can really turn into major explosions!), nor how Alice came up with one main aspect of the problem—that *she* was ready to go to sleep!

February 10th

I've been having trouble lately leaving Alice with other people. She's been so upset at my departure that it's made baby-sitting very difficult for whoever is with her. It's also made *me* worry a lot about it. Active Listening and "I-messages" have not seemed to alleviate the problem, and problem-solving doesn't get off the ground. So I've been trying to figure out at least why *I* have been so upset about it. I've become aware that I was feeling *really* anxious, nervous, unsure. Obviously, this wouldn't be hidden from Alice—and would compound the problem: She sees how anxious *I* am about leaving her, and becomes more anxious herself (there must be something really scary about Mommy's leaving). So this won't help.

Why am I so nervous about it? I think a lot has to do with trying to be the *perfect* mother. An unrealistic goal, what? But one that has been very real to me. Am I really so powerful a force in her life that she can't handle some of these things by herself?

Obviously I *am* important to her as a mother still, but can't I allow her that independence and encourage that responsibility of herself which I say I really want for her?

Something else: Why do I feel I should leave her? This is a question referring to those times when I leave her, thinking it's something *she* needs—that she *should* have her own time away from me. My needs to do anything in particular are not all that well-defined. Why should she have her own time away from me if she doesn't like it? Do I feel pressure from others that I should be able to leave her, even if I don't always feel *my* need to be alone? Is that some idea I've adopted about what's a "well-adjusted" child?

I enjoy being with Alice a great deal of the time. And I don't feel anxious about leaving her when I have a definite need (e.g., doctor's appointments, social engagements, P.E.T. classes). Then there usually isn't any problem for her—she accepts that Mommy is gone for a while. But I can see that when I try to leave her for the sake of leaving her and *my* need isn't legitimate, I'm as nervous as a witch, and the whole thing probably doesn't seem quite right to her. Nor to me, as I think about it. What the hell, if she needs me with her in those situations, *I'm* really more interested in filling her needs, rather than vacuuming a living room or whatever! My being with her is more important to me and to her, too. Wow! That's a load off my mind! Not that she isn't going to still be unhappy when I leave her, but at least my needs and priorities are becoming clearer to me, and it takes the edge off the problem. I guess I've been accepting certain social pressures and theories as my needs. Actually, *my* needs—my very own needs—are a far cry from what I've been trying to fulfill. I can start again from here!

February 14th

Alice accepts my apologies. I blow up, feel bad about it, tell her how sorry I am, that I'm feeling under a lot of pressure. She comes over to me, gives me a hug and pats me on the back. I really appreciate that. She makes me feel good.

February 15th
    I have a problem with P.E.T.! My conscientious self has overdone it again! I am so darned aware of what I say, what I want to say or don't want to say, what others say, how they probably feel, how I feel, etc., that sometimes I feel like I'm going to explode. But I don't. I cry.
    I've really made it a burden. I feel responsible—totally—for any and every relationship I have. Ordinarily a feeling of responsibility would be healthy and realistic. But I think I've gone too far! I also feel lonely in it. I know more when someone doesn't understand how I feel. The skills have made it more obvious. Then again, I know more when I *am* understood and when I understand others. The positive sides of learning P.E.T. methods have been pretty evident from the start. I'm just learning what the problems are that I as an individual am having in implementing these methods. They are serious enough so that I want to take a new close look at what P.E.T. means to me, what I want from it, what I can get from it.

February 19th
    Interesting! It's been four days since I wrote the last entry, and I feel very different about P.E.T. now. The biggest problem I have with it has come to light: The burden and loneliness, responsibility and self-consciousness, I think had arisen from the fact that a true feeling of caring—real empathy—has not always been present when I Active Listen or problem-solve. Obviously, such a host of overwhelming emotions within me have more to do than with just P.E.T. and me; a lot of other factors are involved. But as for these skills, I really think that my levels of empathy, of caring, have not matched the verbal skills acquired. For me, this is *not* P.E.T. I think a real caring without any communi-

cation skills would be a lot more effective in building relationships than the utmost in perfected methods.

The last couple of days I have noticed that when I tried to Active Listen or problem-solve, I was really more concerned with *my* ideas and feelings about the situations than with trying to really understand the other person's feelings. With that awareness I was able to shut off my feelings for a while and really listen empathically, method or no method. This, for me, is the crux of P.E.T. It's my particular problem. Sure, it's nice for me to feel understood, but just like the book says, if I can turn off all the jabber and preconceptions inside my head, and really listen *with care,* then the understanding I gain of the other person will most likely be appreciated and reciprocated. It's been one thing to read it and another to really experience it!

The importance of empathy as prerequisite for Active Listening has been mentioned repeatedly in the text and by the instructors. Intellectually I understood it, but it hasn't been until the last few days that I have really seen and experienced what it's all about. Halfway caring, halfway listening, with a lot of my own ideas and strong emotions dominating my vantage point, sure don't do the trick! It's only by leaving my own "mind" for a while, that I can really listen and come to know the other. For me, *that* is caring, and that is what is necessary for implementing the P.E.T. skills. Otherwise, forget it!

February 22nd

A problem-solving situation in which I learned a lot about how *not* to go about it! One evening last week, after putting Alice to bed and then doing some dishes, I sat down exhausted next to Joe, who was watching TV, and was tired, too. I said there were some things bothering me and could we talk about them? Total disaster! My mistakes: *I* was too tired to discuss anything very intelligently; *he* was tired, too. I can see now that's something which can't be ignored! Also, after sort of going around in circles with one problem (my "I-messages" were lousy, and I wasn't

Active Listening!), I brought up not only a second problem, but then a third! It's hard to believe I could have been so totally out of it. Of course he felt, and rightly so, that I'd just come over to complain about him. What a lesson!

February 23rd

I try to Active Listen now only when I *really care* about the other person and his problem. I sort of feel myself out when the occasion presents itself, to see if I have the empathy I know is required for me to be an effective listener. If I find I *do* care, that I really *do* want to listen, then I shut off (as much as I can) all the verbiage inside my mind. Then the Active Listening takes on dimensions it never did before. Not only is the other person able to explore his own problem, but the warmth and closeness that I come to feel for him I find extraordinary. This kind of communication and communion with another human being is the greatest treasure I have found through P.E.T.

February 25th

"Modification of self": Am I trying to fulfill myself through my children? Sometimes I wonder. I seem to spend a lot of my efforts making my way of life adjust to my child's needs—and to my husband's for that matter. I feel often that my needs aren't being met, though I can't even readily define precisely what my needs are. I just have this feeling of unfulfillment. This is *my* problem, something within me, not caused by other people's unacceptable behavior. It's something I feel I had better look into before I start resenting my time spent as a mother and a wife. I immensely enjoy my child and love my husband, but I also feel some creative energies wanting a means of expression.

February 26th

To continue the same line of thinking as in the last entry— There are needs of my own, creative personal needs—exploring myself, my capabilities, getting involved with areas of my own personality, perhaps communicating this part of myself to others in some way—which are vitally important for me as a growing person to experience. My strongest social relationships (my family, close friends) perhaps shed light on parts of this very personal "me," but I must have time alone to fulfill this part of myself. It's not something my husband or my child can do for me. My relationship with them is strongest when the needs that I can fulfill within myself have been met. I cannot demand from them that which only I can fulfill. I am happiest—feel accepting toward both myself and others—when I feel satisfied in meeting my own needs for creativity and self-expression.

February 27th

I find that when Alice and another child are fighting over a toy, and they realize that I am not going to solve their problem for them, they become somewhat more accepting of each other—the problem loses much of its urgency! Alice also is more willing to let the other child continue to play with her toy if she sees I'm not going to interfere in any way.

February 28th

I've been thinking about "negative" behavior more in terms of fulfillment of needs or a difference of values. Take, for instance, those occasions when Alice cries when I leave her. If somehow that crying behavior, which I don't particularly like, were to be extinguished (by reinforcement of noncrying behavior, or whatever), would that necessarily mean that her feelings of unhappiness would also be gone? Perhaps—she's pretty "up-front." But how much do I want to manipulate her behavior? I don't like her screaming when I leave, but if that's the way she feels, I *do* like her to let me know. So, can I change her feelings? Do I want to? Can I allow her to have "negative" feelings along with the "positive" ones (as if I had any control over it, really!)? Can I allow *myself* to accept her "negative" feelings? Are they in fact negative, or is that just the way they appear in my system of values?

March 2nd

More thoughts about "negative" behavior: These days I see unacceptable behavior being truly an expression of personal needs. In that light, the behavior loses a great deal, if not all, of its unacceptability. Not that I find everything acceptable, but in seeing the behavior in terms of needs, my level of acceptance is substantially increased. The instructors have spoken of this, but it's really something inside of me now.

A direct outgrowth of this feeling is that I'm not as afraid of "negative" behavior as I have been. When Alice cries when I leave, I don't feel so uncomfortable and anxious about it. This seems to have an immediate effect on her: Last night I was going out and leaving her with Daddy. She wasn't too happy and started crying, "Mommy, no class!"

"You don't want Mommy to leave you, and it makes you very unhappy," I said.

"Yeah . . . (her lower lip quivering) . . . Mommy home!"

"You want Mommy to stay home with you, but I *do* have to go to my class."

Her lip starts to quiver some more, and she looks as though she's holding back a cry—something I don't think I've ever seen her do before! I say, "Alice, it's OK to feel unhappy. You can cry if you want."

She cries for a minute, then runs to Daddy, very excited, saying, "Daddy! Train!" (I had told her they were going to play with a train while I was gone.)

March 4th

I feel strange. I feel uncertain. I feel like I've lost a grasp on my conception of "me." Upon clarification of some values I've held as my own, I find that either I've felt pressured into accepting these values by individuals who are important to me or that I don't find certain values valid to me anymore.

For example, I have valued frugality. I tend to save my dollars rather than spend them on something I might enjoy. I believe I acquired this value from my father and perhaps from philosophical concepts I entertained during my teen years. But my frugal behavior makes me feel tense. I don't like feeling tense or self-constricting. Under scrutiny, I find I don't even value saving my dimes and nickels anymore. I love the freedom to spend without feeling guilty. I've been maintaining a value now archaic to my person.

I find this is true with other values I've held. It's exciting to feel a change, to chuck values that no longer pertain to me. On the other hand, it's scary to be aware of so much of myself that I feel is no longer me and to let it go flying out the window. The letting go is fun, but then I get a sudden feeling of emptiness, of not knowing who I am or what is important to me. It's like demolishing a building and having only a wasteland left after the building is gone and before another has been erected. What kind of a structure am I going to build? It's wonderfully exciting, the possibilities—even the idea that I can tear it down and start over again when it no longer suits me.

March 6th

Possibilities! What new me is coming to life? I don't know. It's like spring before the new growth has appeared. You feel it there, as a surging force about to push its way into existence. It's fun to let my fantasies run free, to see what they bring me. I feel a strong sense of being able to choose what feels good or right to me. I can try on new values and see how they feel. And I can try new behaviors that I never dreamed could emanate from me. What a joy to change, and forever change!

STRUGGLES AND STROKES

I have been struggling for days to find a starting point for writing this. I want to begin with some pre-Parent Effectiveness Training accounts of our family life, but the analogy of childbirth keeps crossing my mind. It is almost impossible for me to remember the pain of previous family interactions. Our family today consists of four people who have grown this past year beyond my highest hopes. Even our vocabulary, our way of talking with each other, has taken on a foreign sound to observers unfamiliar with P.E.T.

An example immediately comes to mind. Our son Walter, age six, and his friend Robert were recently playing upstairs. I overheard Robert say to Walter, "We might get into trouble if we do that," to which Walter replied, "We don't get into trouble in our family. We have conflicts."

Trouble used to monopolize a great deal of time and energy in our household for both the culprit and enforcer. During the past year we have learned some skills to deal with needs, conflicts, and problem ownership, and we no longer view stress in our relationships as trouble but rather as opposing ideas which need resolution. We have all been working as a unit to establish feelings of caring and trust in our new ways of interacting, and of late we have all been experiencing some of the strokes of this struggle. Now the bulk of our time and energy is invested in making our family relationships sources of joy and growth rather than sources of trouble. This has been a piecemeal and painstaking process.

Brent, our other son, is an extremely energetic eight-year-old. On the bus ride to school each day a group of boys, including Brent, can usually be counted on to test the patience of the driver and the bus mother of the day. Recently, a neighbor of mine who had ridden the bus with the children said to me, "I don't know what you do to Brent to keep him in control, but whatever it is, it sure works!" Apparently Brent had been getting rowdy and excited on the way to school and my neighbor mentioned to him that she would be seeing me the next day and she would not want to have to inform me of his misbehavior. Brent gave her a smile, turned around, and suggested to the other kids that they continue their game at recess. For the remainder of the ride Brent sat and chatted with his friends in a pleasant and congenial manner.

When Brent arrived home that next day I told him

that my neighbor had told me about the bus ride incident and how delighted I was to hear that he had been able to accept the responsibility of his behavior, especially with his friends right there. I told Brent that it seemed to me that he was caring about how I would react when told he was misbehaving. Further, it seemed that he was not willing to suffer the consequences, which would be my feeling disappointment. Brent acknowledged that the thoughts of causing me feelings of disappointment were the governing factor in his settling down on the bus. These feelings of care for one another did not suddenly emerge one fine day but rather have been the result of diligently using our P.E.T. skills.

To explain. A few months ago Brent came home with a note from school saying that he and two other boys had been sent out of physical education class for being repeatedly disruptive. They had to stand in the hall for the remainder of that class and bring a note home to be signed. Brent thrust the note at me, saying, "You're going to be mad at me."

He was absolutely right and I told him so. Brent asked me if his father would give him a spanking. I told him that the matter of the spanking was between him and his father, but I could see that he was afraid of the consequences of his dad's anger. Brent was panic-stricken as he asked, "What are you going to *do* to me?" This question opened up a most profound conversation, one to which we often refer and one that has been the foundation for an atmosphere of caring and trust.

By using my Active Listening skills I learned that Brent was feeling guilty about his behavior and wanted to be rid of it, pay for it, and be done with the whole thing. I explained to him that I was not interested in having a pound of his flesh. I was feeling disappointed that he wasn't willing to be responsible for his behavior.

"I don't know what you mean," was his candid response.

Then we began talking about self-control. Brent

defended his behavior by falling back on the safety-in-numbers routine—"Well, I wasn't the only one kicked out of class . . ." Further Active Listening disclosed that his real concern centered around the spanking business. I said that I felt that a spanking was a real cop-out; that I was optimistic this situation could be avoided or at least minimized by talking things out; by looking at how we feel about it and trying to focus on what could be done to help Brent in similar situations.

Brent exploded with a statement about how hard it is to be a kid because grown-ups can do anything they want and kids always have so many people around telling them what to do all the time. I agreed with him that this was a good point but that I didn't feel he had the whole picture. I talked about how adults must be responsible for their behavior, too, and that adults also have to accept the consequences of their behavior. Then I shared with him my feelings about my wanting him to learn responsibility so he could learn to live a full and rich life in our society.

However fruitful this line of conversation was proving to be, it did not deal with Brent's primary concern: what he could expect to happen to him as a result of the problem in school.

I said, "What am I going to do? I'm going to stress to you how disappointed I am. I'm asking you to own your behavior, own your problem. I'm asking you to consider what was behind your behavior in school and how you might go about changing it since it does seem to be causing you a problem. If you don't know how to behave in more acceptable ways, I want you to know that we're more than willing to talk it over with you. I'll work at making myself open and available to you for these kinds of conversations."

Then we talked about how the note Brent brought home was in effect saying "Okay, parent, do something about this kid!" I continued, "Now I'm putting it on you. Okay, Brent, do something about this behavior. I care about you and I'm feeling like you don't care about me."

Brent was concerned about how he could get back

in the good graces of his teacher. *He* suggested writing an apology, which he did, and I suggested that his cooperation and self-control in class would prove that his apology was genuine. Our discussion never got back to the issue of a spanking. There just wasn't any place for it and it ultimately was ruled out as an appropriate way of handling the situation. Interestingly, it hasn't been considered appropriate in our household for months.

When Brent's father hit the front door that evening, Brent was truly scared. Raymond was furious, disappointed—and caring. He and Brent went into the bedroom and, after a lengthy exchange, they came out with an understanding. It was another step that has helped us become a working and growing family. (At that time Raymond was taking Parent Effectiveness Training, and it was instrumental in the positive kinds of things to come out of their father-son interaction.)

Getting back to the bus incident in which my neighbor commented on our control "over" Brent. I know that Brent was caring about his behavior, willing to try and change it, and accept the responsibility for it. Parents often say, "You can't follow kids around all the time to control their behavior. Threats and punishments are necessary ('spare the rod and spoil the child') to teach kids right from wrong." I most definitely agree that parents can't follow their children around, but Brent has elected to take us with him everywhere he goes. He is learning that he has our trust, concern, and love wherever he is, while at the same time he is learning the skills to act on his feelings in responsible ways. Raymond and I are learning how to have a positive influence on our two sons, an influence that functions both in our presence and in our absence.

More struggles and strokes. Homework, an issue that has been known to throw usually perfectly rational and civilized parents into moaning fits of anguish! I had taken three weeks of my Parent Effectiveness Training course when I knew that the homework problem in our home had deteriorated into an all-out war. The battle lines were drawn up as follows: Brent hated doing his homework; it had a zero priority in his daily routine. Raymond and I played the united front game in the name of parental responsibility to see that Brent did his assignments. The major thrust of our campaign depended on the hurtling of such clichés as: "You'll feel better when it's done"; "You can have fun if it isn't hanging over your head"; "Every kid has to do homework"; and, "When I was a kid . . ."

At first my plan of attack was to get at the homework thing fast, right after school, so we could blast away at the daily confrontation in hopes that I could enjoy my evening. Brent hated tackling his homework right after school, especially on nice days; he wanted to be out with his friends. On rainy days he wanted to watch television; doing homework distracted him. I used every threat and reason in my command to get the homework done right after school, but Brent was wearing me down with crying, fussing, tantrums, and the like.

Enough was enough. I decided it wasn't fair for me to take all this abuse alone, so I called in the big gun. Raymond was arbitrarily put in charge of the homework dilemma after dinner each night. We clearly saw this as a discipline problem requiring more force. After a few weeks of this, Brent was barely speaking to anyone and made sure that we all shared his misery.

One night I just dumped the whole mess into the laps of the people in my P.E.T. course. By using their new skills with me, they helped me zero in on the homework predicament. I realized that we were directly involved with an issue of problem ownership and, indirectly, with an issue of values. The homework problem that Raymond and I had taken on in the name of parenthood was in fact between Brent and his teacher. Granted, Raymond and I put a high premium on a child's doing his/her homework because of what we valued as goals, but when all was said and done, the problem was Brent's.

I discussed these feelings with Raymond (who was not then destined to take P.E.T. for several months, which is another story), and he let me know in no uncertain terms that he considered my new views irresponsible and permissive. I finally convinced Raymond to try handling the matter my way since we really had nothing to lose at that point.

Next I sat down with Brent to review my new insights with him. I explained that I accepted the fact that all the pressure, force, and general unpleasantness over the homework was a mistake. I told him that I viewed his homework as something that was between him and his teacher, but would be very willing to help him with a reminder and with his spelling if he asked for these. But force was a thing of the past.

I called his teacher and explained that henceforth Brent would be responsible for his assignments and asked her to please deal with related problems in any way she saw fit. I shared the content of this conversation with Brent.

At this, Brent was delirious with joy. He concluded that he had clear license to call the shots with his parents and that he was being excused from homework for life. For a couple of days he merrily trotted off to school without his assignments. Ah, but on the third day he came charging through the front door hysterically screaming about his hatred for his teacher. It seems she did not share Brent's philosophy toward homework and had given him an extra heavy assignment of copying spelling words over, twenty-five times each, because Brent had been remiss with his homework.

I Active Listened Brent's feelings about his teacher. He felt that she was picking on him, she was unfair and just plain didn't like him. He obviously was taking this extra assignment quite personally and hadn't as yet made the connection between it and the consequences of his behavior.

After an incredibly long evening Brent finished the grueling work and came in to complain to us about his sore fingers. Further Active Listening helped Brent to realize what was really behind his ailments. Sure, his fingers did ache but he verbalized that it would be much easier to do the regular assignment than to have to go through the extra writing every night.

The stroke. The homework issue is no longer an issue. We merely say "Homework, Brent?" every night. He nods agreement or grunts dissatisfaction, but he learned a very real lesson in problem ownership, consequences, and responsibility. So did his Mom and Dad!

In our household, shopping with Walter was always a problem. This thankless chore had to be done during the day to fit in with my schedule and Walter had to be dragged along. Inevitably our Number Two son would see a goodie or a toy that he just had to have. I could be counted on to sneak in a lecture about tooth decay, and even in our pre-P.E.T. days I was very aware of Walter's facial and bodily expressions, which communicated "Yeah, yeah. So get your sermon over, already."

The desired toy was usually beyond my financial means at the time and I would try to explain that what *we should do* is plan the purchase and save up for it, using Walter's allowance plus my contribution. The ride to the store was miserable for both of us, Walter displaying his disappointment and resentment and my anger simmering at having this reoccurring headache to deal with.

After talking the problem over with Raymond, we decided that Walt and I might benefit from using my newly acquired P.E.T. problem-solving skills. So before departing for our next shopping excursion I asked Walt if we might try applying some new skills I had learned. I explained how the process works: both of us listing our needs, both of us making suggestions about how these needs might be met, and forming some ground rules to use during shopping.

I listed my needs to get the shopping done, being limited in finances, having to say NO! when the toy was too expensive, my feelings about candy and suggesting a piece of fruit as an alternative. Walter said that he needed to go off alone to browse in the toy aisle, then to show me the things he would like to buy, and for us not to be in such a big hurry to get home.

I said this wasn't so good for the ice cream in my shopping cart, but that we could work out that part somehow.

We were anxious to try out our new agreement so we jumped in the car and left to meet our destiny. I attached myself to a shopping cart, bid Walter farewell, and off he went to the toy aisle. I shopped and really enjoyed Walter's absence and his running commentary about his having to endure this chore. When I arrived at the toy section, Walter was very excited about showing me three toys of special interest. We went over the prices and Walt made this tremendous concession of deciding he only wanted "one little model, just one."

I felt that I was getting a con job.

"Walt, I'm feeling pressure from you and disappointment that our agreement is being trashed. I expected to talk about the things you want to buy. I thought we would plan to save up for things. Now I think you are not willing to talk about this as we agreed. You're falling right back into the game of having it now or you'll put on your long lip."

Walter expressed his desire to have the model and wound up by telling me that I had lots of money and that he hated me. I said I could see that we needed to get back to the drawing board and work through problem-solving again.

Home again. What went wrong? I had read Gordon's book, taken the course and used the skills. Where was my miracle?

Walter came in the house, threw his coat on the floor, kicked the cat, and went upstairs to find solace with TV cartoons. While putting the groceries away I mentally reviewed the situation and decided that not only was the supermarket unacceptable; Walt himself was unacceptable. Why didn't he live up to our agreement, the little monster? I credited myself with posing a good question.

After a while I was feeling calm and open-minded, so I went upstairs to talk with Walter. I walked

into the room, switched off the violent cartoons he
was watching and announced my concern about what
had happened in the store. I asked Walt how he
felt about all this. He ran off into his bedroom, crying.
He crashed onto his bed and pulled the pillow over
his head. I lovingly tried to remove the pillow to establish eye contact. He was sobbing and telling me to
go away. I was telling him that we had to talk about
this and come to some understanding. This was just a
hopeless mess. Walt didn't speak to me the rest of the
evening.

The next morning I talked about this situation
with a good friend who is also committed to P.E.T.
principles. She Active Listened my frustration and
helped me to realize that I had blown the whole thing
beginning with my ignoring Walt's need not to be
rushed by me out of the store. I had given him the message that my butterscotch ripple ice cream was more
important to me than he was. Then, at home, I had
swished into the room like Loretta Young and had
turned off his television program without considering
his needs. Finally I attempted to force my good intentions on him and POW! I had fallen flat on my face.

My friend and I role-played this situation, and
some points were made hard and clear to me. Walt
probably felt like a loser all the way. Well, so did I.
Back to the basics, but where to begin?

I decided to ask Walt if he would let me share
with him the experience I had had with my friend
earlier in the day. He was willing. I explained to him
that we had talked about the shopping episode and that
I really wanted to apologize to him for being the cause
of so much of his sadness. I suggested to him that
maybe he couldn't trust me to live up to our agreement.
For the first time since the conflict Walter began to
respond. He said that I was unfair, that he didn't
have a chance, and that my turning off the TV proved
it. He told me that I "do stuff like that all the time."

I told Walter that I needed for him to call me on
things like that. I told him: "I need to know what
you're thinking and feeling about the way we behave

toward each other. If we can learn to talk with one another and speak up our hurt feelings, then we have a better chance of meeting what each of us needs."

At this point we could hear kids playing outside and I suspected that Walter had mentally joined them. I bypassed my usual demand that he hear me out and suggested that perhaps he was anxious to join his friends but that I hoped we could talk more later. Walter lit up and yelled a warm "Okay!" over his shoulder on his way out the door.

The next day, at my instigation, we got back to our conversation. Walter wanted to know, "Why do we have to keep talking about this?" I explained to him that he was very important to me and how vital it was that we talk about how we feel about each other. Walter wanted to know if "this feeling stuff" was why I was going to school (my P.E.T. course). Absolutely. And I admitted to him my feelings of dissatisfaction with the way things were going in our family: "I'm trying to learn new ways to be a friend to you as well as your parent. In class we talk about kids who fire their parents because they feel that their parents don't understand them or listen to them. I don't want you to fire me, Walter, and I don't want you to give up on me, either. I think that's what happened the other day in the supermarket. We gave up on each other. I tried to make you listen when you wanted to be alone. It's hard for me to back off because, like many parents, I often think I know what's best for you and I overlook your rights."

Walter wanted to know what I meant by "rights." I realized that he had no understanding, no sure feelings about what was expected of him. We had either gone along with no problems at all or we got into all-out war, but we had never learned to exchange ideas or express our feelings about our family relationships.

This conversation opened up a whole new method of communication between Walter and me. When Walter expressed frustration over my "never" giving him what he wanted to eat for lunch, I could deal with my defensiveness, anger, and wanting to yell, "So I'm not a mind reader! Tell me what you want! Give me a clue. Just a little one." Instead, I learned to ask him what he'd like for lunch and we could discuss choices.

We eventually got back to the shopping incident and after a lengthy discussion about money I came to understand Walter's belief that parents had an unlimited source of money. After all, when had we ever taken the time to explain our finances? We had assumed that a five-year-old would not be mature enough to understand such matters. I realized that I was guilty of selling our children short with such an assumption. In fact, not only could they understand the concept of a budget; they accepted the need for planning and thinking about purchases.

Now when we go shopping, Walter and I beforehand decide whether it's a "looking day" or a "planning day" or a "buying day." Stroke.

Another time Raymond and Brent returned home from a wrestling match and they were themselves wrestling with a tense problem. Raymond, a Marine, must attend all sports events in uniform, which adds pressure because Brent's behavior is of utmost concern to his father. Apparently Raymond had been upset about Brent's behavior in the field house that evening, and when they got home he sent Brent to his room. I Active Listened Raymond as he discussed his unwillingness to take Brent to future sports events until "he learns how to behave."

Having just recently lived through the shopping problem with Walter, I shared with Raymond the potential benefits of establishing ground rules and using problem-solving skills. These were, at that time, new concepts for Raymond, but he was willing to give it a try. Father and son had a problem-solving session that night.

Before leaving for a sports event the following weekend, Raymond and Brent reviewed their newly negotiated agreements. Raymond stated his need to be able to sit in one place and not have to get up and down to keep Brent out of restricted areas. They discussed which areas were off limits to spectators. Also, Raymond needed not to be bothered by Brent for more money to use at the concession stand. Brent said that he needed the freedom to sit where he chose, be able to go to the concession stand alone, and to move around at will. Raymond re-emphasized his concern that Brent not disturb other spectators and they talked about when moving around would be least disturbing for other people. With the ground rules clearly understood, they left for the match.

At dinner that evening Walter and I were treated to a very animated account of the wrestling match. Instead of a strained atmosphere in our home, we all enjoyed a hassle-free family interaction.

I have been relating experiences that primarily involved me and one of the boys. But it is important to stress that other kinds of things have been happening in our family. For many years I played the role of umpire between Brent and Walter, usually daily. Since they are close in age and the same sex, I had fallen into the habit of seeing "the boys" only as they engaged in activities and not as two separate and entirely different people. Example. Both boys were signed up for swimming lessons, both joined Y-Indian Guides; at Christmas Santa would bring two trucks, two pairs of ice skates, and two games. I automatically thought in terms of the number "two," and I am confident that I helped ingrain this attitude into them.

When a fight occurred between Brent and Walter, my umpire conditioning demanded that I be fair, so my procedure was to break up the physical contact, demand silence, hear their arguments one at a time, pass judgment, and impose sentence. However, in many situations I could not decide who was to lose (in all fairness, that is) and the only way to handle the problem was for me to remove the object of contention, say a basketball. This simply meant that either one kid lost or they both lost.

A side effect of my method of maintaining the status quo was that it compounded rivalry between them for my favorable judgment. I was teaching them to worm their way into the good graces of my role as official at the expense of the other guy. Ultimately, they were unable to discuss a conflict rationally and coherently because they knew that at any moment I would swoop down on the scene to end the problem and they had to have a good case against the other guy to get off. Struggle.

When I first began to employ Active Listening skills in these triad situations, I was tempted to bring a box lunch. The time involved was incredible! Being a newcomer to P.E.T., I would patiently await the miracle of harmony and bliss between the brothers. As communication on a one-to-one basis (me and whoever) began to flow, I naturally assumed that these new skills would spill over into the interactions between Brent and Walter. This just wasn't happening.

I was tempted to conclude that P.E.T. skills are limited to adult-child interactions—and then the miracle began to happen. My miracle was realized for several different reasons. First, because I was not taking on their problems (a learned skill). Second, because I was learning to really hear what they were saying (a learned skill). And third, because I was learning to trust my utilization of the skills even when things weren't happening fast enough to suit me.

I saw that Brent and Walter were beginning to grow in their individual relationship with me because I repeatedly acknowledged my caring about (and trust in) them and because my level of acceptance had expanded, allowing these feelings to be felt by them. I could also see that a pattern of competition had been firmly established between them and I had to accept that this attitude toward each other was not going to suddenly disappear. But I was optimistic that I was wandering down the right path. I believed that my "spillover" would be forthcoming, but it would require adamant patience on my part.

In short, I realized that trying to instill P.E.T. skills into the relationship between my two sons in the heat of conflict was not going to gain any ground. Each was still very much concerned with being Number One in my eyes, and I had led them to believe that this was a realistic goal. They were not able to I-message their feelings about each other because they found that dumping on each other helped them to feel better about themselves. Something along the lines of "Well, if I dump on him before he dumps on me, then I'm obviously a better person." I actually became physically sick when I realized this. Then I had an idea.

Brent and Walter never discussed their feelings about each other, in good times or bad. I began to initiate open conversations about such safe topics as what meals we liked best, which TV program was most interesting to us, just anything that could get us talking comfortably. When either boy would try to belittle the other's opinion ("How could you like that show? It's so dumb"), I'd ask to be heard and suggest that what we had was merely a difference of opinion and not a right versus wrong situation.

This was initially a very difficult concept for them to accept. I would periodically use my relationship with Raymond as an example, pointing out how many, many things we disagree on, but if Raymond used force or rudeness to win, I'd be a black and blue and a very unhappy mess. They'd giggle when they imagined these scenes.

These kinds of conversations have helped us to get into feelings of self-worth and how it can (and has to be) a fact of life that someone, somewhere, is always going to disagree with us about something. This is okay as long as others don't try to force their opinions on us or demean us as people for our opinions. We were in the talking stage and that was at least something.

It was a couple of months before I felt the stroke of all this, but what a fantastic stroke it was! I was in the kitchen one morning, dashing back and forth between the eggs in the frying pan and the sandwiches for lunch. Morning is not my best time of day anyway, and at one point I tripped over a cache of Walter's GI Joe gear, which he had left by the back door. Brent had just entered the kitchen telling me that Walter was upstairs getting dressed.

"Well, go up and tell him to get down here this

instant or I'm going to throw him and his toys into the trash can." Brent responded, ever so calmly, "Looks like you're not having a good morning."

I ranted and raved something about wanting to break Walter's neck and about the horrible time I was having. Brent started to pick the toys up, but I stopped him by yelling that the mess was Walter's and he was jolly well going to pick it up. Brent looked me square in the eye and said, "I don't mind helping my brother. Seems to me that you're gunning for Walter this morning. I'll help. Isn't that what we've been talking about?"

How very sobering that comment was! From this time on I have been aware of some effort, not all the time by any means, but some effort being made to actively care about each other.

As a family we have been truly growing now for well over a year and the few situations I've described here are but a glimpse of our struggles and strokes. In my role of mother I experienced feelings of doubt that I was even equipped to be a mother, feelings of tension in having to deal with recurring problems, and frustration with not seeming to make noticeable headway with these problems. My self-esteem was suffering and my level of acceptance was decreasing as Brent and Walter got older.

In summarizing some of the results of my Parent Effectiveness Training, several points must be emphasized.

As I was attempting to use my newly acquired skills with my family, Raymond was expressing his concerns about his perceptions. For instance, Walter would ask me to tie his shoes. Walter is perfectly capable of tying his own shoes, but many times I would happily and willingly comply with his request. I liked this kind of interaction. However, I found myself being overwhelmed by Raymond's barrage of "You're being permissive!" accusations. Not so, but this was what he was concluding.

After a while Raymond began to realize that as my level of acceptance toward Walter was increasing, Walter's level of acceptance toward me was in turn in-

creasing. Walt began to respond positively to many of
my needs and he began doing such things as hanging
up his coat, putting his lunch box away, and offering
his help in the kitchen. At the same time, Raymond
became aware of changes in the tone of our own dis-
agreements as a result of my using my skills. He was
motivated to read Gordon's book, and after smothering
me with "Well, what if . . ." kinds of questions, he
decided that his most expedient course of action would
be to take the course himself, which he did. Now
our family has both parents using similar communication skills, which lends an element of continuity to
all our interactions.

An analogy to a mathematical progression comes
to mind. As I learned to be more accepting of myself,
my husband and our two boys, they also began to
grow. For many years Raymond and I had assumed
that as parents we had the right to demand respect
from our children and that their trust in us would
naturally follow. Earning and being worthy of another's respect and trust, including those of children,
was a new concept for us.

Tied in with this, we realized that we had to re-
define the two key words "attitude" and "discipline."
As responsible and involved parents, we were and are
very concerned that our boys be disciplined, but we
have come to realize that the way we were going about
instilling discipline was creating a family attitude of
fear, tension, distrust, and resentment. Brent and Walter
are both strong-willed, healthy, active boys, and it was
becoming more difficult to control them. Unbeknownst
to either of us, Raymond and I were caught on the
treadmill of assuming the children would be responsible while we were demanding that we have their respect as our payment for being their parents. We have
now learned that authority by influence is far more effective for all concerned and that it is ultimately futile
to try to control another's behavior by force.

As individuals and as a family, where are we
going? Our behavior has changed because our attitudes have changed. By using the skills, we are all

learning to trust each other—to be honest about trying to share what our feelings really are, rather than trying to concoct feelings of what we think they should be. Are we as parents taking a risk? Yes, and so are Brent and Walter. The risk is that we are exposing ourselves with such openness that we stand to be rejected as well as accepted. We are putting our money on being accepted. We are risking an involvement, with all the pain and joy that this can bring. We have learned that this risk can and does grow into trust and that this has to be a two-way street in any relationship.

While I have been working on this account, my typewriter has been in a prominent place on the dining room table. Brent wanted to know what I was working on. I told him that I was writing up our Parent Effectiveness Training experiences. He said, "Oh, I know. You're writing all that stuff about how we used to be." Stroke.

A FAMILY TURNS AROUND

My story begins four years ago. It was a few weeks before Halloween, a cold damp night with the feel of winter in it. I had been to a Cub Scout Den Mothers' meeting and when I arrived home, I found my husband, two of our older sons, Steve and Mike, and our fourteen-year-old daughter, Lisa, at the kitchen table, with the tension so thick it was suffocating.

The boys were so concerned about Lisa that they had decided to tell us that she and her friends were into drugs—pot, speed, and LSD, primarily. We felt sick, yet it only confirmed the gnawing suspicions we had had for nearly a year. Lisa was an attractive girl with long shiny brown hair and dark-brown eyes. She was a good student, played several musical instruments, and had always seemed well liked by her friends. She had been school captain of her elementary school. When a girl with so much to give begins having trouble at school and flying into a rage at the slightest criticism at home, there is something terribly wrong. We told her how worried we were, and Jim, my husband, insisted she stop seeing her crowd of recent friends completely. Seething with resentment and rage, she announced that we were not going to tell her who her friends should be, left the house, and disappeared.

The next day we tried to locate her, but without any results. We had figured she would probably stay at the home of a friend. But when phone calls to most of the logical places failed to turn up a lead, we were worried sick, wondering where she was, whether she was safe.

The second night she called us to ask our permission for her to stay in a house for runaways in the inner city. We said no and begged her to come home. She hung up and disappeared again.

A few days later, a member of the staff at her school called to say that she had gotten in touch with him. He was the one person she seemed to feel she could trust not to force her to do anything. He had made arrangements for her to stay in a private home and said she would be willing to enter family counseling if we would. We agreed and during the next two weeks had several sessions with a psychologist.

Jim and I finally reached the point where we felt we were doing all the giving and we resented Lisa's continued refusal to come home. In addition, we could ill afford the cost of the counseling. So she moved home and an uneasy truce was established. We had little reason to trust her. One morning I saw her heading away from school, so I got out the car and drove her there—only to find out later that she had immediately left school by another door and spent the day at a friend's house. Not long after that a counselor brought her home from school suffering from an overdose of speed. There were few days without crises.

While this alone would have been enough to worry us sick, our sixteen-year-old son, Bill, was also having problems. He was sick much of the time, probably from drugs and from not eating right, and was finally hospitalized and treated for a possible ulcer, although the tests were negative.

Back in school, he dropped further and further

behind in his work. He cut classes frequently or fell asleep in them. Eventually he got caught smoking and was suspended for the next two weeks. His behavior was erratic and he tended to disappear for a day or two at a time, telling us ridiculous stories about his whereabouts when he wandered home.

Bill was a gentle person, timid as a small child and sensitive. He had many fears. I had worried about his ability to cope with school, but he seemed to do well enough if the pressure wasn't too great. He had grown into a tall, good-looking youth with light hair and corn-flower blue eyes. He loved music, but not the discipline of practice or being in a band. He was not a person who would hurt others deliberately, but he was certainly destroying himself.

My frustration and feeling of helplessness had my stomach tied up in knots, my head throbbing, and my heart breaking. My depression was so overwhelming that I did not want to talk to anyone, even to reach out for help. Our family doctor suggested P.E.T., but I could not believe a course could help my needs. So things continued through a shaky Christmas and then, the week after New Year's Eve, the nightmare resumed. Bill took an overdose of LSD. He couldn't stop hallucinating and finally came to me for help.

Jim was out of town, so Mike and I drove him to the hospital, where he was admitted to the security end of the psychiatric ward. I will never forget the sound of the metal door being bolted behind us.

In the next two weeks he began to see the hospital as his escape. All the pressures were off, he was being waited on, he had a private room, his own stereo and snacks any time he wanted them. But his doctor told us he was completely uncooperative and recommended having him declared incorrigible and sent to a state school. Somehow, we didn't see how that would do anything but increase the problem. So at the end of the second week we brought him home.

The stage was set for the final act. Jim had gone back to work, after driving us home from the hospital. Bill and I were in the kitchen, having some soup, and I told him I'd take him to school after lunch to find out where he stood and what he would have to do to catch up. But he wouldn't buy that idea. He became hostile and incoherent and said he was leaving. With that, Lisa appeared and said she'd go with him. She had cut school and was sulking because, the night before, we had told her she would have to wait until summer to take Drivers' Education. The two of them packed a duffel bag, being careful to include only the belongings they felt were really theirs. Before they left, I said, "Are you sure you know what you're doing?"

Lisa replied, "I know we may be making a mistake, but we have to find that out for ourselves." And off they trudged across the ice and snow of the park behind our house. It must have been ten degrees that day and my insides felt almost that cold and numb with fear for them.

This time there were no phone calls, nothing. Even their friends were frightened. There was no sign of either one after they left the house, although I did find out they had withdrawn Bill's savings from the bank. The days stretched into a week and, on the tenth day, we received a letter from Lisa telling us they were in California living on a farm and would like us to send Bill's driver's license and their social security cards. We did.

A few weeks later, about the time we were beginning to get used to the situation, an earthquake hit southern California in the area where we knew they were living. They had no phone. We were frantic! That afternoon I received a call from our local police asking if we had a son, Bill, sixteen, and a daughter, Lisa, fourteen, in California. My insides contracted with terror! But the terror quickly gave way to relief as the officer explained that they were all right and were being held in a detention center near where they had been living. The night before, Bill had been discovered by the police wandering in the sheriff's parking lot. He had sent the police to the commune where Lisa was. Apparently, he couldn't stomach the situation any longer. Their money and most of their belongings had been confiscated and they weren't eating very regularly. The house was dirty and in poor repair and there was no plumbing. The detention center must have been something of a relief, but the two of them were kept separated and neither knew where the other one was until after the earthquake. The detention center was damaged but Bill and Lisa were not hurt and were later transferred to Los Angeles.

My husband got into the car almost immediately and drove the two thousand miles to L.A., stopping only once, briefly, for Coke and gas. Bill and Lisa were relieved to see him and must have realized how very much he cared about them to have put aside everything else to make that long, arduous trip. The journey home was surprisingly tranquil, the conversation relaxed and quite normal. Back home, they both seemed somewhat subdued and more willing to live within our regulations.

Bill was so far behind at school that he dropped out and went to work full time as a bag boy. I was glad he had something constructive to do, but wondered how long he would keep his job, because he was late for work frequently or didn't show up at all. We were not letting him use the car very often because we knew he was drinking, but he was riding with friends who were equally irresponsible and that was a worry.

Lisa went back to school and quickly made up the work she had missed. But she was restless and ill at ease. She was cutting school a lot and turning in most of her work late, and we were concerned about what she and her friends were doing during all those hours they weren't in school. If we questioned her about the slightest thing, she'd fly into a rage, and we were afraid we were making things worse. In a sense, we were letting her blackmail us into staying out of her affairs completely. The tensions began to build up again. Somehow we survived that spring, but we recognized our need for help. Our doctor continued to urge us to take P.E.T., and in May I found a class and we got started.

My climb up out of the depths of despair began.

I began to grow as new insights and understandings tumbled in on me with each week of classes. I felt as though I was slowly emerging from a closed-in shell into a beautiful sunlit world full of color and music.

What did I actually learn that could cause such a transformation? The first startling discovery was that I did not have to "own" my children's problems. I did not have to find solutions for all the problems of all my seven children. Secondly, I learned how to develop a separateness from my husband and children. Until this time, I had been upset if any of them were upset and, with such a large family, it wasn't very often that somebody wasn't upset.

With me, being upset meant feeling cold and clammy, having stomach cramps and diarrhea, not wanting to move. Fixing meals and caring for the children took a tremendous act of will. Nothing seemed worth the effort of doing it. I learned about my need to have everybody in the family happy and productive to feel good about myself, and I suppose that was the key to freeing myself from it; to learning how to feel "OK" about myself so that I could help the others when they were feeling "not OK."

It didn't happen overnight. Earlier I described the situation with Bill and Lisa when we began P.E.T. I suppose at first they suspected that we were learning some new way of controlling them. But when we began to tell them about what we were learning, they gradually came to see P.E.T. as a way of improving all the family relationships, reducing the tensions that had been upsetting them as much as us.

We began by talking about feelings, and I put one list of feeling words on the refrigerator door and one in my pocketbook. When somebody started talking about a problem or seemed upset in any way, I would quickly refer to the list and say, "You're resentful." "You're disappointed!" "You're furious!" or whatever seemed appropriate. This usually produced laughter and teasing, which is not the normal goal of Active Listening, but it succeeded in relieving the tension and making everyone feel better and that was a step in the right direction. Eventually, I managed to use AL with more skill and, once the children had experienced how nice it was to have me really hearing them, they felt less wary of it. It's become the most valuable skill I learned.

I remember before P.E.T. when Bill told me he'd been suspended from school. I hugged him and cried. I felt bad for him, but I felt just as bad for myself, as if I were to blame somehow. How much more helpful it would have been if I had let him know it was his problem and that I had confidence he'd be able to solve it himself; if I had Active Listened to him, letting him know I would help in any way I could if he wanted me to. One night after I had learned about AL, he came into the kitchen seething with resentment because his father had not let him take my car because he got in too late the last time he'd had it. He exploded with, "I'd like to take the car and smash it into something!"

A year before I would have thought, "It'll be a long time before he gets his hands on my car again!" Instead, I said, "You're really mad!" and he began to pour out all his grievances. I continued to Active Listen and within half an hour he was talking calmly and munching on a sandwich, the hostility completely dissipated.

With Lisa, Active Listening was quite threatening at first. There were a lot of things she did not want to reveal to us in those troubled days, but eventually she felt desperate enough to unload it all. By that time we were ready to handle it.

Our other children were also pleased with the changes that were taking place. You can't have so much tension in a family without everyone being affected by it to some degree. The older children were involved with school activities and part-time jobs and weren't home much except to eat and sleep. But I was very much concerned about the younger ones—Lanie, Rob, and Carol—feeling insecure and developing problems. So I made a special effort to Active Listen to their feelings and to try to get in touch with their needs.

Our six-year-old daughter, Carol, was only two when I first used Active Listening with her. My husband had driven off with her two older sisters and she began to cry. I was going to suggest watching TV or something when I remembered AL. So I said, "You're upset because Daddy left you home." She stopped crying and looked up at me with such love that I was overwhelmed. She knew that I understood how she felt and that was her need, to have me know how she felt. She has become increasingly aware of her own feelings and the feelings of others. She will tell her friends and teachers when something makes her uncomfortable or shy or embarrassed. And sometimes she'll say to me, "You're upset" or "You're angry."

My efforts to Active Listen had some very unexpected benefits. For instance, Steve, our oldest son, had never had any serious problems, but he had never talked to us much, either. So one day when he came in looking smugly pleased about something, I said, "You seem awfully happy today." To my amazement, he flopped down in a chair and spent the next half-hour telling me about how well things were going at work. He hadn't talked that much in years.

Mike, too, had needs I'd never thought about before. He was an excellent student and very much involved in band and student government and was extremely self-sufficient, so I'd never had any worries about him. But I suddenly realized that, operating under such tremendous pressure, he really appreciated an interested ear to help him unwind occasionally.

Lanie was concerned with fairly typical sixth-grade girl problems; too old for some things, not old enough for others. She was either very happy or very unhappy, and I probably got more practice using AL with her than any of the others. And it worked. The problems that upset her were her problems and AL let her keep the ownership of them and find solutions to them that really satisfied her. Naturally, she made mistakes, but she learned from them. For instance, she was a school patrol captain and didn't like telling the other patrol members when they weren't doing their jobs right. This reluctance got her in trouble with the advisor. By being allowed to keep the ownership of the problem, she was able to solve it herself. I was just there to listen while she talked it through.

The hardest skill for me to learn was sending "I-messages." I had always felt reluctant to complain about the annoying little things the kids did because I didn't like to nag. So I would let the little things build up until I finally erupted over something relatively unimportant, simply because I'd become saturated. There was no more room and the irritations wouldn't go away just because I ignored them. For example, one wet towel on the bathroom floor, one glass left in the living room, or one box of crayons left on the kitchen table right before dinner, were no great problem individually but after a whole day of silently taking care of such little things, I would have so much resentment built up that if anyone looked at me the wrong way during dinner, that's when I'd explode. Using "I-messages," I try to keep up with the little things so they don't build up and take control of me.

My husband had a problem with "I-messages," too. He was terribly frustrated by the idea that you could tell the kids how you felt—yet you had to let them decide what *they* were going to do about it. It was very hard for him to accept the fact that there was no way he could force his decisions on them short of escorting them everywhere and chaperoning them constantly. But he kept trying to avoid the Roadblocks and gradually his efforts were rewarded. We had problem-solved what hours our kids should be in at night, and they gradually became more cooperative about observing them. We limited ourselves to what our fears and worries were when they were out late—the accidents that could happen and the possibility they could be picked up by the police for violating the curfew—

and what our legal responsibilities were. Or you might say we let them know what tangible effects their behavior could have on us.

Problem-solving by Method III also became a part of our "modus operandi." Lisa hated cleaning her room, but she liked to cook and didn't mind giving Sharon her bath, so we would trade jobs. Most of the things we use Method III for are little problems like Rob and Lanie and Carol deciding who is going to watch what on TV, or how we're going to get Lanie to work and Rob to his football practice at approximately the same time but in opposite directions. But we also used it to plan an unexpected vacation. We had not made any summer plans because we'd all been too busy with the daily routine and, one day in late July, we decided we needed a change. So Jim and I rounded up the family and began by telling them we wanted their ideas about where we should go and what we should do. We all entered into the discussion without any preformed decisions since it was such a sudden idea. We ended up spending a really memorable week in a spectacular area in northern Minnesota. We stayed in a cabin, but Bill, Mike, Lisa, and Lanie went on a three-day canoe trip, portaging between the lakes and camping in wilderness at night. It was a wonderful chance for them to strengthen the bonds between them.

I have recounted only a brief chapter in the lives of our family, but it was a period of dramatic change. The changes continue day after day.

Bill has grown a lot in four years. He decided to go back to high school the fall after he dropped out, and has since graduated. He has outgrown his need for drugs, has a responsible job, and is engaged to a girl we're very fond of. He stops in to see us often, and our relationship is full of love and warmth. He has returned to our church and wants to be married there. Most important, he's making value decisions as he runs into problems, and he is acting on them.

Lisa, too, has changed. I enjoy having her around now. I feel comfortable with her again. Gone are the tense, cold barriers that seemed to rise between us in the past, making conversation stilted and awkward, if possible at all. She is working in a state hospital for the retarded and plans to go into nursing. She, too, comes home often and expresses her love for us in many ways, doing things for us, bringing flowers or applesauce cake.

Perhaps the following will show how much P.E.T. has become a part of our everyday lives. A few days ago, Bill had to back out of a date to take Carol bowling, and she began to cry. So I said, "You're disappointed."

"Yes," she answered, "nobody ever wants to do anything with me."

"You feel left out of things," I replied.

"Maybe Daddy will take me," she said.

"Well," I answered, "Daddy has been out of town all week and got home very late last night, so he may not want to go out."

(More sobs.) "It's not fair! You get to spend more time with Daddy than I do, 'cause I have to go to bed early."

"You'd like to do more things with Daddy," I answered.

"Yes. I like to do things with Daddy. I miss him when he's gone."

"I think Daddy would like to have you tell him that," I said.

She had brightened up by this time and she heaved a sigh and said, "It sure feels good to get all that off my chest."

There is such joy and understanding in our relationship. I'm always comfortable with Carol, never afraid she won't understand me. How different things might have been if I had understood the skills and human psychology that P.E.T. has taught me before we had our older children. It would not have prevented problems; these seem to be part of our human condition. But perhaps we would all have suffered less.

XV

THE CREDO FOR PARENTS

At some time during the evolution of the P.E.T. course, I don't remember exactly when, I began to realize that all that we taught parents could be integrated into an underlying philosophy of parent-child relationships. We were not teaching disparate and unrelated skills, but offering a total philosophy of relating to children, new to most parents.

I tried one day to formulate that philosophy as succinctly as I could. My description somehow took the form of a parental declaration of intent—a statement of the kind of relationship a P.E.T. parent would want to foster with his or her children. Eventually it became "A Credo for My Relationships with Youth." And soon it was printed in the Parent Workbook issued to all participants in the P.E.T. course. It was later included in the last chapter of the first P.E.T. book. We began to receive requests from parents for reprints of the Credo, some wanting it for their friends and neighbors and others wanting to tape it up on their refrigerator door as a daily reminder to themselves and their children of how they wanted to relate to each other. A few parents even had their reprint decoupaged for hanging on a wall. One parent I know

343

decoupaged the reprints and gave them as Christmas presents.

You can undertsand my reactions when I learned that several P.E.T. instructors included the reading of the Credo in their wedding ceremony. After all, they explained, this was the philosophy they wanted to live by in their marital relationship, too. My own daughter, Judy, my collaborator on this book, asked me just last year to read the Credo at her wedding to John Sands, who has since become a P.E.T. instructor.

Because the Credo obviously has had much meaning and value to so many, I want to include it here for those who have not yet had an opportunity to read it. You, too, might find that it defines the kind of relationship you want to foster and maintain with others, as well as with your children.

A CREDO

For My Relationships with Others

You and I are in a relationship which I value and want to keep. Yet each of us is a separate person with unique needs and the right to meet those needs.

When you are having problems meeting your needs, I will try to listen with genuine acceptance in order to facilitate your finding your own solutions instead of depending on mine. I also will try to respect your right to choose your own beliefs and develop your own values, different though they may be from mine.

However, when your behavior interferes with what I must do to get my own needs met, I will tell you openly and honestly how your behavior affects me, trusting that you respect my needs and feelings enough to try to change the behavior that is unacceptable to me. Also, whenever some behavior of mine is unacceptable to you, I hope you will tell me openly and honestly so I can try to change my behavior.

At those times when we find that either of us cannot change to meet the other's needs, let us acknowledge that we have a conflict and commit ourselves to resolve each such conflict without either of us resorting to the use of power or authority to win at the expense of the other's losing. I respect your needs, but I also must respect my own. So let us always strive to search for a solution that will be acceptable to both of us. Your needs will be met, and so will mine—neither will lose, both will win.

In this way, you can continue to develop as a person through satisfying your needs, and so can I. Thus, ours can be a healthy relationship in which both of us can strive to become what we are capable of being. And we can continue to relate to each other with mutual respect, love, and peace.

APPENDIX

This book is based principally on reports of actual parents who had completed the twenty-four-hour, eight-session P.E.T. course, designed by the author and taught by other seven thousand specially trained instructors.

In this section I will describe the methods that were used to obtain the reports; how the data were coded and analyzed; and relevant information about the parents who shared their opinions, feelings, and experiences in the interviews.

METHODS

Interviews

Ninety-two P.E.T. graduates were interviewed in sixty-seven in-depth interviews, each lasting from one to two hours. All interviews were conducted by Judy Gordon Sands, a member of the staff of Effectiveness Training and a trained P.E.T. instructor. All interviews were tape-recorded and later transcribed in full, word by word.

Parents were assured anonymity, and their permission was obtained to use interview material in the book. Interviews for the most part were conducted in the home of the parent. The sample of interviewees included:

24 couples, both parents P.E.T. graduates

42 mothers:　20 husbands had taken P.E.T.
　　　　　　 16 husbands had not taken P.E.T.
　　　　　　 6 were single parents

2 fathers: wives of both had taken P.E.T.

Some parents were selected for interviews by randomly picking names from class enrollment forms. Some (thirty-six in all) were identified by P.E.T. instructors whom we had asked to choose people who they thought would be willing and able to provide us with specific examples and experiences. Interviewees were contacted by phone to obtain their permission and set a date for the interview. All interviewees received a letter, explaining the purpose of the project and the types of questions they would be asked.

A number of parents expressed no interest in granting an interview, giving such reasons as: inadequate use of the P.E.T. skills, unwillingness to "be in a book," incompetence as a P.E.T. parent, paucity of real-life incidents, too busy, bad time, and so on.

Although the interviewer did not rigidly follow a set schedule of questions, she guided the interviews so that the parents would provide data in the following categories:

1. Why did the parent take P.E.T.? What was the family like before they enrolled? What did the parent hope to get from P.E.T.?

2. What experiences did the parent have with the P.E.T. skills while taking the P.E.T. course? What worked, what did not?

3. What experiences did the parent have with the P.E.T. skills subsequent to completing the course?

4. Description of critical incidents in which the parents felt very successful and critical incidents in which they felt very unsuccessful.

5. What from P.E.T. is the parent most grateful for? What was most disappointing?

6. What is the family life now?

7. What is it about the family that has changed the most?

The interviewer not only asked such questions as these, but also probed for specific illustrations or for more detail in incidents reported. The interviewer used a lot of Active Listening to clarify and to accept parents' feelings.

The 92 parents interviewed had a total of 217 children, ranging in age from less than 1 year to 32, with an average age of 11.4 years. Thirty-one were no longer living at home.

The parents' ages ranged from twenty-five to sixty-four years, the average age being around thirty-six years.

The distribution of the parents with respect to the highest educational level attained is as follows:

	Mothers	Fathers
High school	7	3
Some college	20	10
College graduate	22	19
Some graduate school	8	5
M.A. degree	6	10
Doctorate	2	14

Within the parent interview sample were parents who had taken P.E.T. as long as ten years prior to the interview and as recently as a few months, with the average being around two years prior to the interview.

Of the six single parents, five were separated or divorced and one was widowed. In the sample of married parents, twelve were in their second marriage and one in the third.

Only thirty of the parents were not employed (homemakers or students); the remainder had part-time or full-time employment. Of the fathers, all but one (a student) worked full time.

Questionnaires

A questionnaire was designed for P.E.T. instructors, asking for names of parents whom they would recommend for interviews or written case material. We asked for the names of parents they judged "successes," "poor successes," and "special families" (single parents, foster parents, etc.). Instructors were also asked to write out in detail one critical incident in which they used P.E.T. skills (a success) and one critical incident (a failure); fifty-eight were returned out of a thousand mailed.

A questionnaire was designed for parents identified by the instructors. They, too, were asked to write out two critical incidents (a success and a failure), and to write their "favorite P.E.T. story." Of 129 questionnaires mailed, 20 were returned.

Many of the critical incidents furnished by instructors and P.E.T. graduates were used in the book.

Essays

Because we wanted some extensive accounts of the overall impact of P.E.T. on families, we conducted an essay contest. Flyers announcing the contest were mailed to all seven thousand P.E.T. instructors, inviting them to enter the contest and asking them to distribute the fliers to parents in their classes or to P.E.T. graduates.

The fliers invited parents to submit a long essay or "short story" that described "what happened to my family as a result of P.E.T." The winning essays would be those judged by a committee of our Effectiveness Training staff to be of sufficient dramatic interest to be included in the new book.

We received thirty-four essays; four were selected as winners (prize: $250 each) and three as runner-ups (prize: $25).

Tape-Recordings

Instructors and P.E.T. graduates were asked to submit tape recordings of dialogues in their families to illustrate use of P.E.T. skills. Requests were made in the newsletter that goes to all instructors, in a flier that went with all questionnaires, and at each interview with parents. Eleven tapes were submitted.

Anecdote File

Over the years we have built up a file of written anecdotes and incidents submitted by parents and instructors. These were added to the reports from the sources above.

CONTENT ANALYSIS AND CODING

The reports, incidents, and illustrations from all sources (except the tapes) were subjected to a content analysis. This proved to be a long and arduous task. Judy read each page of every interview and every incident described in the questionnaires in order to identify *themes, ideas,* and *issues.* Each such passage (or segment) was classified according to its particular content and then assigned a code. Over seven hundred themes, ideas, and issues were identified.

These were then combined into 133 categories, which in turn were classified under 19 major topics—such as, The Role of the Parent, Reasons for Taking P.E.T., The Course Experience, Attitude Changes, Limitations of P.E.T., Active Listening, I-Messages, Method III, Values, Use of Power, Roadblocks, etc. A card catalogue of the original seven hundred themes, classified as described above, enabled us to locate any particular passage in the interviews and incidents.

We collected far more rich data than we could possibly use. It would take a second book to deal adequately with all that we found out in this study.

Certainly this was not a research study in the strict scientific sense. Our sample of parents was not selected using a systematic or random method. While the sample contains many different kinds of parents (from forty-five communities in four states), it is not a representative sample of the 250,000 parents who have taken P.E.T. in fifty states and several foreign countries.

And our study provided only *reports* from parents about their reactions and experiences, as opposed to results from evaluation instruments.

Our purpose, however, was limited: to find out from parents what P.E.T. had meant *to them* and what impact they felt it had on themselves and their families. We wanted to put together a book of cases, drawn from the experiences of some parents who took P.E.T., hoping that other parents might derive benefit.

GUIDE TO RELATED READINGS

Axline, Virginia M. *Play Therapy*. Boston: Houghton Mifflin, 1947.

    The first book describing the application of the client-centered approach to therapy with children. Demonstrates use of Active Listening. Deals with concept of limits. Presents a variety of case material and recorded interviews. Techniques described may be applied by parents in the home.

————. *Dibs: In Search of Self*. New York: Ballantine Books, 1969.

    A moving story of a child's growth and change in the process of therapy with the author, who is one of the pioneers in client-centered play therapy. Demonstrates active listening and the power of the language of acceptance.

Bach, George R. and Herb Goldberg. *Creative Aggression*. New York: Doubleday, 1974.

    Discusses suppressed and released aggression, and some exercises and suggestions for uncovering suppressed aggression in a nondestructive, even creative manner.

Baruch, Dorothy W. *New Ways in Discipline*. New York: McGraw-Hill, 1949.

One of the most widely read books for parents. Written in simple style. Illustrates use of Active Listening. Deals with problems of reward and punishment. Shows how parents can apply methods of play therapy at home.

————. *How to Live with Your Teenager*. New York: McGraw-Hill, 1953.

Author incorporates same ideas and principles as were in her 1949 book. Focus is on special problems of teen-agers.

Briggs, Dorothy D. *Your Child's Self-Esteem*. New York: Doubleday, 1970.

Focuses on the child's self-esteem, its importance in relation to health, its antecedents, and methods parents can use to foster positive self-esteem. Mrs. Briggs, an early P.E.T. instructor, uses P.E.T. concepts and methods, weaving them creatively into her own unique organization of ideas about self-acceptance, love and self-esteem. The book adds meat and life to the methodology and theory stressed in P.E.T. Enrollees will find this book a most helpful supplement to the textbook.

Button, Alan DeWitt. *The Authentic Child*. New York: Random House, 1969.

A penetrating analysis of the characteristics of the child who becomes authentic from his relationship with authentic parents. Stresses the importance of parents' acceptance, honesty, and willingness to be human. Will help parents see beauty in their children and experience joy in a mutual, nonpower relationship. Rejects pat solutions in parent education in favor of developing spontaneously open relationships with children.

Carson, Rachel. *The Sense of Wonder*. New York: Harper & Row, 1965.

A beautiful book with pictures and ideas

for parents and children about nature and the importance of the sense of awe and wonder in a child's learning experience.

Comer, James P. and Alvin F. Poussaint. *Black Child Care*. New York: Simon & Schuster, 1975.
A question and answer guide for black parents that covers the parental facts of life, emphasizes the impact of racism, aggression and self-esteem in bringing up black children.

Donovan, Frank R. *Wild Kids*. Harrisburg, Pennsylvania: Stackpole Books, 1967.
An eye-opener for people who are unaccepting of today's children and their behavior. Shows how kids have been rebelling against authority throughout history. Shows how children have been exploited and dominated by adults in all generations.

Faber, Adele and Elaine Mazlish. *Liberated Parents —Liberated Children*. New York: Grosset & Dunlap, 1974.
With humor and honesty, this book affirms that given skills, parents can give up self-defeating patterns and help themselves and their families live together in mutual dignity.

Frank, Lawrence K. and Mary Frank. *Your Adolescent*. New York: Viking Press, 1956. Also a Signet Key Book, published by the New American Library.
Written for parents, this paperback will be useful for parents wanting to understand the dynamics of adolescence and how parents can develop the hidden potentialities of children for creative and constructive behavior.

Fromm, Erich. *The Art of Loving*. New York: Harper & Row, 1956.
A classic volume that examines the senti-

ment of love between man and woman, parent
and child. Relates the capacity to love to one's
inner strength, the love for oneself and one's pro-
ductivity. Excellent to help parents understand
the true psychological meaning of "loving one's
children."

Ginott, Haim G. *Between Parent and Child*. New
York: Macmillan, 1965.
      Excellent for showing importance of listen-
ing. Deals with special problems of sex education, jealousy, serious emotional problems.

Gordon, Thomas; *P.E.T.: Parent Effectiveness Training*. New York: New American Library, 1975.
      The basic text for the P.E.T. course that has
been taught to over a quarter of a million persons. A step-by-step presentation of the P.E.T.
philosophy and the specific skills parents need to
raise responsible children in a happy family. Rich
in examples and case histories illustrating the
new methods.

Holt, John. *How Children Fail*. New York: Dell,
1964.
      A teacher provides a penetrating analysis of
what teachers and classes do to children to make
them fail—even children who get good grades.
Shows effects of evaluation. Shows how schools
make children bored, afraid and confused. Parents, as well as teachers, will find this book fas-
cinating.

Hymes, James L. Jr. *Understanding Your Child*
(1952) and *Behavior and Misbehavior* (1955).
Englewood Cliffs, New Jersey: Prentice-Hall.
      These two books are well written and based
upon sound psychological principles. Both provide parents with fuller understanding of the parent-child relationship.

————. *The Child Under Six*. Englewood Cliffs, New Jersey: Prentice-Hall, 1963.

Easy to read and helpful to parents in understanding children and their psychological needs. Incorporates many of the ideas and principles of the course.

Jourard, Sidney M. *The Transparent Self*. New York: D. Van Nostrand, 1964.

Offers the hypothesis that man can be healthier, more fully-functioning and more helpful to others if he gains courage to be his real self with others. Concealing our feelings and thoughts prevents intimate relationships and brings on emotional sickness.

Maslow, Abraham. *Toward a Psychology of Being*. New York: D. Van Nostrand, 1962.

Excellent presentation of a positive and optimistic philosophy that people have an urge to grow and to actualize their potential and that this tendency is facilitated when they are accepted as they are.

Missildine, W. Hugh. *Your Inner Child of the Past*. New York: Simon & Schuster, 1963.

Excellent for understanding the effects of various parental patterns on the child's personality and his later adult ways of coping with problems.

Neill, A. S. *Summerhill*. New York: Hart Publishing, 1960.

Report of a pioneering school in England in which an attempt has been made to incorporate in an educational institution the principles of democracy and the elements of a therapeutic community.

————. *Freedom—Not License*. New York: Hart Publishing, 1966.

A sequel to *Summerhill*. More of Neill's philosophy. Excellent for reinforcing some of the concepts in P.E.T. Recommended very strongly.

Powell, John S. *Why Am I Afraid To Tell You Who I Am?* Chicago: Argus Communications, 1969.

A beautiful, easy to read book on the risks of revealing our real selves to others in open communication.

Putney, Shell and Gail Putney. *The Adjusted American.* New York: Harper & Row, 1964.

One of the best books for understanding self and others. Clearly written, insightful and penetrating. Shows parents how they contribute to child's maladjustive behavior. Will help parents understand their relationship with their own parents. Recommended strongly.

Rogers, Carl R. *Client-Centered Therapy.* Boston: Houghton Mifflin, 1951.

The basic text on client-centered therapy— the theory, practice, research foundations and applications to groups, teaching, leadership and administration and play therapy.

———. *On Becoming a Person.* Boston: Houghton Mifflin, 1963.

A collection of Rogers' papers, most of them unpublished, covering his thinking about therapy, education, the self, the healthy individual, the helping relationship, etc. Useful to parents wanting to understand the broader implications of client-centered therapy and to capture the essence of Rogers as a person.

Russell, Bertrand. *Marriage and Morals.* New York: Bantam Books, 1959.

A classic treatise on the economic, religious and cultural foundations of the family. Shows the changing roles of father and mother in different societies. Excellent for showing changes in attitudes toward sex in the family. An eye-opener for parents who believe there are fixed and absolute standards for morality.

Satir, Virginia. *People Making*. Palo Alto, California: Science and Behavior Books, 1972.

Describes the coded interactions of people communicating with one another, and suggestions and exercises on opening true lines of human communication.

Simmons, J. I. and B. Winograd. *It's Happening*. Santa Barbara, California: Mare-Laird Publications, 1966.

A book for parents who want to understand the present generation of youth with their protesting, drugs, freer sex, and anti-war attitudes. Reveals the kids' side of the story.

Stone, Joseph L. and Joseph Church. *Childhood and Adolescence*. New York: Random House, 1957.

Presents a philosophy similar to the course. Shows parents ways of avoiding stress of adolescent period. Helpful for parents who are finding adolescence puzzling and bewildering.

Thomas, Marlo (editor). *Free to Be You, Free to Be Me*. New York: McGraw-Hill, 1974.

A delightful book (also a record album) for children dealing with feelings, prejudices and the joy and gentleness of living.

INDEX

ABOUT THE AUTHOR

DR. THOMAS GORDON, a licensed clinical psychologist, received his Ph.D. from the University of Chicago, where he later served on the faculty. He is a Fellow of the American Psychological Association and a past president of the California State Psychological Association. He is the founder and president of Effectiveness Training Inc., a nationwide network of professionals offering training programs for parents, teachers, administrators, and others working with children and youth. He is author of *P.E.T.—Parent Effectiveness Training and T.E.T.—Teacher Effectiveness Training.*

THE P.E.T. COURSE

This is an educational program taught in thousands of communities in every state and in Canada by specially trained and authorized Instructors.

Parents attend one night each week for eight successive weeks in small groups of 15-30, usually in churches, homes, or public meeting rooms.

Parents get coaching and practice in putting the skills to work immediately.

More than a quarter of a million parents have completed the course.

FOR INFORMATION ABOUT ENROLLING
IN P.E.T.:

Mail in the above coupon.

Look in the white pages of your telephone directory under P.E.T. or Parent Effectiveness Training.

Bantam
On Psychology

☐	01419	**IF YOU CAN HEAR WHAT I CANNOT SAY . . .** Nathaniel Branden	$8.95
☐	23043	**ACTIVE LOVING**—Ari Kiev, M.D.	$2.95
☐	22576	**PATHFINDERS**, Gail Sheehy	$4.50
☐	23234	**PASSAGES: PREDICTABLE CRISES OF ADULT LIFE**, Gail Sheehy	$4.50
☐	23006	**THE FAMILY CRUCIBLE**, Dr. Napier	$4.50
☐	20300	**A YEAR IN THE LIFE**, W. Bridges	$2.50
☐	23399	**THE POWER OF YOUR SUBCONSCIOUS MIND**, Dr. J. Murphy	$3.95
☐	23125	**FOCUSING**, E. Grendlin	$3.95
☐	23079	**LOVE IS LETTING GO OF FEAR**, Gerald Jampolsky	$2.95
☐	22503	**PEACE FROM NERVOUS SUFFERING**, Claire Weekes	$3.50
☐	20540	**THE GESTALT APPROACH & EYE WITNESS TO THERAPY**, Fritz Perls	$3.50
☐	20220	**THE BOOK OF HOPE**, DeRosis & Pellegrino	$3.95
☐	23449	**THE PSYCHOLOGY OF SELF-ESTEEM: A New Concept of Man's Psychological Nature**, Nathaniel Branden	$3.95
☐	23267	**WHAT DO YOU SAY AFTER YOU SAY HELLO?** Eric Berne, M.D.	$3.95
☐	20774	**GESTALT THERAPY VERBATIM**, Fritz Perls	$3.50
☐	22870	**PSYCHO-CYBERNETICS AND SELF-FULFILLMENT**, Maxwell Maltz, M.D.	$3.50
☐	20873	**THE FIFTY-MINUTE HOUR**, Robert Linder	$2.95
☐	22794	**THE DISOWNED SELF**, Nathaniel Branden	$3.50
☐	23553	**CUTTING LOOSE: An Adult Guide for Coming to Terms With Your Parents**, Howard Halpern	$3.50
☐	20977	**WHEN I SAY NO, I FEEL GUILTY**, Manuel Smith	$3.95

Buy them at your local bookstore or use this handy coupon for ordering: